KLAN OF DEVILS

KLAN OF DEVILS

THE MURDER OF A BLACK LOUISIANA DEPUTY SHERIFF

STANLEY NELSON

LOUISIANA STATE UNIVERSITY PRESS | BATON ROUGE

Published with the assistance of the Mason C. Carter Fund and the John and Virginia Noland Fund

Published by Louisiana State University Press
lsupress.org

Manufactured in the United States of America
First printing

Designer: Mandy McDonald Scallan
Typeface: Sentinel
Printer and binder: Sheridan Books, Inc.

Maps by Mary Lee Eggart

Jacket photograph: The patrol car driven by deputy Oneal Moore the night of June 2, 1965.
Photograph courtesy FBI.

Names: Nelson, Stanley, 1955 September 18– author.
Title: Klan of devils : the murder of a black Louisiana deputy sheriff / Stanley Nelson.
Description: Baton Rouge : Louisiana State University Press, [2021] | Includes bibliographical references and index.
Identifiers: LCCN 2021010931 (print) | LCCN 2021010932 (ebook) | ISBN 978-0-8071-7607-8 (cloth) | ISBN 978-0-8071-7646-7 (pdf) | ISBN 978-0-8071-7647-4 (epub)
Subjects: LCSH: Moore, Oneal—Death and burial. | Ku Klux Klan (1915–) | United States. Federal Bureau of Investigation. | Center for Investigative Reporting (U.S.) | Police murders—Louisiana—History. | Sheriffs—Louisiana–Biography. | Murder—Investigation—Louisiana—History. | Investigative reporting—United States. | Louisiana–Race relations–History.
Classification: LCC HV8145.L8 L46 2021 (print) | LCC HV8145.L8 (ebook) | DDC 364.9763–dc23
LC record available at https://lccn.loc.gov/2021010931
LC ebook record available at https://lccn.loc.gov/2021010932

I used to think maybe there was some good to the Ku Klux Klan, but they're nothing but a pack of no-good devils.

—A white woman in Bogalusa, Louisiana, whose husband was abducted and beaten by the Ku Klux Klan in 1964

CONTENTS

KLAN OF DEVILS

INTRODUCTION

Almost six decades ago on a quiet Wednesday night, June 2, 1965, a sheriff's office patrol car eased through the village of Varnado around 10:15. Located in the southeastern corner of Louisiana, Varnado is seventy-five miles north of New Orleans. Following behind was a black pickup first observed a few minutes earlier by the two African American deputies inside the police cruiser. As they crossed the railroad tracks on Main Street, gunshots rang out when the pickup began to pass. Suddenly, the patrol car swerved off the street and crashed into an oak tree. Inside the bullet-riddled vehicle, the driver, Oneal Moore, a young man with a wife and four daughters, was dead. His partner, Creed Rogers, a few years older, was seriously injured but survived. Within minutes, parish and state police officers arrived at the scene along with FBI agents. One of the biggest tasks for investigators was to solve the main puzzle: Who were the occupants of the pickup?

Less than an hour later, based on a description provided by Rogers, police officers in Tylertown, Mississippi, spotted the vehicle racing through town. Quickly apprehended was the pickup's driver and owner—a forty-one-year-old white paper mill worker from Bogalusa—Ernest Ray McElveen. He was alone. The only person ever charged in the murder of Oneal Moore, McElveen refused to talk to the FBI or to reporters from across the nation who contacted him periodically over the thirty-eight years between the killing and his death in 2003. McElveen had returned home from World War II a decorated war survivor. Soon afterward, he began a quiet family life in Bogalusa and a terroristic personal life, involving himself in vigilante justice, working to disenfranchise hundreds of Black voters from the voting rolls of Washington Parish, serving as president of the local chapter of the white Citizens' Council, and later becoming a member of the Original Knights, the largest Klan group in Louisiana, which spawned the White Knights in Mississippi in 1964. He was held in jail eleven days before his release. Although the sheriff charged McElveen with murder, the district attorney never asked a grand jury for an indict-

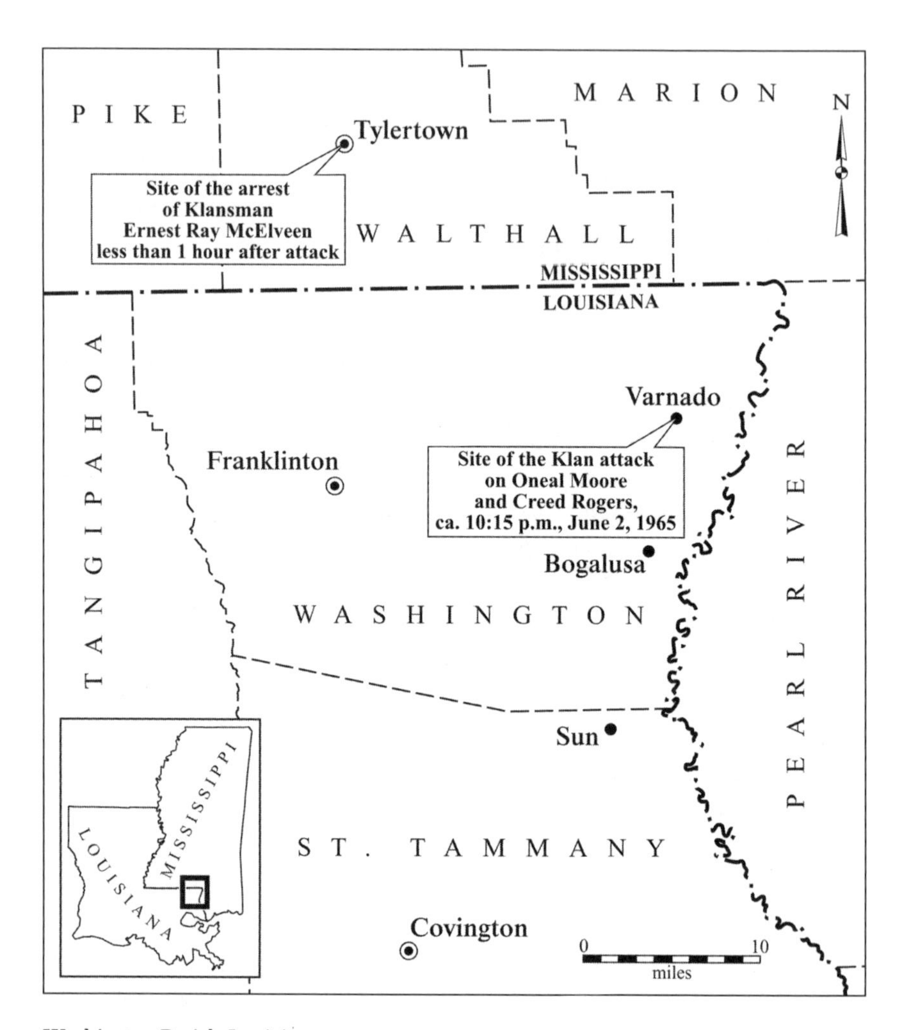

Washington Parish, Louisiana

ment because Rogers, the key eyewitness who identified the truck holding the attackers, never got a clear view of the occupants. He could not identify McElveen as the driver or as a passenger. Behind the scenes, several grand jurors, friends of the defendant, pushed to hear the case so they could reject an indictment and clear McElveen's name. Additionally, fear of the Klan made the work of the law enforcement even harder. Witnesses in both the white and Black communities whose testimony in court may have assisted in identifying all of the killers refused to do so.

The two deputies had been on the job for a year and a day when the shooting occurred. Each had been hired by the white sheriff, Dorman Crowe. His decision enraged members of local units of the Original Knights. The hiring also was historic: Moore and Rogers were the first Black men to serve as deputies in Washington Parish. And the case stands out in another way: it appears to be the only one during the civil rights era in which the Klan targeted Black law enforcement officers.

Six miles to the south of Varnado is Bogalusa, where news of the shooting resulted in more bloodshed in the city streets. For months, the Bogalusa Voters and Civic League, allied with the Congress for Racial Equality and the Deacons for Defense and Justice—an armed group that protected Black neighborhoods and activists from the Klan—had led multiple marches and demonstrations seeking to desegregate the mill town and to have the mandates of the Civil Rights Act of 1964 fully enforced. Disrupting these events were the Original Knights in Washington Parish, home to the largest concentration of Klansmen in Louisiana. The situation in Bogalusa, made all the more volatile due to the shooting of the deputies, became perhaps the greatest challenge of the first term of Governor John J. McKeithen, who came from northern Louisiana, where the Original Knights had first organized in 1960 in Shreveport-Bossier. McKeithen met with civil rights leaders and with Klan leaders in attempts to quell the violence. His last visit with Washington Parish Klan leaders came during a secret meeting in Bogalusa two days before the shooting of the deputies. McKeithen thought he had convinced Klansmen to stay off the streets and end the violence. Consequently, the reality of the shooting of the deputies stunned him and opened his eyes to the fact that violent Klansmen could not be trusted or managed. As a result, McKeithen, who had sought the governorship as a segregationist, moderated his position on race and came to understand that enforcement of civil rights laws was a necessity.

Historian Adam Fairclough noted in his epic study of the civil rights movement in Louisiana that Bogalusa, because of its geographic location in a parish bordered on the north and east by Mississippi, was more like a Mississippi town than a Louisiana one. In Mississippi, where the White Knights had launched a statewide reign of terror, one of the most iconic Klan murder cases of the era involving three civil rights workers (Michael Schwerner, James Chaney and Andrew Goodman) in Neshoba County in 1964, was still being intensively investigated by the FBI and continued to hold the attention of a shocked nation. Fairclough opined that had the same crisis in Bogalusa occurred in Mississippi it was improbable that "it would have been tackled with the same combination of constructive mediation from the governor" and "resolute intervention by the Department of Justice."[1]

The attack on Moore and Rogers also holds another distinction: it resulted in the FBI's most intensive and longest investigation of a Klan murder in Louisiana and one of the most intensive in the South. From 1965 until the case was closed in 2016, the FBI followed scores of leads and developed two dozen suspects. The Justice Department, which launched lawsuits against the Klan, restaurants, and city officials in Bogalusa seeking enforcement of civil rights in the mid-1960s, also convened numerous secret federal grand jury investigations into the Oneal Moore murder over the following decades.

Early on, the FBI determined one thing about the black pickup: that it was occupied by at least three Klansmen—one driving, one who fired a high-powered rifle multiple times, and one who used a shotgun. There also was evidence that another wrecking crew—a Klan hit squad—working in conjunction with McElveen's, was gunning for the deputies that night as well and if the opportunity had arisen would have launched the ambush attack. These facts confirmed for the FBI that this was a highly coordinated military-style attack.

In 2007, the FBI, as part of a national initiative, reopened multiple unsolved civil rights–era cold cases involving more than one hundred killings in the South for review or investigation. The following year, Congress passed the Emmett Till Unsolved Civil Rights Crime Act, named after a Black teen from Chicago killed in Mississippi in 1955 for allegedly whistling at a white woman. The Till Act authorized the FBI and Justice Department to investigate cold case murders of African Americans occurring before 1970. All of the cases opened as a result of the initiative have since been closed.

Twelve unsolved murders made the FBI's list in Louisiana, the Oneal Moore case being the last to be closed. While much more will be written in the future about the civil rights era, the possibilities of shedding new light on these killings based on the memories of living eyewitnesses is fading fast. But a few are still around. Chronicling their memories and their knowledge of these killings is a task that journalists continue to pursue.

Because the FBI's investigation into the shooting of the two deputies was so long lasting, the bureau and the Department of Justice over the decades had made few investigative documents—all heavily redacted—available for public consumption. But after the matter was officially closed in 2016, the Center for Investigative Reporting in California, at my request, successfully filed suit in federal court for an expedited release of the case file. Soon we learned that the file contained almost forty thousand pages. Monthly releases of documents soon followed. The pages reveal a massive FBI investigation that was both intensive and creative. The documents also provide new insight into the Original Knights formation and operation in Louisiana.

I grew up in Louisiana during the 1960s and recall watching the evening news on television featuring reports on the murders of the three activists in Mississippi in 1964. I was ten years old in 1965 when the two deputies were shot in Varnado, although it was years later before I heard about this case. While in my teens, the school I attended was integrated in the years after passage of the Civil Rights Act of 1964. A few days before school started, the Klan dropped letters into our mailbox and those of our neighbors demanding that white parents not send their children to a school also attended by Black children. This reality, the one thing Klansmen and segregationists feared the most, came about even as white segregation continued in private schools. Until integration, the majority of Black and white students at my school had never been in the same room with someone from the other race. This was a transformative event for me and my classmates as well for the country, although it did little to resolve the issues of equality and justice for African Americans.

Bob Lawrence, a reporter for the *Bogalusa Daily News* during the 1960s, said the city was "totally segregated" up until the middle of the decade. He recalled in a book on his memories of Bogalusa that he had known only five African Americans while growing up there—the family maid and cook, a handyman, twins who worked at the grocery store, and a hospital porter. "I never had occasion to speak to a black person other than those few," he said. "The degree of separation was infinite."[2]

Having investigated civil rights–era murder cases for years, I have long sought out retired FBI agents who investigated the Klan and Klan homicides at the time they occurred. Only a few retired agents who served the bureau during those days were still alive. I found two, Ted Gardner and Milton Graham, who were each on the ground in Washington Parish in the 1960s. Both recounted their many experiences, including harrowing encounters with Klan suspects and the daily grind of investigating the murder while also enforcing the newly passed civil rights laws.

While the Klan's desire to defeat civil rights was fueled by the common themes of racial hatred and the desire to preserve white supremacy, local issues often triggered Klan attacks. For years before the assault on the deputies, the Citizens' Council and the Klan in Washington Parish tried to defeat Sheriff Crowe and put a Klansman in the sheriff's office. During the election of 1964, Klan candidates ran for every office in the parish as well as for district offices. Klansmen were elected to the school board, the police jury, and multiple other local offices. Twice during the 1960s, the Klan had put up its own candidate against Crowe and both times Crowe won narrowly, depending on the Black vote for his victory margins. Klan leaders believed that as the chief law enforcement officer of the parish, the sheriff was best positioned to fight civil rights and the federal government, and because of this, the office was considered crucial to achieving the Klan's goal of preserving white supremacy in Washington Parish. But Sheriff Crowe stood in the way.

The 1960 and 1964 sheriff elections were bitterly fought and further hardened feelings segregationists already held against Crowe. Without Black support, the Klan would have won the sheriff's office and who knows what chaos would have followed. After the 1964 election, the Klan's bitterness turned to rage when Crowe hired the two Black deputies in June 1964. From day one, Crowe stood behind Moore and Rogers and once attempted to have a game warden, who also was an officer in the parish Klan, relocated elsewhere in the state after the man accosted and harassed the deputies. Decades after the shooting, Creed Rogers would publicly thank Crowe for hiring the two men, calling the event life changing. He also expressed his love and respect for Crowe. Yet Rogers was profoundly saddened and disappointed that the murder of his partner was never solved.

In the months leading up to the shooting of the two deputies, the Original Knights had undergone a major statewide revamping as original leaders were ousted and hardcore violent men—including one who had killed four Black men in 1960—assumed the reins. By 1965, the Klan's membership had dwindled due to the infighting and the lack of political success in halting the steady march forward of civil rights and because the average member feared the new leaders. The Klan left standing plans to go to war against Blacks and against the federal government. Ray McElveen was among the Klansmen encouraged by the new Klan leadership and its focus on violence to win the war. He found himself on the front lines again—not in Saipan this time, where he was wounded during World War II—but at the center of the Klan's war against the sheriff and to eliminate the Black deputies from the sheriff's office either through politics, intimidation, or violence. This fight was a local one, and before the 1964 election, Klansmen in Washington Parish were focused only on their home turf. They had no interest in what was happening in Neshoba County, where the three civil rights workers were killed, or the bombing murders of four schoolgirls in Birmingham or Klan murders or crimes elsewhere in the South. They circled their wagons with a goal of taking absolute control of Washington Parish by winning the sheriff's office. They'd think about the rest of the South later.

Through the years, the primary goal in my investigation of all murder cases has been to figure out what happened, why it happened, and who did it. In Mississippi, arrests in several civil rights–era murders during the 1960s and over the past decades resulted in convictions of several Klansmen. But in the Louisiana cases, there was no justice.

In Washington Parish, the sheriff had charged McElveen with murder but the district attorney (DA) could not make a case. The FBI and Justice Department, despite a half-century investigation, could not make a case either. This alone means that to a degree, McElveen and Klansmen were victorious in getting away with taking the life of Oneal Moore and spilling the blood of Creed Rogers. The Klan's price: eleven days in jail for McElveen. The icing on the cake for Klansmen followed: during the next election in 1968, Sheriff Crowe was defeated, although it was not by a Klan candidate.

But by no means did the Klan win the war. Many of the suspects in the killing of Oneal Moore, including McElveen, may have felt like fugitives for the rest of their lives when periodically over the decades they were surveilled by FBI agents or subpoenaed to testify before federal grand juries. They were always looking over their shoulders. Several were so paranoid they hired lawyers.

Some Klansmen were good criminals. Good criminals keep their mouths shut. Consequently, many carried their secrets to the grave.

Or so they thought.

The FBI documents and the memories of FBI agents on the ground and the survivors of the era provide answers and a compelling list of suspects, some of whom confessed to their wives or confessed unaware they were being secretly recorded as they discussed their involvement in the attack on the deputies. The identities of those involved and the conspiracy that led up to the shooting can now be revealed and the motives explained. More than five and a half decades after that June night in 1965, the secrets of the assassins and the mysteries of the black pickup are finally unraveled.

1

"NEED HELP QUICK AT VARNADO"

The fragrance of the approaching summer overwhelmed the Louisiana air in early June 1965 as gardeners prepared to harvest the season's first tomatoes and ranchers baled hay for their livestock. Bees hummed and flitted about the fruit trees and patches of clover. In the little town of Varnado in Louisiana's Washington Parish, located at the top corner of the toe of the boot-shaped state, Maevella Moore's day was winding down in her kitchen. Two hours before midnight she was preparing a fried catfish supper for her husband and his work partner. She was expecting them to pop in at any moment for a quick bite before finishing his shift four hours later.[1]

Oneal Moore and Creed Rogers had made history a year and a day earlier on June 1, 1964, when they became the first two African American deputies for the Washington Parish Sheriff's Office. A white sheriff hired them. Their employment didn't draw print from the two local newspapers or the city papers in Baton Rouge or New Orleans. But the hiring infuriated the Original Knights of the Ku Klux Klan. Its membership had tried for years to defeat Dorman Crowe—the man who hired them—as the parish's top law enforcement officer.

Oneal and Maevella were the parents of four daughters. He was a carpenter, mowed yards, and had busied himself before his shift began by putting a roof on his father-in-law's carport.[2] Creed Rogers, who worked as a plumber on the side, ran errands that day, gave a hitchhiker a lift, and bought groceries. He also purchased a load of topsoil and transported relatives to a nearby Mississippi town where they sold their first crop of cucumbers to a company that brined them into pickles.[3] He didn't feel well and complained that his stomach ulcers were acting up.[4]

It was 9:30 p.m. when they departed the sheriff's office in the parish seat of Franklinton en route to Varnado. There was very little traffic. Churches had already completed their midweek prayer meeting services. They slowly made their way north and east to Angie, where they took a right turn onto Louisiana Highway 21. Angie was just south of the Mississippi line, and Varnado five miles below Angie. They were working the 6:00 p.m. to 2:00 a.m. shift. It was Oneal Moore's week to drive the patrol car—WP-14—and when he left home earlier in the evening, he had radioed the sheriff's office that the deputies were going on duty. A short distance down the road, he picked up Rogers.[5]

Bogalusa, a mill town located six miles south of Varnado, is the parish's biggest municipality. Both towns rest in the Pearl River basin. For decades the Crown-Zellerbach paper mill had employed hundreds of families, Black and white, thanks to the abundance of the longleaf yellow pine. The northern half of the parish, marked by rolling hills and small creeks, was home to a thriving dairy industry that also fueled the economy.

On Highway 21, the deputies observed a burning pile of brush to their left on the east side of the highway. As Moore slowed the vehicle—a 1964 white Chevrolet four-door sedan with a red light mounted on the top—and steered to the right shoulder, the men noticed the lights of a dark pickup that had appeared behind them seemingly out of nowhere. There was nothing menacing about the truck. Although the nights and back roads were typically quiet, everyone knew that Klan night riders were about. But now on a paved highway on the eastern side of the parish, and only a short distance from Moore's home, the deputies were tired, hungry, and relaxed. Bars were closing and a few fox hunters were following their dogs in the woods, but the children and old people were in bed, and just about everybody else was planning to join them. As the truck passed by, the deputies looked over and could barely make out the driver's outline. The pickup eased on, but for some reason pulled off on the right shoulder about one hundred feet ahead without stopping, only to return to the highway and continue south at a snail's pace.[6]

Moore then made a U-turn and drove two hundred yards back to the scene of the trash fire. The deputies looked it over. Satisfied that the fire was contained and would not spread, Moore drove back onto the highway and continued south to Varnado, about two miles distant. The deputies never lost sight of the pickup, and at Miley's Tavern they caught up with it and began to pass. As the patrol car came abreast of the truck, the two men looked to their right. Rogers observed a white male driving. He saw no passengers either inside the pickup or in the back.[7]

Down the road the deputies recognized an acquaintance preparing to enter the highway from the left side just north of town. Moore blew the siren as a greeting. In Varnado, population 330, Moore turned on his left blinker and steered east. Rogers saw two or three Black men working on a pulpwood truck at Rester's service station. The dark pickup turned left, too, as the patrol car traveled along at twenty-five miles per hour. The pickup was about fifty yards behind them and gaining as they slowed to pass over the double railroad tracks that crossed Main Street. Moore planned to turn left on Pearsoll Street just a few feet ahead en route to his home. At that moment, Rogers heard an explosion—it sounded like a rifle shot—just as he observed a hole appear in the middle of the dashboard between the two men.[8]

The thirty-four-year-old Moore immediately wondered aloud if their car had backfired. But the forty-two-year-old Rogers immediately knew the two deputies were in trouble. By now the truck was beginning to pass the cruiser. "Someone is firing at us," Rogers shouted to Moore. "Speed up!" At that moment he heard a second blast and watched Moore's body jerk and slump over the steering wheel, the left side of his head blown away. A volley of shots followed, accompanied by flashes of light. Windows in the vehicle shattered. The patrol car swerved to the right. Rogers felt a pain in his left shoulder and tried to brace himself before WP-14 crashed into an oak tree on the south side of the street. His head slammed into the windshield. For a brief period, time stood still. Then Rogers—dazed and bleeding—reached for the microphone, uncertain that the police radio would work in the wrecked vehicle.[9] Olin Harmon, a preacher working as a dispatcher for the sheriff's office, looked at his watch as a call came in at 10:18 p.m.: "WP-14 SO. Been shot. Need help quick at Varnado." Harmon recognized the voice as that of Creed Rogers. The dispatcher alerted all police units of the shooting and contacted a state trooper who was near Varnado. The trooper radioed for an ambulance.[10]

Rogers had gotten a good look at the dark pickup, a Chevrolet. It appeared dark green but could have been Black. He thought it was likely manufactured in the early to mid-1950s. A Confederate flag license plate was mounted on the right side of the front grill. The bed of the pickup had wooden side panels, also known as sideboards, approximately six to eight inches high on the body of the bed. The driver was described as white.[11] The Louisiana State Police quickly broadcast a description of the truck, which was later picked up by Mississippi authorities. Police radios came alive, and the chatter was at times confusing. In Bogalusa, a green pickup was pulled over, but the Black driver was sent on his way.[12]

Only two witnesses would claim to have seen the shooting. Daniel "Scraps" Fornea, a forty-eight-year-old teacher and coach at Varnado High, lived on

Pearsoll Street, which led to Jones Creek Road and Moore's home. Scraps had been watching TV until about 10:15 p.m. when he went outside to put his car in the garage. While on the porch, he looked approximately one hundred yards toward Main and saw the patrol car and behind it a dark-colored pickup nearing the railroad tracks when suddenly shots rang out.[13] He estimated that eight to ten shots were fired in a matter of seconds and two days later told the *New Orleans Times-Picayune,* "The first shot was a real bang. It sounded greater than an M-1."[14] As the truck passed the car and the vehicles left his line of sight, Fornea heard sounds of the impact. Barefoot, he raced up the street to Main, where the patrol car had crashed into a tree. The pickup was nowhere in sight.[15]

Fifty-year-old housewife Jessie Bell Thigpen, whose mobile home sat fifty yards off Main Street, was inside reading a book when she heard a gunshot that sounded close. Racing outside, she looked up Main, where she too saw the pickup behind the police car at the railroad tracks. She estimated five or more shots followed as the truck passed the car. Thigpen described the pickup as black in color with a spare tire mounted on the left side behind the cab door. When the patrol car swerved right and slammed into a tree in front of the vacant L&M Grocery Store, the pickup continued down the road before making a right turn and disappearing. Thigpen yelled for her daughter to call the police. She thought the sides of the bed of the pickup were six to twelve inches higher than a standard truck bed, but she didn't see sideboards.[16] Scraps Fornea didn't see sideboards either. And neither saw the shooters, although he thought the shooters fired from the cab. As Scraps reached the driver's door of the patrol car, he saw that the driver was dead. He went over to the passenger side where he recognized Creed Rogers, who told Scraps he didn't think he was hurt bad. Rogers had just reported the shooting over the police radio. Realizing that Moore was the driver, Scraps told Rogers that his partner was dead. Not sure whether the shooters would return, Rogers handed Scraps his handgun and pulled a shotgun from beneath the seat and handed it over. Scraps hid behind the big oak as Rogers slumped down in the seat playing dead, the body of Moore leaning against him.[17] Rogers would make two more calls on the radio.

After the first dispatch, Deputy Doyle Holliday was contacted about the shooting. As he headed for the scene, he heard Rogers over the radio: "WP-14 . . . I'm shot up bad and my partner appears dead." Holliday radioed a deputy to locate the sheriff.[18] At the sheriff's home, Dorman Crowe's wife, Helen, answered the phone. Their son Bobby, who would be elected sheriff decades later, heard his mother say, "Oh, my goodness!" She told Bobby that

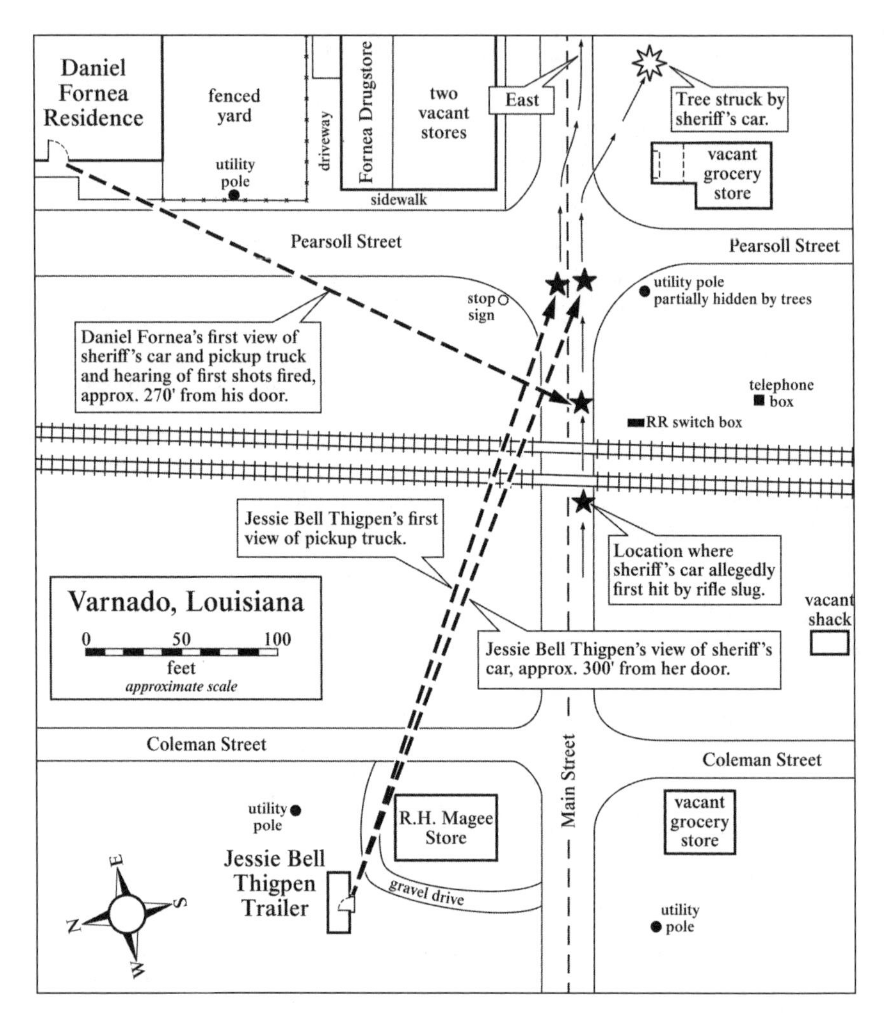

The crime scene

Oneal Moore was dead. Dorman was at his fishing camp on the Bogue Chitto near the town of Sun, which could be reached only by boat.[19]

Once at the scene, Holliday observed WP-14 rammed into a big oak tree. A Falstaff beer sign was nailed to the tree. By then Moore had been placed in the ambulance, and Holliday helped load the blood-soaked Rogers into another. Rogers was suffering from a bullet wound in the left shoulder. Glass shards were imbedded in his face, hands, and wrists from the impact with the windshield. He couldn't see at the time and would permanently lose sight in his right eye. Holliday asked Louisiana State Police officers and parish deputies to hold back the gathering onlookers while contacting a wrecker to remove the patrol car and a local photographer to make crime scene photos. A trooper handed Holliday five spent .30.06 cartridge hulls that had been picked up in the vicinity of the crash.[20]

Less than fifteen minutes after the ambush, the FBI was notified, and agents were quickly on the ground. Twenty-five minutes after that an off-duty Mississippi Highway Safety Patrol officer received a call from the Brookhaven substation. He was told to be on the lookout "for an old dark colored Chevrolet pickup with a rebel tag on the front."[21]

The patrolman relayed the report to Tylertown, located thirty-five miles northwest of Varnado in southern Mississippi above the Washington Parish / Louisiana line. Immediately, night marshal Vern Brumfield picked up Walthall County Sheriff's Office special deputy Jack Cantwell. They proceeded east on US 98 to the Magee's Creek Bridge when at 11:10 p.m.—less than an hour after the shooting—they observed a pickup fitting the description enter US 98 from Mississippi Highway 48. The driver ran a stop sign and proceeded west at speeds of sixty to sixty-five miles per hour. Brumfield turned around and chased the truck, pulling it over a half mile outside the town limits at Wynn's Texaco service station. The officers observed no vehicles proceeding or following the truck.[22]

They approached the pickup slowly and ordered the stranger out. The white man told the officers he had two weapons inside. His driver's license identified the suspect as forty-one-year-old Ernest Rayford McElveen of Bogalusa, an employee of Crown Zellerbach. He had brown hair, a three-inch scar on his right temple, and another on his right index finger.[23] Almost anyone who knew him knew he was a Klansman and a decorated World War II veteran, wounded in the Battle of Saipan in the Pacific.

The pickup, painted black and covered with several pitted rust spots, had 56,047 miles on the odometer and a half tank of gas. Inside were a .45 caliber Webley revolver and a .22 caliber automatic pistol, both fully loaded. There was spare ammunition for both guns, several .16 gauge shotgun shells, a walkie-talkie radio, electrical wiring, and firecrackers. An electrical device used to illegally electrocute fish was found hidden beneath the gas tank. A rifle cartridge clip, which appeared to be from a US Army M-1 Garand, was found on the seat.[24]

At the police station, McElveen emptied his personal belongings on the counter and was searched. His wallet contained twenty-eight dollars and membership cards for the Citizens' Council of Greater New Orleans, National States' Rights Party and National Rifle Association. Another card revealed that he was a special deputy for the Louisiana State Police effective November 8, 1962. After McElveen was placed in a cell, Brumfield heard the prisoner heaving and vomiting on three occasions. The toilet was flushed several times. McElveen washed his hands more than once. A good while later, he was photographed and fingerprinted and had paraffin wax impressions made of his hands.[25]

Over the course of several hours he was questioned. Where was he going? He wouldn't answer. Where had he been? He said a "secret meeting about 10 miles back," but would not describe the location.[26] He later told Deputy Holliday that he had spent most of the day at his fishing camp on Pushepatapa Creek in the State Line community in Washington Parish near the border with Mississippi, not far from Tylertown.[27] Asked if he was ill, he refused to answer. He complained of back pain.[28]

The pickup fit the description detailed by Creed Rogers. The spare tire was mounted on the truck bed behind the driver's seat just as Jessie Bell Thigpen said. But police were puzzled. Where were the wooden side panels? Mississippi Highway Safety Patrol investigators observed that "the body of the truck had four holes, one at each corner, for the placement of a stake body or side rails. Examination of these holes indicated that the inside of each was shiny, indicating that some kind of post or side rail had been inserted within the recent past."[29]

McElveen admitted his truck once had sideboards. When were they removed? He refused to answer. Law enforcement knew that McElveen could not have fired a weapon killing Moore and wounding Rogers while driving the pickup at the same time.

Who else had been in the pickup with him?

Where were they now?

McElveen was done talking and asked for a lawyer.[30]

In the hours after the shooting, US assistant attorney general John Doar, having been briefed on the assault, requested a full federal investigation. Information on the matter was furnished to the White House and the general counsel of the President's Council on Equal Opportunity.[31] From that point, things moved fast. An army of FBI agents was assigned to the case and in Washington, FBI director J. Edgar Hoover pressed the New Orleans field office to hit the ground aggressively, urging supervisors to "press vigorously."[32] Doar and legendary FBI case inspector Joe Sullivan were soon on the scene in Bogalusa, where Blacks were infuriated by the attack on the deputies. Officials feared this, along with Klan threats, would result in more violence on the city's streets.

By the end of the month, Doar and Justice Department attorneys were in US District Court in New Orleans filing injunctive proceedings against public officials in Bogalusa. In court, the feds showed a film revealing city law enforcement officers and Louisiana State Police troopers looking away as whites attacked pickets and demonstrators. Louisiana State Police superintendent Thomas Burbank saw the film in court and was incensed by the scenes. Inspector Sullivan wanted Burbank to have a copy and also thought it would be a good idea for the film to be used by FBI trainers for recruits because it "shows very clearly what can happen because of inaction by the police." With the uproar over the racial attack on the deputies, FBI agents, most from the North, were equally outraged: this was an attack on law enforcement. In hindsight, it appears it was the only Klan attack on Black deputies during the era.[33]

Among the first agents on the ground was Milton Graham, a thirty-one-year-old New York State native who was physically well suited for the job: he stood six feet, six inches, weighed 230 pounds, and had spent a decade playing professional football in Canada and in the United States after graduating with a degree in geology from Colgate University. After joining the FBI in 1964, Graham's first assignment was in Detroit before he was sent to New Orleans, where the bureau was still investigating the murder of President Kennedy and deeply involved in investigating Ku Klux Klan crimes and civil rights and voting rights violations and murders.[34] In Louisiana, there were several unresolved racial murders, including the killing of four sanitation employees gunned down by a Klan leader in Monroe in the northeastern part of the state in 1960. In 1964 in Concordia Parish, also in northeastern Louisiana, a shoe shop owner had been killed by arsonists in Ferriday, Louisiana, and a young Vidalia motel porter was kidnapped on the highway by policemen and Klansmen and hasn't been seen since that day more than a half century ago.

In recent years, Graham recalled that most Washington Parish Klansmen held down jobs and had served in the military: "They would not burn the flag and would fight for their country. But they were bigots, narrow minded and trashy in many cases, but some were intelligent," while only a "few were capable of killing and burning and beating people." Confrontations between agents and Klansmen were not common but happened. One Klansman ordered his dogs to attack Graham and another agent while another shot at their feet with a shotgun.[35] Agents dealt daily with taunts and veiled threats.

Agents were aware they were dealing with dangerous men, some who had no fear of the federal government. They found themselves in a fight with a well-organized Klan that had transitioned from a large political organization in 1962 to a much smaller one in 1965 that considered violence the only means to preserve white supremacy. The Klan had met its match in Bogalusa, where strong local Black leadership followed by fearless activists took on Klansmen in the streets as they pushed for civil rights. Bogalusa had been in crisis for months and had captured the attention of the nation. A federal court in New Orleans would determine that Washington Parish since its formation had been "segregated from cradle to coffin."[36] When Congress passed the 1964 Civil Rights Act, the Black organization known as the Bogalusa Voters and Civic League launched an aggressive campaign demanding that local officials recognize their constitutional rights. Black activists held voter registration drives and picketed businesses that refused to provide them equal service and accommodations. They also petitioned Bogalusa officials to end the city's discriminatory policies.

While Bogalusa had long been in the spotlight, the countryside of Washington Parish was a different environment. In many of the small towns and communities families, white and Black, lived in poverty and isolation. Many were uneducated. Some lived in shacks that had no indoor plumbing or electricity. Computers and cell phones didn't exist, and not everyone had a landline phone inside the home. Newspapers, magazines, and television were the only outlets for news. Many didn't have access to transportation. They lived along dirt and gravel roads in forested hills and lowlands, pathways that weren't marked on maps. For months, through intimidation and threats, the Klan had owned these communities. Most everyone was afraid.

Urgent teletype messages were exchanged between the New Orleans and Jackson, Mississippi, field offices and FBI director J. Edgar Hoover throughout the night of the murder and for days to come. A look into the FBI's files reveals that McElveen had been on the bureau's radar for a number of years. In 1959, Sheriff Crowe and other local law officers had told agents that McElveen and his friend Saxon Farmer, a Conoco Oil distributing agent who owned a gas station in Bogalusa, were "sufficiently anti-Negro" to be considered logical suspects in the murder of Mack Charles Walker across the Pearl River in Poplarville, Mississippi. Crowe said numerous Black men had complained to him that Farmer had beaten them because they were unable to settle debts Farmer claimed they owed.[37] Also in 1959, McElveen and Farmer had led the local effort by the parish white Citizens' Council in purging hundreds of Blacks from the Washington Parish voting rolls, part of a plan to strip Sheriff Crowe of Black support in his reelection bid against the Klan's candidate. Federal District Judge Christenberry in New Orleans would opine that Farmer "seems to have an uncanny capacity for being present whenever there is racial trouble" in Bogalusa.[38]

Additionally, Bogalusa police reported that in early summer of 1954 McElveen and two other men, all armed, had kidnapped a man and forced a "shotgun" wedding with their relative, whom they claimed was pregnant with the man's child. Both McElveen and the others were charged with simple battery and simple kidnapping, but the victim later dropped the charges. McElveen claimed it was simply a "family matter." In 1962, McElveen served as president of the parish Citizens' Council, and informants told the FBI he "had a high degree of potential for violence." By 1963, McElveen was a member of the Original Knights of the Ku Klux Klan.[39]

A coroner's hearing on June 3, the day after the Moore murder, determined he died as a result of gunshot wounds to the head and left shoulder from a .30.06 rifle.[40] The FBI investigation would determine that a shotgun was used in the ambush as well. On that same day, a murder warrant was issued in Washington Parish charging McElveen with Moore's murder. Louisiana governor John J. McKeithen dispatched Colonel Thomas Burbank, head of the Louisiana State Police, to Washington Parish along with a squad of troopers. McKeithen had been involved behind the scenes trying to bring peace to Bogalusa and convince radical whites that no good would come from attacking civil rights marchers. The governor also called Joe Sylvester Jr., assistant special agent in charge of the New Orleans field office, to ask that he come to Baton Rouge to talk about the case. But the governor was told Sylvester was too busy and that the FBI "was conducting a full investigation" and was "not in a position to furnish any facts . . . at this time."[41] The two men did, however, meet at the Bogalusa airport on June 5 when McKeithen arrived for a press conference.

In a message marked "urgent" to the FBI director from the New Orleans office, Sylvester outlined McKeithen's comments. Sylvester was the number two man at the New Orleans field office and was admired by the agents he supervised. The document provides a clear picture of McKeithen's understanding of the reality of the situation and his personal desire to solve the murder quickly, a task he felt only the FBI capable of achieving. McKeithen arrived in Bogalusa shortly before 6:00 p.m., where he was greeted at his plane by Sheriff Crowe, Deputy Holliday, and District Attorney Woodrow "Squinch" Erwin. The governor asked Sylvester and Colonel Burbank to join him and the local officials for a brief conference. McKeithen advised that the state would offer a $25,000 reward for information leading to the apprehension and conviction of the murderers of Moore. Looking at each of the lawmen assembled, he said he wanted evidence promptly gathered and the guilty party prosecuted. But he said with confidence that only the FBI and Burbank had the training and expertise to resolve the case. Afterward, he pulled Sylvester to the side and asked for assurance that the FBI was making the case a top priority. Upon reading the teletype at his office in Washington, DC, Hoover underlined this part of the report and noted in the margin: "We will look after our own responsibilities & don't need the governor's stimulations." McKeithen told Sylvester he didn't want what happened in Georgia, Mississippi, and Alabama to happen in Louisiana. In those states, the governor said, arrests had been made in racial cases, but convictions were not forthcoming. Sylvester assured the governor that the FBI was working to solve the case with all the might of the federal government.[42]

Before the press conference, McKeithen made an intriguing comment to reporters that he had made a "secret trip" to Bogalusa two days before the murder to persuade unidentified white residents that "the course they were pursuing could lead only to disaster." For months, McKeithen said, Bogalusa had been "in a racial uproar," and there was a dangerous chance of "open warfare" between whites and Blacks. He thought progress was being made, only to see the two Black deputies attacked in the shadows of Bogalusa.[43] Who was at the secret meeting? FBI files released for the first time in 2018 would reveal that McKeithen was in the company of some of the very men who would become suspects in the murder. But because of the FBI's standard tight-lip stance, the governor may never have known this.

The *Times-Picayune* quoted McKeithen as saying that the state was shocked "by the dastardly, heinous, cowardly deed. . . . The murder of this officer of the law and the attempted murder of his associate is a blot on our history and a disgrace to us all. The sad, sad part of it is that a few, just a very few, misguided souls were determined to wreck us all. . . . The guilty parties shall be found. They shall be brought to justice and we shall demonstrate to the world that Louisianans are law-abiding, God-fearing citizens and that our state is no haven for cowards and murderers."[44]

The newspaper also reported that Moore's wife, Maevella, who had heard the shots that killed her husband, said Oneal "loved his job" as a deputy and was dedicated to his family. Her four daughters—ages nine months to nine years—"will never see their daddy again. They just don't quite understand." Among the visitors to the Moore home was Archbishop John P. Cody of the Catholic archdiocese of New Orleans. He also visited Creed Rogers in the hospital. "If every Louisiana citizen could have visited the widow of Deputy Moore and their four children as I did and look into the eyes of Deputy Rogers there would be no further violence," he told the paper. "No man with human feelings could stand before these people and not be moved to compassion."[45]

Reporters John Fahey, Joseph A. Lucia, and Wiley S. Masters Jr. of the *Times-Picayune* filed several stories about the investigation and covered the funeral, reporting that 450 attended, although many were unable to get inside the packed building. Heavy rain poured beginning at 2:10 p.m. and "sent those outside the church scurrying for shelter." A hailstorm greeted the cortege at the cemetery located a mile from the church, the rain falling so hard that it flooded several streets in Bogalusa six miles to the south. "Sheriff Crowe," the paper reported, "who angered the Ku Klux Klan last year by hiring the two Negro deputies, stood outside during the services." With Crowe were two members of his staff as well as the ten-member all-white delegation from the National Council of Churches.[46]

Messages of condolences came in from across the country. The national leader of the Congress of Racial Equality (CORE), James Farmer, attended the service but did not speak. Later, he called Moore a "a casualty of hate and his death the Klan's bloody answer" to demands that the city of Bogalusa hire Black police officers. Pastor Rev. A. I. Owens told the congregation that Moore "enjoyed a wonderful reputation in the community. He successfully held many offices in the church because he was a Christian gentleman. He was devoted to his family and lived for them." Born across the Pearl River in Poplarville, Mississippi, Moore had grown up in the White Sand community, where he had been involved in church activities since his youth. He served as president of the Jones Creek PTA and had served in Germany and France during his service in the US Army from 1952 to 1954. He and Maevella Nichols were married on August 15, 1954, in the church where his funeral service was held.[47] In 2018, looking back on their life, Maevella recalled that they had met as teenagers and had a long courtship. He was a "good kisser," she said, and "so handsome . . . a good husband."[48]

The printed obituary distributed at his services noted: "He was employed June 1, 1964, by the Washington Parish Sheriff's Department under the leadership of Sheriff Dorman Crowe. He served well his host of duties and was admired, respected and deeply appreciated by those who really knew him." Moore had kissed his wife twice before he left for work on the evening of the murder and by all indications was "happy and at peace" with his life.[49]

Two days after the shooting, on June 4, Sheriff Crowe and Deputy Holliday transported McElveen from Tylertown to the two-story parish jail in Franklinton. The *Times-Picayune* reported that McElveen's wife, Doris, was waiting for her husband when he arrived at the courthouse. McElveen's civil attorney, John Gallaspy, told the paper that the suspect "seemed in good spirits" and "expressed concern for his family." Gallaspy said McElveen denied involvement in the murder and was in Tylertown on the night of his arrest to see a doctor about severe back pain.[50] McElveen claimed to have spent the afternoon working at his camp in northern Washington Parish, not far from Tylertown. But the FBI quickly found McElveen's doctor, who reported his patient had not made an appointment or contacted him in any way.[51] McElveen would soon get a new lawyer, his third in three days. Ossie Brown, who seven years later would be elected district attorney of East Baton Rouge Parish, is mentioned in FBI investigative files as having Klan connections and sympathies.

Hours later, the FBI's Sylvester was awakened by an agent in Bogalusa with news that an attempt had been made on Deputy Holliday's life, an attack that also endangered his family. After forty-eight hours with little sleep, Holliday was sitting in the living room with his family when he heard an explosion. Two days earlier Oneal Moore had thought the first shot fired by his attackers was the sound of the car backfiring. Holliday thought the first shot he heard was from also from a car backfiring until he heard "gas escaping from an air-conditioner that had been hit." That was followed by five additional shots. Holiday grabbed his magnum revolver, ran outside and shot six times at a fleeing vehicle. It was too far away for him to identify its make or the number of occupants or whether his bullets connected. The taillight on the car led him to believe it was a 1958 Chevrolet or a 1957 Pontiac, but he was uncertain. A half hour or so after the shooting, Holliday's son answered the ringing phone in the house that would soon fill up with FBI agents. The caller said, "Did we get you?" Holliday's son initially thought the caller was a teenager disguising his voice. FBI agents pulled slugs from the house that appeared to be from a small-caliber firearm. Soon this shooting was made a part of the FBI's Oneal Moore murder investigation.[52] Were Klansmen angered that Holliday and the sheriff's office were actively involved in probing the murder? Were the sheriff and other deputies at risk as well?

Earlier in the day, as FBI agents covered Washington Parish from top to bottom, Creed Rogers was transferred from the Bogalusa Medical Center to the Flint Goodrich Hospital in New Orleans, where state police guarded his room. Dr. George Ellis reported that Rogers had "sustained injuries from a gunshot to the extent that included lacerations of the left wrist, scalp, face and a rifle wound in the right shoulder. He had a head injury and contusions of the right eye with severe intraocular hemorrhage and a detachment of the retina." He couldn't be moved and would remain hospitalized for weeks. That meant the only eyewitness was unable to testify before a grand jury any time soon.[53]

Rogers never got over the attack. He felt guilty that he survived and realized that had it been his week to drive the patrol car he would have been dead. Over the weeks to come Rogers would be interviewed multiple times by the FBI. He would ride the route he and Moore had taken the night of the murder and would return to the crime scene, where he would become so emotional that the agents transported him home. He would in time return to the sheriff's office, from which he would retire decades later. Over the years many individuals offered Rogers their unsolicited thoughts on the murder and the people they suspected.

Rogers and Moore felt indebted to Sheriff Crowe for choosing them to serve as the parish's first Black deputies. Unknown until the FBI files were released in 2018 was the fact that Crowe, once he hired the two men, would stand behind them firmly despite constant attempts by the Klan to get them fired. Newspapers in the parish provide a clear picture of how Crowe came to be elected sheriff of the parish in 1948 and remained there longer than anyone to this day. For three straight elections, from 1956 to 1964, the Klan would back the same candidate each time to bring Crowe down. But Klansmen couldn't do it even though they came ever so close on two occasions. When Crowe gave two Black men the power of an officer of the law in 1964, the Klan couldn't believe it even though Crowe had promised he would do just that following his 1963–64 reelection campaign. As much as the killer Klansmen despised Moore and Rogers, they had a bitter hatred for Crowe. How could a white man give a Black man law enforcement authority over whites?

There would be constant dead ends for a half century, and two dozen suspects would emerge, but to the credit of the FBI, the bureau followed every lead and every trail.

It would be an epic investigation.

"SETTING OFF A TIME BOMB"

On June 3, 1965, the day after the attack on the deputies, FBI agents quickly fanned out across Washington Parish in search of related evidence and witnesses to the ambush. They sought to learn everything about Ray McElveen, beginning with his activities on the day of the murder. His Klan past would offer many leads, providing the bureau a sense of the depth of McElveen's passion for white supremacy. Although there had been other cases of Klan violence in Louisiana, this attack on law enforcement was intolerable to the FBI and in Washington at the bureau's headquarters, Director J. Edgar Hoover pushed the New Orleans field office for quick resolution. In Louisiana, Governor John J. McKeithen had early on made it clear to law enforcement, including the FBI, that he wanted the case solved immediately, and he told the press the same. FBI agents in the field were particularly incensed that their brothers in law enforcement had been targeted. Agents would work multiple hours of overtime investigating this case during the immediate years after the attack from 1965 through 1967. They never complained.

In the months leading up to the attack on the deputies, the *Bogalusa Daily News* published stories reporting nocturnal attacks believed executed by Klan nightriders. One occurred on April 12 when twenty-eight-year-old Jerry J. Varnado of Bogalusa, a white man who had recently separated from his wife, was abducted while leaving his apartment. In a front-page story headlined "Bogalusa Man Is Beaten by 3 Black-Hooded Men," the newspaper reported the kidnappers forced Varnado into a car, drove him to a secluded place on Crown-Zellerbach property and whipped him.[1] Klan hit squads—known as wrecking crews—were directed by their leaders to attack African Americans primarily because of their skin color or civil rights activity, but they were also told to attack whites. Immorality—ranging from drinking too much to not properly providing for their families—was the common allegation behind the attacks, especially on poor white men, some who suffered from alcoholism. These attacks were as old as the Klan and designed to create fear and in some cases to engender obedience from impoverished or ignorant whites. Some victims threatened by the Klan showed agents copies of letters they received. Each contained the identical message: "In consideration of your family welfare and decent support we have investigated this matter and find neglect on your part. You better get a job and give decent support or you will have to suffer a price you won't like. Unless you go to work soon you will be seeing us. You are being watched."[2]

Varnado was told he was being punished for neglecting his family, but he told the newspaper he was a working man who was on his way to his job when abducted. Notably, he didn't accept the Klan's judgment without a fight. As the newspaper went to press, it reported that Bogalusa police and Washington Parish Sheriff's Office deputies were interviewing Varnado. But several details of the beating were not provided to the *Daily News.*[3]

Interviewed after the murder of Oneal Moore, Varnado told FBI agents that when the three hooded men attempted to force him into their car, he punched one in the face so hard with his fist that it knocked the man to the ground. In return, Varnado was struck in the head by the butt of a pistol and knocked unconscious. At the beating site, Varnado was forced to lie across the hood of his abductor's car. While two men pointed pistols at each side of his head, the third man beat him with what felt like a strap or piece of hose. Unlike many victims, Varnado reported the incident to the authorities. Because the men wore hoods, he did not see their faces and did not recognize their voices. But police had an idea of who may have been involved. While at the police station one of two suspects had a black eye. Varnado told the FBI that police identified the man as Ray McElveen. No charges were ever filed.[4]

Although McElveen resided in Bogalusa, he had friends and family in the northern and central portion of the parish, where he spent part of his childhood. He was born in the parish seat of Franklinton in 1923. His parents were Diaz Dewitt McElveen Sr. and Lena Sumrall McElveen. McElveen was the youngest of three children. Diaz was self-employed as a farmer and merchant. By 1930, when McElveen was six, the family lived in Orange, Texas, where Diaz worked as the manager at a bag factory and Lena was a billing clerk. A few years later, the family had returned to Washington Parish to Bogalusa when a fourth child was born. For many years, Diaz and Lena operated the Credit Bureau of Bogalusa. Diaz kept close ties with family in the Franklinton area, a place son Ray visited regularly throughout his life. Diaz had a reputation as a staunch segregationist and as a drinker.[5]

Friends and family members said McElveen had remained under his father's influence until Diaz's death in 1967. A bar owner in Bogalusa whose establishment was frequented by Diaz said that one rarely saw the father without the son and that when Ray was not with Diaz, he was usually alone.[6] In 1943, McElveen was inducted into the US Marines. At the time, he was working at a cotton gin. FBI agents took note of McElveen's service specialty: he was an automatic rifleman. In 1944, he was shot in the shoulder in Saipan. For his action on the battlefield, he was awarded a Purple Heart, a Gold Star, and a Presidential Citation.[7]

Known by some of his Bogalusa neighbors as a quiet man, few knew him well. He attended the Presbyterian Church, was involved in a few veteran organizations, and attended most military celebrations and ceremonies. One neighbor called him mild mannered. A friend said he was a good father. But McElveen had another side. Other neighbors and coworkers said he was nervous and sickly. One saw him walking along the highway near the town of Varnado in the middle of the night. When the acquaintance pulled over to ask if he was okay, McElveen said he was fine, just unable to sleep. On many occasions, due to his nervous disposition, he was seen running in a field near his home. He told those who inquired that he was simply relieving tension.[8] For years, McElveen had suffered from severe stomach pain. He was treated at the Ochsner clinic in New Orleans over a three-year period until February 1965, four months before the shooting of the deputies, when he underwent surgery for an ulcer and the removal of his appendix.[9] McElveen told coworkers that more than 60 percent of his stomach had been removed. But the stomach pain continued. Two weeks before the attack on the deputies, he sought a doctor's care in Bogalusa. In the weeks before the murder, he was treated twice in Tylertown for a low back condition.[10] A relative told agents that McElveen might at times have been overmedicated. He drank beer and smoked cigarettes.

McElveen also had multiple problems relating to his war injury. Before his discharge from the marines, he told doctors he suffered from shortness of breath and pains in his chest. He complained that he could no longer perform certain physical activities that he found easy prior to joining the marines. The gunshot to the shoulder in Saipan also fractured three ribs and caused bleeding around his lungs, causing the Veterans Administration to grant him a 50 percent disability, amounting to $144 monthly.[11] In addition to his job at Crown-Zellerbach, McElveen also sold home, fire, and casualty insurance out of his residence on Border Drive. When applying for his insurance license in

1956, he listed fifty-eight-year-old Saxon Farmer, a Klan leader and member of the white Citizens' Council, as a character reference.[12]

McElveen was known for his extreme segregationist views, especially concerning politics. If a candidate were not emphatic and vocal in his opposition to integration, McElveen would not only vote against the candidate but would actively campaign against him. The co-owner of a car dealership in Bogalusa told FBI agents that McElveen was so violently opposed to integration that almost everyone but Klansmen avoided discussing the matter with him. When the Rotary Club scheduled Louisiana labor leader Victor Bussie, head of the state's AFI-CIO, as a speaker, the Klan was outraged. In the Klan world, some unions were too sympathetic to integration. McElveen demanded the club cancel the speech. A Marine Corps League functions, McElveen got into heated and loud arguments with others over segregation. He seethed with rage when anyone voiced openness to integration.[13]

He often tried to seed racial hatred and vowed that the league would never allow Blacks to join. One businessman told the bureau that McElveen was "one of the most radical elements" in town.[14] Many remembered that he had gone to Oxford with other Klansmen in 1962 to oppose the enrollment of African American James Meredith into the University of Mississippi. During spring of 1965, while he was recovering from surgery and not working, he was seen sitting in his pickup on Columbia Street as white men, mostly Klansmen, did all they could to disrupt peaceful civil rights marches and demonstrations. In the back of his pickup were several teenagers singing "Alligator Bait" as marchers walked by.[15]

The FBI found sources and informants in the Klan who said that McElveen was not one to discuss his personal affairs. If ever asked, "Did you do it?" concerning the murder of Moore, he would neither confirm nor deny it. There would be little or no response, which in part would explain his refusal to answer a few questions from law enforcement on the night of his arrest. At a meeting of the Original Knights Unit 1 in Bogalusa three days before the Moore murder, McElveen distributed literature by radical conservative Robert Welch, the founder of the John Birch Society who advanced various conspiracy theories with communists at the center. McElveen also said at the meeting that a future speaker would inform the Klan how to start its own newspaper.[16] Klansmen despised the *Bogalusa Daily News* and its publisher, Lou Major, who consistently criticized the Klan and, consequently, he was threatened by Klansmen many times, including by burning crosses in his yard. Major was also among a handful of white men who urged white Bogalusans to accept the changes that were coming through federal civil rights legislation, but he also thought the presence of CORE was inflaming racial tensions in town.

A Louisiana State University (LSU) journalism graduate, Major had joined the local newspaper in 1951 as a cub reporter. Over the years, he was promoted many times until he was named publisher in 1963. On April 20, 1964, a few days after Klansmen abducted and beat Jerry Varnado, the *Daily News*'s most read story of the day was headlined: "Klansmen Threaten Daily News Publisher: Reporter Is Beaten." The story noted that Major had been warned the night before that he would be assaulted unless he left the state. Journalist Bob Wagner, a correspondent for WDSU, a radio and television outlet in Baton Rouge, issued the Klan warning. Wagner had been working on a documentary about the Klan with Robert Schaefer of United Press International when the men located thirty armed Klansmen meeting in a well-guarded farmhouse in a heavily wooded area near Jackson in East Feliciana Parish. As Wagner alone filmed while hidden in a grove of trees, a Klansman suddenly stuck a pistol in Wagner's back and told him to kneel. Placing the barrel of the pistol between Wagner's eyes, the man said, "You've reported your last story." But instead of shooting, he called some of the other men over. They took Wagner's camera, and several men took turns beating him with a leather strap. For a while, they held him in a dog cage mounted in the back of a pickup. The younger men in the group wanted to kill him, but the older ones ruled against it. They knew Schaefer was waiting nearby in his car but decided to let him go. Wagner was released. He reported the beating to police and said the Klansmen told him to pass along a warning to Lou Major that he would "get the same" unless he left Louisiana.[17]

Two weeks before the ambush of the Black deputies, McElveen had traveled to Covington to speak with the publisher of the *Mandeville Bantam* about starting a second newspaper in Bogalusa. McElveen and the men with him said the *Daily News* gave too much space to the "nigger agitators." The publisher also told FBI agents that McElveen discussed guns, mentioning that he "had a carbine and preferred that weapon to all others." One week before the murder, McElveen attended a Klan meeting with representatives of the White Knights of Mississippi who were interested in bringing Bogalusa Klansmen into their fold. McElveen's friend Saxon Farmer presided over the meeting. McElveen, dressed in a black robe and armed with a .45 caliber automatic pistol, served as an inner guard.[18]

Another white man in Bogalusa who took a stand that outraged McElveen and the Klan was a forty-four-year-old Arkansas native, Ralph Blumberg, who moved to Bogalusa in 1961 to purchase the local radio station, WBOX, which played country music and counted Klansmen among its listeners. In the fall of 1964, Blumberg, local attorney Bascom Talley, and publisher Lou Major were among a small group of white men that thought it would be a good idea to invite Brooks Hays, a former Arkansas congressman, to address an interracial meeting about the newly passed Civil Rights Act of 1964, specifically the integration of public accommodations. Hays served as head of a federal agency created to help southern communities accept and adapt to the changes. Because this was to be a federally sanctioned meeting, it had to be open to all races. The local group thought that because Hays had once served as president of the Southern Baptist Convention white citizens would hear him out. The group advised Mayor Jesse H. Cutrer Jr. that they were seeking support from town officials, professionals, and businesses to attend the Hays meeting in December. The mayor told them he feared the Klan would violently object but agreed to support the visit.[19]

Among the officials meeting with the local group was city attorney Robert T. Rester, who also secretly served as exalted cyclops (head) of one of the Klan units in Bogalusa. Rester dutifully leaked details of the mayor's meeting to fellow Klansmen. Two hours later the pastor of the Episcopal Church, where the meeting was to be held, was approached by a Klansman who proclaimed the meeting was a mistake. Soon it was apparent that no public official in town and no local business or church in the white community would host the venue in fear of the Klan. The Klan seized on the issue to galvanize white support in Bogalusa as activists prepared to test the new civil rights law beginning in January 1965. If white people attended the Hays meeting, a Klan pamphlet claimed, then they would be showing their support for total segregation, just as they would "by sitting in church with the black man, hiring more of them in your cafes, and allowing your children to sit by filthy runny-nosed, ragged, ugly little niggers in your public schools." Cutrer feared the Klan was preparing to hit the streets violently in the days ahead. To avoid trouble, he met with Klansmen at the Disabled Veterans Hall attended by 150 robed and hooded white men. He accomplished nothing and would acknowledge that he was terrified looking into "150 pairs of eyes." The Brooks Hays meeting was canceled.[20]

But Blumberg didn't cower. In early 1965 he editorialized on the Hays affair and said the new civil rights law had to be complied with. These words, he told the House Un-American Activities Committee investigating the Klan in 1966, had the effect of "setting off a time bomb." Immediately, threatening calls came in to his home and radio station. There were death threats against him and his family. A man came to the radio station and harassed his wife. His car windows were smashed. Tacks thrown in the driveway ruined his tires. Blumberg sent his wife and children to stay with family outside the state. Someone fired a volley of bullets into the radio station's transmission tower. A Klan economic boycott against his station had reduced him to near poverty by March when his seventy-five traditional advertisers eroded to six. Outside donors kept him going for a short while. Blumberg told the House Un-American Activities Committee that ultimately this was a battle for freedom of speech and the Klan knew that if it could control politicians and the media the segregation battle would be won. He tried to reason with Klansmen but finally concluded that he could not "compromise with the devil . . . because there is no compromise with this sort of evil." Bogalusa officials, he told the committee, so feared the Klan that they would take no action without first considering how Klansmen would respond.[21]

Following surgery for his stomach ulcer in February 1965, McElveen had been on sick leave until three days before the murder. He returned to work at Crown-Zellerbach on Monday, May 31. Two days later, on Wednesday, he completed his eight-hour shift around 2:00 p.m.[22] The chemical plant manager, McElveen's boss, told the FBI he overheard McElveen telling others that he planned to spend the afternoon at his fishing camp located at the northern end of the parish near the Louisiana-Mississippi border in a community known as State Line.[23] McElveen's unfinished camp on Pushepatapa Creek stood on poles approximately ten feet off the ground and consisted of one big room. There was no plumbing or electricity.[24] Ever since he bought three acres for the campsite in 1962, he had spent as much time as he could fishing in the creek. He told people the camp offered him a peaceful haven from Bogalusa. McElveen also told his mother he was going to the camp on the day of the deputy's murder.[25]

Around noon, McElveen's eldest son and a friend delivered a small load of building material to the campsite. They left Bogalusa in McElveen's pickup, stopping for gas along the way. It was a forty-five-minute drive from Bogalusa to State Line. What was a simple errand took much longer than expected because the gate to the campsite was locked and the boys didn't have the combination. Unable to find help, they eventually removed the hinge pins and took the gate off the fence, drove the pickup up to the camp, and unloaded the material. Hot and thirsty, they drank water from the creek. By the time they got back to Bogalusa, it was around 3:00 p.m. The friend said the truck didn't have sideboards. And he also recalled there was no walkie-talkie in the truck. (One of the two receivers was found in McElveen's truck upon his apprehension hours later in Tylertown.) The friend said he saw the pickup at 7:30 p.m. at the McElveen residence, but hours later, when he drove by around 10:00 p.m. the pickup was gone. He did not see McElveen that day.[26] A friend of one of McElveen's younger sons said he was at the house during the early afternoon. He didn't see McElveen either. Another friend said McElveen once asked him if he "liked the Klan." The boy said he didn't answer and McElveen dropped the subject. But the child also volunteered an interesting piece of information. He said the McElveen boys had purchased the walkie-talkies in May and recalled that they had a range of half a mile.[27] This news resulted in two questions for investigators. Where was the other handheld receiver? Did McElveen use it to communicate with accomplices in another vehicle working with him on the night of the attack on the deputies?

Only three witnesses reported seeing McElveen—ironically around the same time of the afternoon—and all said he was in his pickup. S. D. Crain told the bureau that around 4:00 or 4:30 p.m. he was walking home along a road near Varnado when McElveen and his eldest son offered him a ride to his house. He said both McElveen and his son were laughing and relaxed. The man had no doubt that new unpainted sideboards were mounted on the pickup bed.[28] But a friend and relative of McElveen's, Albert Burt, who operated a service station in Bogalusa, said McElveen came by sometime between 2:00 and 5:00 p.m., guessing it was close to 4:00 p.m. He said McElveen's gas tank was empty. He filled it up and purchased a quart of oil. While the attendant at the station said McElveen stayed about twenty minutes, Burt said McElveen stayed possibly as long as an hour, sitting in the rocking chair inside. Neither Burt nor his attendant observed sideboards on the truck.[29]

McElveen had spent time shortly before the murder ensuring his old pickup was running its best. He had the Chevrolet dealership in Bogalusa remove and replace the spark plugs because, he told a mechanic, the engine was sputtering. A day or two before the murder, he brought the truck in again for an adjustment to the brake cylinder.[30] From the time he left work at 2:00 p.m. until he was arrested at Tylertown nine hours later, only three witnesses—

the hitchhiker, the gas station owner, and his attendant—reported seeing him between the time he left work and the time he was arrested. Hours after his arrest at Tylertown, McElveen told Deputy Holliday that he had been at his camp on that afternoon and injured his back during a fall. McElveen suggested he was racing through Tylertown trying to find his doctor, but his doctor told agents he had not heard from him.[31] The FBI would find no evidence McElveen had been to his camp that afternoon although he told coworkers and family that that was where he would be. Was he establishing an alibi?

One friend of the boys at the McElveen's home that day said that at 2:00 p.m., a tall slender man in his early thirties arrived alone in McElveen's white Ford. The boy left the house and returned around 3:30 p.m., and the tall man, who had a deep voice, was still there but McElveen was not. The bureau was never able to identify that man with certainty but believed he may have been involved in the ambush.[32] More intriguing tips came in. A sergeant with the Bogalusa Police Department said a confidential source told him that McElveen's wife, Doris, had called one or more men at the paper mill the day before the murder asking them to attend a meeting at the McElveen home that night.[33]

New Orleans pathologist Dr. A. B. Friedrichs, with Washington Parish coroner Dr. H. A. Stafford looking on, performed the autopsy on Moore on the afternoon of June 4 at Richmond Funeral Home in Bogalusa. The left side of the skull was "completely fragmented," with two small pieces of lead embedded in bone. The left side of the brain was gone. A piece of glass one-fourth inch in diameter was removed from the right side of the brain, where much of the skull was cracked but intact. Friedrichs ventured that either a high-powered rifle or a shotgun blast at short range caused the immense destruction. Bullets also penetrated Moore's upper left arm and left shoulder blade.[34] Three bullets entered the patrol car's trunk bed from the rear, one entered the rear bumper, and a fifth struck the rear bumper but did not penetrate. Lead buckshot was found in a hole in the left rear door window frame. Fragments of copper jacketed bullets were found in the trunk and interior, while steel core fragments from a high-powered armor-piercing rifle bullet were found on the rear floor and near the emergency brake. Creed Rogers's gunshot wound was caused by a rifle bullet. Twenty-three residents in Varnado told agents they heard the shots from their homes but did not see the shooting. Some described the first shot as the loudest.[35]

While a shotgun was used in the attack, multiple bullets were fired from a military rifle, specifically a .30 caliber. Agents sought the opinion of Benjamin Miller, a respected antique gun collector in Bogalusa with knowledge of military weapons and ammunition. Shown photos of Moore's autopsy, Miller believed the massive head wound was caused by a shotgun blast fired at close range, while a rifle bullet caused the wound to the left arm.[36] The bureau determined the ammunition used in the rifle was .30.06. All five rifle cartridges found at the murder scene were fired from the same weapon. Each was headstamped with a code that denoted the year it was made. The Winchester Division of Olin Matheson Corporation in St. Louis, Missouri, manufactured three of the cartridges in 1956. These had been loaded with copper-jacketed armor-piercing .30 caliber bullets. The other two cartridges, manufactured in 1953, were originally loaded with cooper-coated steel-jacketed bullets with lead cores, commonly known as "ball" ammunition. Markings on the cartridges suggested they were fired from an M-1 Garand with a rifling of two lands and two grooves. A bullet when fired is given a spinning motion by the spiral grooves cut inside the barrel. The raised metal between the grooves is called a "land." A hole in a hollow-point bullet enables it to expand when it strikes a target, while a copper-jacketed bullet is one that enables greater penetration into a target. An empty cartridge clip found in McElveen's pickup was from a US Army M-1 Garand. The two handguns found in McElveen's truck—a .455 caliber Webley Mark VI revolver loaded with six cartridges and a Hi-Standard "Sport King" semiautomatic pistol with clip and twelve cartridges—were not used in the shooting, the FBI determined. Additionally, because McElveen had washed his hands—at least three times prior to being fingerprinted and before paraffin casts were made—no significant residue was discovered on hands.[37]

On June 7, McElveen's attorney, Ossie Brown of Baton Rouge, filed a motion for a preliminary hearing asking that his client be discharged and released on bond. A vocal segregationist who represented Klansmen in a federal suit in New Orleans, Brown would go on to serve two terms as the elected district attorney of East Baton Rouge Parish. He would also gain national attention when representing one of the defendants in the My Lai Massacre in Vietnam. On June 9, Brown filed an application for habeas corpus, claiming McElveen was being held illegally and that there was a lack of sufficient evidence to hold him. The judge ordered the sheriff to have McElveen in court on June 15 and told the district attorney to be prepared to respond. But on June 11, District

Attorney Woodrow Erwin told the bureau he had reached an agreement with Brown to release McElveen on $25,000 bond, which McElveen was having difficulty raising.[38]

Erwin had two main witnesses. One was Scraps Fornea, the first on the scene at the shooting. Fornea was prepared to testify, but the other key witness, one of the two victims in the ambush, was not. Creed Rogers was still in the hospital. His doctor said he could completely lose use of his right eye if he was moved before surgery. Rogers was also suffering from the rifle wound to the right shoulder and lacerations of the left wrist, scalp. and face caused when his head collided with the windshield on impact.[39]

Moving forward with a grand jury, however, presented Erwin with a major problem: Rogers could not identify the man driving the truck as McElveen, nor had anyone else been linked to the murder although suspects were emerging. Erwin told the bureau he was looking for a means to deny Brown's request for a preliminary hearing and hoping Rogers's inability to testify would give the DA more time. But Brown contended that Rogers could give a sworn statement from his hospital bed. Erwin preferred a grand jury indictment but under law "it would be necessary to either move on the writ of habeas corpus or for an immediate preliminary hearing or permit McElveen to get out on bond."[40]

The DA asked the FBI whether McElveen's release would affect its probe. The bureau remained as taciturn as McElveen, telling Erwin that this was his decision alone. Considering the situation, Erwin advised that Judge Jim Warren Richardson release McElveen on a $25,000 bond.[41] On June 11, several well-wishers were on hand at the courthouse to greet McElveen. The *Times-Picayune* ran a photo of McElveen and Brown outside the courthouse after he posted bond. Erwin told the paper that "the boy [McElveen] is ill and our principal witness [Deputy Rogers] is in the hospital and will have another operation Monday, so we agreed to the bond."[42] McElveen soon headed home to Bogalusa a free man. Of the thirteen individuals who put up the bail money, McElveen's Klan friend Saxon Farmer accounted for the most, $10,180, almost 70 percent of the total.[43]

In mid-June, agents knocked on Farmer's door on the outskirts of Bogalusa. A short, ornery man, Farmer stood in the doorway holding an infant he identified as his grandchild. He told agents that if they wanted to talk to him they would need a warrant for his arrest, adding that he wouldn't talk even then unless his attorney was present. Agents explained they didn't have a warrant but were seeking any information he might have in connection with the murder of Oneal Moore. But Farmer said he knew nothing and that as far as he was concerned Moore's death was little more than hearsay because he didn't go to the funeral and therefore had not seen a body.[44] For months, Farmer had been the public face of the Klan, particularly in Bogalusa. He spoke at Klan rallies and had raced to city hall to berate the mayor when the Klan felt local officials were giving in to Black demands. But many Klansmen didn't like Farmer's abrasive personality, and many said he wasn't the power behind the Klan in Washington Parish outside Bogalusa.

After the FBI visit, Farmer immediately phoned state police chief Thomas Burbank, complaining of Blacks calling him and accusing him of being the cause of the murder and the civil unrest in the streets of Bogalusa.[45] He also asked Sixth District congressman Jimmy Morrison to run the FBI out of Washington Parish.[46] Blacks despised Farmer, who had a reputation of violence against them. He was often armed and kept a .38 caliber long barrel revolver on his desk. At a Klan rally across the Pearl River in Crossroads, Mississippi, a sixteen-year-old Bogalusa youth gave a brief talk on the Klan's version of the Bible and how it supported segregation. He was a member of Farmer's youth group of local teens that he was mobilizing to battle Blacks on the streets of Bogalusa. The teen told Klansmen at the rally that if they were arrested for violence in Bogalusa they were not to worry because Farmer had promised he would make their bail.[47]

After numerous calls, public officials expressed little sympathy for his complaints. The one person Farmer never called for help was his next-door neighbor, a man both he and his friend Ray McElveen detested—Sheriff Dorman Crowe.

3

"ELMER, EITHER GIVE ME THE BADGE OR I'M TAKING IT!"

The homes of Sheriff Dorman Crowe and Klan leader Saxon Farmer were four hundred yards apart. Despite the close proximity, the two men were not the kind of neighbors who visited one another, shared wild game from a hunt or vegetables from the garden, or even stood along the fence line to chat. They were not friends. After all, for much of the late 1950s and early 1960s, Farmer and his buddy Ray McElveen spent their time and money trying to get Crowe out of office. It was an odd situation. One day the Crowe children heard a .22 rifle being fired. A short time later, their pet Chihuahua returned from the Farmer property riddled with bullet holes and soon died. On another day, one of Bobby Crowe's dogs wandered onto the Farmer property, walked under a chicken wire cage holding quails, and began to bark. The dog so terrified the quails that they attempted to fly away but instead crashed against the cage wire. Some died. When Sheriff Crowe got home that day, Bobby told his father what had happened. On Crowe's direction, Bobby walked over, apologized, and offered to pay for the dead birds. Farmer let it go. On another occasion, Bobby and one of Crowe's deputies stood in the yard and listened to the sounds of a saw cutting lumber. Farmer and others were building Klan crosses.[1]

The fence that separated their properties was symbolic of the beliefs that separated their views of life. Crowe, in hiring the two Black deputies, demonstrated that he was accepting that the world was changing and that integration, not segregation, was the future. He was guided by a strong moral compass that meant he would do the right thing, and as sheriff he intended to set the example for others to follow. Farmer, on the other hand, would accept no rule and no movement that would place Blacks on an equal footing with him. He had no respect for the law and followed a broken moral compass. He was willing to kill to protect and uphold segregation.

The sheriff and the Klansman became neighbors by coincidence. Born a few miles outside Franklinton on May 20, 1915, Crowe grew up in the country.

His father, Gordon, was a logger who used mules to drag logs out of the woods. Later, Gordon and wife, Luna, moved the family to Bogalusa, where he worked for the paper mill. When their son Dorman was in the army serving as a physical training instructor in San Antonio, Texas, he courted Helen Marie Moore. The two married in 1944. Afterward, Crowe brought his bride back to Washington Parish, where he went to work for a pipe company contracted by the paper mill. The couple would have four children. Son Bobby recalled in 2019 that his father was a strong, athletic man who "knew how to flip people through his training in the Army." Crowe had huge forearms, and spoke in a loud, deep voice. When he registered for military service, he weighed 210 pounds and stood six feet, two inches. The family eventually settled on the sixteen-acre farm at Lee's Creek on the outskirts of Bogalusa, where they raised cattle and horses and became neighbors with Saxon Farmer. Crowe fattened the cows in the summer and sold them in the fall, saving a bull calf to butcher. He was an avid squirrel hunter and trained dogs to hunt.[2]

In 1948 the incumbent sheriff was up for reelection in Washington Parish. Crowe decided to challenge him. In Louisiana prior to and during World War II, there had been a rise in prostitution and gambling. Brothers Huey and Earl Long during their respective tenures in the governor's office didn't mind gambling at all. The fact was the two enjoyed support from the New Orleans–based Carlo Marcello mob. If the Long brothers would look the other way on gambling and prostitution issues, Marcello agreed to help finance their campaigns and provide other small favors. After all, Earl Long, who was committed to a mental asylum for a brief period during his final years as governor, also was an alcoholic who spent time with strippers. Consequently, in parishes with weak or corrupt sheriffs, slot machines and other forms of gambling, as well as bootlegging and prostitution, flourished as the crime rate grew. Crowe had no use for such vices and wanted the New Orleans racketeers out of his parish. He announced his campaign in the fall of 1947.[3] He looped around the parish to the country stores, shook hands with voters, and visited with the preachers, whose support meant votes.[4]

Shortly before the election, the *Bogalusa Daily News* reported two incidents that highlighted the racial situation in the parish. The story painted African Americans in a particularly menacing way. On December 15, the newspaper's lead story was headlined: "Blackjacks Are Reissued to Police: Wild Night On 4th St. Brings Orders From Police Head." The paper identified a 225-pound Black man, Ellis Spikes, as a "rip-snorting dangerously drunk truck driver from Angie," who had to be "taken by force" by two officers in Bogalusa. One of those officers was Claxton Knight, who in 1965 was Bogalusa police chief. Spikes had reportedly terrorized patrons in Black-owned bars before police were called. The paper reported that force was used only after Spikes "snatched a night stick from Knight and attacked" the officers. Each was reportedly struck during the fight before they took control of Spikes, who outweighed each officer by sixty-five pounds. The twenty-three-year-old suspect was "getting meaner all the time," police said, and now faced multiple charges. The police chief praised his officers and "immediately took checks to offer further protection for policemen."[5]

Fifteen days later, the *Daily News* lead front-page story was headlined: "Negroes Run White Man Off Own Land With Guns." The paper explained that two Black men from Angie—sawmill hand Clarence Abrams and farmer Will Roberts—were accused of taking a shotgun away from a white farmer on his land near the community of Angie. T. E. Pope, the white farmer, said he heard his hogs squealing in the swamps and went to investigate, thinking a pack of dogs were after them. Instead he said he found two armed Black men who cursed him, threatened his life, and forced him off his own property. It was believed the Black men were in the swamp to steal the hogs, the paper reported. A deputy sheriff and state trooper arrested the two. Pope said he feared for his life as the Black men verbally abused him and threatened all whites in the parish by saying it was about time "we Negroes did something about you white. . . ." (The men allegedly referred to white people with a vulgar word which the paper chose not to print.)[6]

During the 1948 democratic primary, Crowe, then thirty-three, finished second in the seven-man race for sheriff. For decades in Louisiana, the Democratic primary winner faced little opposition from the Republican Party, which rarely fielded a candidate in the general election. Two-term incumbent Loyd Mulina finished first in the primary. In Louisiana at the time, Democrats and Republicans voted in their own primaries and runoffs before the two winning candidates elected by each party met in a general election. In advertisements in the local newspapers, Crowe identified himself as an independent and said he intended to run a clean office, would have an open-door policy, and would uphold the law.[7] At the time, the population of the parish was approximately thirty-eight thousand, including Bogalusa, the largest municipality with a population of just under eighteen thousand.

In the runoff, the *Bogalusa Daily News* reported, nearly eleven thousand Washington Parish voters went to the polls on "a dreary day" and elected Crowe the new sheriff by a 1,312 majority, the first time a candidate residing in Bogalusa won a term in the office.[8] "I will be sheriff of all of the people in Washington Parish without favor and without partiality," he wrote in his thank-you ad.[9] Upon taking office he issued a warning to all slot machine operators that he would be putting them out of business.[10]

Son Bobby recalled that the phone at the Crowe home rang all the time while his dad served as sheriff. Possum in the chicken coop? Crowe would go shoot it. Fight at a bar? Crowe and his deputies would go see about it. He never carried a gun, choosing to keep a .38 special at home and a shotgun in the closet. He enjoyed riding horses and organized a sheriff's posse. Crowe built an arena on donated property and every year would take the family to the rodeo in Baton Rouge and enjoy hot donuts on the way. Crowe made it a practice to have his deputies patrol in pairs. He also opened a sheriff's office substation in Bogalusa.[11]

In 1952, in a reelection ad, the sheriff told voters he would continue to oppose open gambling, slot machines, and the sale of illegal intoxicating liquors and that he would uphold all local and state laws as well as federal statutes.[12] The election would mark the first time in the state's history that voting machines would be used in all parish precincts.[13] The win over Bogalusa service station operator E. B. "Billups" Smith would be the biggest in Crowe's career, with a victory margin of 8,345 votes. The sheriff carried every precinct.[14]

The 1956 election, however, would mark the beginning of a new era in Washington Parish politics as the state and nation grappled with growing racial tensions and with the 1954 Supreme Court ruling in *Brown v. Board of Education* that ordered the integration of public schools. Five candidates entered the campaign in late 1955, and when the votes were counted in early 1956, Crowe led with 5,981 votes. Crowe's five opponents combined garnered approximately eight hundred votes more, forcing a runoff.[15] Charles Tullos, an automobile dealer and the elected finance commissioner of Bogalusa, finished second behind Crowe in the primary and immediately began an aggressive newspaper campaign, alleging in his ads that Crowe was a hypocrite in seeking a third term. Tullos charged that when Crowe sought the sheriff's post the first time in 1948 Crowe "severely criticized" Mulina for seeking a third term.[16] Tullos questioned whether Crowe was running the office in a fiscally responsible manner and whether he was enforcing liquor laws. He also claimed that Crowe employed four "close relatives" in the sheriff's office.[17] One of his employees was deputy Doyle Holliday, who had gone to work for Crowe in the early 1950s. Holliday was married to Crowe's sister.

Tullos also alleged that Crowe was conducting a "whispering campaign" that Tullos would be too occupied with his business interests to serve as sheriff. He assured the voters that his sons would handle his business affairs.[18] While Tullos ran on a campaign of change, Crowe ran on his past record and cited improvements he made to the office. The day following the February 23 election in 1956, the count revealed that Crowe was the victor by 910 votes. He also made history by becoming the first person ever elected to a third term in the parish. But the election also showed that Crowe was vulnerable. The *Bogalusa Daily News* pointed out that Tullos "made amazing gains since the first primary little more than a month ago, picking up almost a four-to-one margin over the sheriff over-and-above what each candidate had in the first primary."[19]

But other forces were at work in Washington Parish politics in the mid-1950s as the issue of race came to the forefront. The *Era-Leader* in the parish seat of Franklinton reported in June 1950 that a group of Black citizens brought the registrar of voters to court, alleging that he refused to register them because of their skin color. A month earlier, the paper had reported that approximately fifty Black citizens, male and female, approached the registrar, Curtis M. Thomas, who had set up office for a day at the Bogalusa City Hall specifically to register voters. When the Black citizens asked to be registered, Thomas shut down shop and was taken to a hospital because he reportedly suffered a "nervous upset."[20] Afterward, a member of the group, Joe Dean of Bogalusa, filed a complaint in federal court.[21]

In July, Judge Skelly Wright of New Orleans ordered Thompson to register all qualified Blacks in the parish. Wright in his order wrote that Thomas declined to register the group because of their race, noting that this violated equal protection under the Fourteenth Amendment and the right to vote under the Fifteenth Amendment. Thomas told the paper he would abide by the judge's ruling, but race had nothing to do with it. He said that as registrar he "has the right to request proof of identity."[22] In the meantime, two Black men who were registered to vote were selected to serve on a grand jury.[23]

Soon, two rulings by the US Supreme Court in *Brown v. Board of Education* would bring the issue to the forefront not only in Washington Parish but also nationally. In the first, the justices ruled that public education in the country separating the races in the classroom was anything but equal. For six decades the Supreme Court ruling in *Plessy v. Ferguson*—a New Orleans case concerning seating on street cars—created the "separate but equal" system and opened the Jim Crow era. However, the modern court ruling of May 17, 1954, determined that the practice violated the equal protection clause under the Fourteenth Amendment and therefore was unconstitutional. On May 27, the *Era-Leader* ran a front-page story on Governor Robert Kennon's assessment of the ruling. The headline said it all: "Kennon Says State Will Continue Segregation in La."[24] But months later, a front-page story on October 21 in the same paper rocked the parish and infuriated staunch segregationists. The article was headlined "Negroes Present Petition to the School Bd. Asking Hearing on Attending School." Twenty-seven Black parents of school-age children signed the petition that pointed to the Supreme Court's ruling that segregated public schools were unconstitutional. They requested a hearing to discuss the petition and asserted that children "of public school age attending and entitled to attend public schools cannot be denied admission to any school or be required to attend any school solely because of race and color."[25] But school boards statewide did little and were assured that white politicians would figure things out.

In 1955, the high court picked up the pace when it instructed local school boards, with supervision from the courts, to proceed with integration of schools "with all deliberate speed." In Louisiana, the legislators reacted quickly by creating a joint legislative committee that became known as the "Segregation Committee," chaired by state senator Willie Rainach. A resident of the tiny north Louisiana community of Summerville in Claiborne Parish, Rainach had been born in Kentwood in 1913. Orphaned as a child and later adopted, he became the undisputed leader of Louisiana's resistance to integration but in 1978 killed himself in his backyard with a .38 caliber pistol. He served two terms in the House of Representatives before his election to the state senate in 1948, where he served until 1960. While chairing the Segregation Committee, he also led the Association of Citizens' Councils of Louisiana as the organization's first president. The purpose of the association was to preserve segregation and to go after anyone who expressed support for integration, including university professors and school teachers. The council published a pamphlet in 1956 addressing election laws aimed to purge Black voters from the rolls. Rainach saw to it that the state distributed manuals to registrars in every parish to instruct them on how to preserve segregation. The Segregation Committee also published a pamphlet entitled "Don't Be Brainwashed: We Don't Have To Integrate Our Schools!" The document branded the court rulings and civil rights as communist movements based on "the false promises of socialism." And it asked: "Do we want our youth thrown into close social contact with a people of different racial origin, setting the stage for inter-racial marriages?"[26]

In the November 1, 1956, edition of the Franklinton paper, Rainach ran two ads on behalf of his committee, asking Washington Parish voters to support segregation amendments to the Louisiana constitution. Rainach toured the state seeking support to continue "separate public school systems, in the interest of public health, morals, better education, peace and order." Protecting "Our Way of Life" was another theme. This would ensure "the general welfare and happiness of the people" and continue racial harmony, Rainach said in the ad. Additionally, he asserted that in Louisiana "people of all races have gotten along well for many generations." Amendment 47, he told *Era-Leader* readers, would "protect the registrar of voters from NAACP nuisance class action suits," and Amendment 48 "would protect our segregated education facilities from NAACP racial integration suits."[27]

Segregationists knew that the NAACP was a giant threat to white supremacy. Since the early 1950s, the organization had filed multiple lawsuits across the country with the goal of toppling segregation. Its court successes ultimately led to the Supreme Court rulings of 1954 and 1955. Afterward, legislatures across the South sought to put the NAACP out of business.

On September 12, 1958, a *Daily News* story in Bogalusa was a shocker. Distributed by United Press International, the story was headlined "Supreme Court Orders Little Rock Integration: Arkansas School Board Directed to Admit Negro Students Monday." For weeks, the paper had regularly reported desegregation efforts across the country, including Arkansas governor Orval Faubus's activation of the National Guard to prevent integration by Black students of the whites-only Central High. The story outlined a Supreme Court ruling upholding the 8th US Circuit of Appeals action ordering the Little Rock School Board to integrate the school. African American Thurgood Marshall, the NAACP's chief counsel and a future member of the high court, said the state had exhausted all of its legal avenues and could no longer "pretend not to know what the law is. Anything now done to prevent desegregation in Arkansas is in open defiance of the law."[28]

In 1959, as Sheriff Crowe prepared for his bid for a fourth term, a horrific racial murder across the Pearl River in Poplarville, Mississippi, dominated the headlines in Washington Parish. For days, the *Daily News* ran story after story on the jailhouse abduction and murder of twenty-three-year-old African American truck driver Mack Charles Parker shortly after midnight on April 25. The paper noted that the murder was drawing national attention as the Mississippi Highway Safety Patrol and the FBI sought members of "a masked lynch mob that broke into the Pearl River County Jail, beat up an accused negro rapist with clubs and pistols, and dragged him screaming to a getaway car." The officer on duty at the time of the kidnapping and murder, Deputy Jewel Alford, was later arrested in the case along with others. Parker was to be tried for allegedly raping a young white mother, June Walters, in the presence of her four-year-old daughter. Sheriff W. Osborne Moody said Parker shouted to the other prisoners as he was abducted, "Help me, don't let them run over me this way!" The rape victim had once lived in Bogalusa.[29]

A few days after the abduction, Parker's body was found two and a half miles south of the Pearl River bridge in Bogalusa. He had been shot twice while on the bridge, his body weighed down with logging chains and tossed over the railing. Several men were arrested in the case, but no indictments were forthcoming in either Mississippi or federal courts. Milton Graham, the former pro football player turned FBI agent, recalled that in 1965, six years after the Parker murder, Klansmen and segregationists would still joke "about a black guy drowning in the Pearl River who must have stolen a bunch of chain and was trying to swim with it." Graham said those comments "were intended to antagonize us."[30]

While the FBI investigated the case in Bogalusa, agents asked Sheriff Crowe whether if he knew of any potential suspects. He told the bureau his next-door neighbor, Saxon Farmer, and Farmer's good friend, Ray McElveen, both despised Blacks and could be considered suspects in the Parker case. Additionally, the sheriff pointed out that both men had been involved in a Citizens' Council campaign to purge Black voters from the voting rolls.[31]

The purge came as Rainach sought the governor's post in the 1959–60 campaign in one of the most racially charged elections in the state's history. Governor Earl Long, whose foul language and crude manners repulsed many, was a supporter of voting rights for Blacks, who tended to vote for him. He once called down Rainach in the legislature, telling the senator that when he retired and had time to reflect on life and politics back home in Summerfield he would realize that "niggers is human beings too." In his characteristically vulgar manner, Long pointed out that Black men were tired of white men having their way with Black women. In his widely read nationally syndicated column, "Washington Merry-Go Round," Drew Pearson wrote that in the weeks after the Citizens' Council began the Black voter purge, the governor "proposed legislation to protect them and his other lower income supporters." WBRZ television station in Baton Rouge filmed a speech made by Long defending the bill. Long said that in the early 1900s his uncle "got drunk one night, went down to the colored quarters in Winnfield, kicked a nigger man out of bed and he got into bed. That nigger man was so enraged he shot my pore ol' uncle and he died. . . . Do you know, that's what the colored people resent now most. They want their womenfolk left alone."[32]

Ray McElveen, who headed up finances in Washington Parish for Rainach's gubernatorial campaign, had a first cousin from Franklinton who impregnated a Black woman in the 1950s. FBI agents visited the woman in 1965. She lived in Franklinton and described the relationship as brief and mutual. She said both were single at the time. As a result of a relationship, a daughter was born, and the daughter had been told who her father was. Once her baby was born, however, the woman never heard from the man who impregnated her again. He was exiled to New Orleans by the McElveen family when the relationship was rumored in the community. She never received support or acknowledgment of the child from the McElveen family. The woman pleaded that agents keep the matter quiet. Otherwise, her reputation would suffer, and she would lose her jobs cleaning houses for white people.[33]

The local Citizens' Council, led by McElveen and Farmer, developed a simple strategy to take down Dorman Crowe in the 1959 election. They moved on two fronts. One was to find a candidate for sheriff supportive of the Citizens' Council agenda in preserving segregation. Secondly, because they knew Crowe would be hard to beat and that his Black support might be the difference in a close race, they decided to follow Rainach's directive to purge as many Black voters from Washington Parish as possible. By March 1959, a month before Mack Charles Walker was murdered, they had begun the purge. The *Era-Leader* reported on March 12 that McElveen and Farmer challenged more than one hundred Blacks in Bogalusa alone during the previous few days. Assisting the two men in the purge were McElveen's father, Diaz, and Farmer's brother, Eugene.[34]

In November 1958, there were 11,444 white voters in the parish and 1,517

Blacks. Seven months later, in June 1959, the number of Black voters had dropped 85 percent to 236. Acting under Louisiana law, McElveen, Farmer, and others filed affidavits of challenge individually against 1,377 Black voters and 10 white voters purportedly based on deficiencies in registration cards ranging from misspellings to inaccurate age information to illegible handwriting. A Justice Department lawsuit against the council pointed out that a random sampling of 200 voters, of whom 198 were white, revealed that 60 percent of these registration cards contained the same "defects and inconsistencies," while the registrar of voters estimated that at least 50 percent of all of the cards on the rolls contained similar "errors and omissions."[35] As the case went through the court process, everyone wondered whether the Black voters would be restored to the rolls in time for the primary election in the fall and the runoff in January.

Now the Citizens' Council, which in the months ahead would lose much of its membership to the Klan, chose segregationist and anti–civil rights candidate Elmer Smith, a future Klan leader, as its candidate. Smith listed his qualifications as thirty-one years in public service, including a quarter century as a policeman and as a fireman and fire chief in Bogalusa. He had finished third in the 1956 sheriff's race that saw Crowe face off in the runoff against Charles Tullos. But before the runoff election, Smith endorsed Crowe. The *Daily News* ran Smith's statement immediately after the fall 1955 primary in which the defeated candidate said he had studied the election returns and "decided to join hands with Sheriff Crowe and to support him in the second primary." In a political move after Smith's statement, Crowe hired Smith as a deputy. But they would soon become bitter enemies.[36]

Crowe's son Bobby said that his uncle, deputy Doyle Holliday, informed the sheriff in the summer of 1959 that Smith was going to challenge his boss, Crowe, in the upcoming election. The sheriff called Smith and picked him up. "They were riding on Columbia Street in Bogalusa when Daddy asked Elmer if he was running," Bobby Crowe recalled in 2019. "Elmer said yes." The sheriff pulled off onto the parking lot of the Columbia Street elementary school. Dorman Crowe looked at Smith and said, "Elmer, either give me the badge or I'm taking it!" Smith handed it over. Bobby Crowe said both families went to the Calvary Baptist Church in Bogalusa, with the Crowe family sitting on one side of the aisle and Smith family on the other. All the while the preacher preached forgiveness and reconciliation, but it would be years before that would happen between Crowe and Smith.[37]

In the *Era-Leader* on November 19, 1959, Smith pointed out to voters, "I am not now an officeholder. Sheriff Dorman Crowe fired me from my position as a deputy, July 27, because I desired to exercise the right that every good citizen has—the great privilege of offering myself as a candidate for public office." In another ad in the same issue, Smith wrote, "Mr. Present Sheriff You know that four years ago in the presence of myself and a highly respected business executive, you said that you would not seek a fourth term as sheriff of this parish, and pledged me your support for this race."[38] Crowe's campaign ads were much like those in past years. He ran on his past record of law and order, honesty, and his continued pledge to keep the gambling forces out of the parish. But a three-term sheriff seeking a fourth term has a long list of enemies, and in the racially charged atmosphere of 1959–60 it was unclear if Crowe would overcome the segregation fever led by the white Citizens' Council.

On December 10, 1959, the *Era-Leader* reported a stunning outcome in the primary—Smith led the three-man race with 5,513 votes, lacking only 366 votes to beat Crowe outright. Crowe polled 4,280 votes. The third candidate, Lacy Richardson, garnered enough votes—1,599—to set up the runoff.[39]

In the governor's race, Quitman, Louisiana, native Jimmie Davis, a country and gospel music singer famous for the song "You Are My Sunshine," led the field in Washington Parish, with Rainach finishing second. Davis would go on to win the election statewide.[40] While McElveen and Farmer's work for Rainach through the white Citizens' Council failed to give Rainach the victory in Washington Parish, their plan to beat Crowe by eliminating his Black support was working like a charm. As the voter purge case now rested in the hands of the federal court, Crowe seemed as good as beat.

On December 17, a few days after the democratic primary, Crowe's ad in the *Era-Leader* thanked his voters and asked for their continued support in the January 9, 1960, runoff. He asked those who didn't support him in the first round to consider him now. Support honesty, he said, and he asked for the opportunity to resolve any grievance a voter might have against him. "Don't let 12 years experience go down the drain," he said. "Vote for the man who will do the most good for all."[41]

But Smith moved in for the kill. In an ad headlined "Shame-Shame, Mr. Dorman Crowe," the challenger continued to attack, claiming that after his "big primary vote," he "is now subjected to an organized, vicious and totally untrue smear campaign by Sheriff Crowe and a small group of his political henchmen." He alleged Crowe was spreading "manufactured falsehoods" that

Smith would not enforce gambling and liquor laws. Additionally, Smith said Crowe had claimed to have turned down $16,000 for his campaign because he feared "it was crooked money." If that were so, Smith asked, why didn't Crowe arrest the crook?[42] An ad from a Crowe supporter countered: "Don't think for one minute that the most aggressive and boldest gang of racketeers and gamblers in the whole United States that has its headquarters less than 100 miles from here, hasn't had their eyes on our lush milk income and the tremendous payroll of Bogalusa! They would pay any price to get a foothold in Washington Parish."[43]

On January 9, 1960, Crowe did the impossible—he defeated Smith by 136 votes, 6,680 to 6,544. Two days after that Judge Wright in New Orleans ordered restoration to the voting rolls of Washington Parish the 1,377 African-Americans whose names had been removed from the registration rolls. The *Era-Leader* reported: "Acting assistant attorney General Joseph M. F. Ryan Jr., in charge of the Civil Rights division, said that 'while the government does not seek the retention of the voting rolls of people who are not qualified under state law, the decision of the court makes it clear that the state may not apply one set of rules as to the qualifications to one race which it does not apply to the other.'"[44]

Judge Wright, who ten years earlier ordered the parish register to enroll qualified Black voters, ruled that the "acts and practices" of McElveen and Farmer in 1959 "were committed and engaged in for the purpose and with the effect of depriving Negroes, solely because of their race or color, of the right to register and vote." In February, Louisiana attorney general Jack Gremillion asked for a rehearing, and the matter eventually went before the US Supreme Court. In the March 3 edition, the *Era-Leader* reported that the "question which has kept Washington Parish in the limelight throughout Louisiana and the Nation during the past several months, apparently has been settled by the United States Supreme Court, when its decision this week ordered returned to the rolls of voters in Washington Parish, the names of approximately fourteen hundred Negroes, whose names were purged from the rolls before the recent primary election and thereby deprived these people to vote in either the first or second elections in 1959 and 1960. . . . It is hoped by most people, white and colored, that this matter has been settled once and for all."[45]

While the effort to remove the Black voters to maintain segregation had failed, the effort to defeat Crowe was still viable. A short time after the votes had been counted in January, Smith petitioned the court, protesting the election.[46] When the district judge ruled against his challenge, Smith appealed to the Supreme Court of Louisiana. He alleged irregularities in Ward 4, which encompassed Bogalusa, and challenged fifty-two voters. Supreme Court Justice Rene A. Viosca discovered that the commissioners serving in the election were primarily "reputable housewives" who served "as a matter of patriotic duty and performed their duties conscientiously and to the best of their ability." He added that "there is not a scintilla of evidence in this record indicating fraud." Any mistakes made by the commissioners were honest, their job more difficult because of the huge turn out and long lines at the polls, the judge said. He found that only twelve votes were cast illegally in the parish and "it was not established for whom these twelve votes were cast."[47]

Crowe had prevailed at the polls. Black voters were back on the rolls. Undeterred, McElveen and Farmer immediately began planning for the next election at a time when the Ku Klux Klan was replacing the Citizens' Council as the leader of segregationists in Washington Parish. Elmer Smith would again be the segregationist candidate. In the days to come, Farmer assembled and lit up scores of Klan crosses, and McElveen became a member of a wrecking crew as they ramped up the war against integration and Sheriff Crowe.

4

"THE WOODS ARE FULL OF PEOPLE LIGHTING CIGARETTES"

In the lunchroom at Crown-Zellerbach in 1963, Ray McElveen fumed about Dorman Crowe as the sheriff's election campaign kicked off. It was no surprise to anyone that he was going all out for Elmer Smith, who in 1965 claimed to the FBI that he had joined the Original Knights of the Ku Klux Klan in 1963 but only for "political expediency."[1] Smith claimed he rarely attended Klan meetings. Others interviewed by the FBI, however, said he attended many meetings and was known to be "hard on Negroes." His Klan membership was a true indication of his racist beliefs, they said.[2]

The world had change greatly between the 1960 and 1964 sheriff elections. Civil rights legislation was becoming more a reality, and segregationists believed the momentum was based in part on the failure of the Citizens' Councils to stop it. Historian Numan V. Bartley has written that in the 1950s the councils "fed on long-developing racial fears and frustrations, and, of course, by feeding on them, heightened them. Fitting the climate of the time, the movement effectively filled a void felt by many white southerners who were often inclined to blame the NAACP (and probably communist) organizational superiority for Negro gains and thus tended to view a white man's organization to counter the threat and reestablish 'southern' values as the obvious solution to the race problem."[3]

The Klan, on the other hand, presented a more aggressive agenda, and its secrecy offered members some degree of anonymity and the chance to hide behind a hood. By 1963, the Original Knights had grown into one of the biggest Klan organizations in the South before violent men with criminal records ousted its leaders. In Bogalusa, McElveen, Elmer Smith, and Saxon Farmer were among the Original Knights' newest members, with Farmer taking a leadership role. They were banking on the Klan vote to elevate Smith into the sheriff's office. Already Klansmen were calling Crowe a "nigger lover" because he welcomed Black political support. During Klan meetings in Bogalusa, McElveen was known to launch into wild tirades. Just put him alone in a room with a few Black troublemakers and he would straighten things out by any means necessary. Others outside the Klan heard these comments too. One of his coworkers at the papermill said that before the attack on the deputies McElveen had become "emotional and confused."[4] The violent sentiments McElveen expressed would explode within the Klan when Crowe dared to do the unspeakable—hire two Black men as deputies and give them the lawful authority to arrest a white man, or worse, a white woman.

The hiring of Oneal Moore and Creed Rogers would be talked about by Klansmen across Louisiana. During this period, the most feared Klansman in the state emerged as a major force. He was a six-foot-one, 220-pound Monroe resident who operated a sanitation business that involved installing and pumping waste from septic tanks. His name was Robert "Shotgun" Fuller, and he personally would demand that the sheriff fire both deputies. Fuller was a dangerous man, and few knew this better than FBI agents.

The need for Black deputies in Washington Parish was more than just a matter of politics. It was a logical move as well. Crowe knew that civil rights was not going to go away, and he knew that most white southerners, including those in Washington Parish, would ultimately follow and abide by the laws of the land even if it ultimately meant the end of public segregation. Most white people opposed integration vehemently. But most would not raise a hand in violence against another person. Ultimately, of the men holding public office in the South, those who served as sheriffs were in the best position to protect the Black community from violence. A fatal shooting involving a young Black man by one of Crowe's deputies illustrated that it was also time to look at a new way to handle crime in the Black community and that hiring Black police officers would be a reasonable way to begin.

In late 1960, one of Crowe's deputies, O. C. "Buddy" McDaniel, shot and killed twenty-three-year-old African American Tommy James Warren in the community of Black Jack in northern Washington Parish. Illegal gambling in the white and Black communities had been a continuing source of complaints. In a front-page story in the *Era-Leader,* Crowe said his deputies had been making routine checks in several rural areas far from the beaten path, including the predominantly African American rural community of Black Jack. Accompanied by Bogalusa policeman Claxton Knight, Deputy McDaniel's first stop at Luther Bickham's place turned up nothing. From there, the officers walked through a field more than a quarter of a mile distant to Hut Dillon's bar, the scene of dozens of raids over the past decade where many crimes had been reported and where illicit liquor sales and illegal gambling were common. Black Jack in Ward 8 of northern Washington Parish and Ward 4 in Bogalusa were the only "wet" wards in the parish. McDaniel entered the front door. Knight entered from a side door. Inside, they discovered an illegal dice game in progress. According to the newspaper, once they entered McDaniel walked toward the men involved in the game while at the same time Warren in a "threatening manner" began walking toward McDaniel when Knight suddenly shouted, "Look out! He's coming for you!" The deputy ordered Warren to stop in his tracks, but he did not respond to the order. When Warren was within a few feet, the officer raised his gun and fired once, the bullet striking Warren in the left eye and killing him. Afterward, fifteen Black men were charged with disturbing the peace.[5] Police shootings were rarely investigated in the 1960s. The case illustrated to Crowe, particularly during the racial tension in the state, that Black officers would be more effective and accepted in such situations.

By the time of the state Democratic primary in fall of 1963, the Washington Parish economy was thriving. Crown-Zellerbach announced a $6,000,000 project to upgrade its pulp and paper mill in Bogalusa, while in Franklinton in the heart of dairy land, the Gulf Milk Association announced there were 450 milk producers in Washington Parish, bringing $20,000 daily into the area's economy.[6] But the *Bogalusa Daily News* in June ran a front-page article headlined "Racial Trouble Remains Nation's First Problem." The article pointed to several violent racial incidents and mass arrests as "Negro demonstrators, backed by US Supreme Court desegregation decisions, sought equal rights in schools, theaters, lunch counters, hotels, parks and other public facilities." Attorney General Robert Kennedy was helping draft "stronger civil rights legislation," which President John F. Kennedy planned to send to Congress. James Farmer, national director of CORE, believed segregation in public places would be eliminated in three years except "in a few hard-core Southern areas. . . . I think we're on the threshold of a full-fledged revolt that will bring down the walls of segregation."[7]

The Kennedy brothers met with theater owners and retail merchants to urge them to integrate their businesses. Vice President Lyndon B. Johnson said that "until justice is blind to color, until education is unaware of race, until opportunity is unconcerned with the color of men's skins, emancipation will be a proclamation but not a fact." While these words encouraged Blacks and civil rights advocates, they repulsed Klansmen. But they found hope from another *Daily News* story that reported Alabama governor George Wallace refused to admit two Black students into the all-white University of Alabama.[8] As the Klan saw it, an evil federal government prevailed as US deputy attorney general Nicholas Katzenbach made sure that both Vivian Malone and James A. Hood were escorted to their respective dormitories and later registered. Maybe, radical Klansmen now believed, the Klan's political efforts should be supplemented by a violent approach to the agents of integration.

It was during this period that the Original Knights of the Ku Klux Klan, long the dominant branch of the Klan in the state, underwent a power purge led by a violent faction in Winnsboro and Monroe, both in northeastern Louisiana. What was originally billed in 1960 as an organization designed to preserve segregation and white supremacy through political activism, intimidation, and dirty tricks morphed into a militant terrorist organization that would use violence to achieve the same goals. In Washington Parish, the Klan decided to take it a step further. Ejecting Sheriff Crowe and others from office and establishing the Klan as a political power was now the major mission. A staunch segregationist sheriff would preserve white control of the parish. Klansmen felt their best approach was to field their own candidates and only support statewide officials who supported the Klan.

At the time Crowe squeaked out a runoff win over Elmer Smith in 1960, the Original Knights of the Ku Klux Klan was chartered in Shreveport. Its leader was Roy E. Davis, a seventy-year-old preacher with a four-decade-long criminal record. Many of his offenses occurred at a time when a man's crime in one region of the country would not necessarily be known in another. A native of Texas, his long rap sheet across multiple states included charges of forgery, theft, fraud, bail jumping, swindling, and wife and child abandonment. He stole from the churches he pastored and disappeared when the congregations reported his actions to the law. He was a member of the Citizens' Council and as far back as the 1920s served as a promoter for the Knights of Ku Klux Klan, based in Atlanta. Membership at that time reached an estimated four million nationally.[9]

Throughout his life Davis preached white supremacy and strong resistance to integration of any kind. In a page-one article in the *Shreveport Times* on April 7, 1961, the paper reported that Davis had been arrested by local authorities following cross burnings in Shreveport, including one in the front yard of

US congressman Overton Brooks. With the story was a photo of Davis being fingerprinted. Police Chief Harvey D. Teasley said Davis's Klan was made up of "debt beaters, liars and drunkards." The paper also reported that Davis had spent much time with John Deason Swenson, a Bossier City dry cleaner picked by Davis as the leader of the Louisiana Realm of the Original Knights. The police chief pressed Davis about Klan finances until the preacher acknowledged that he intended to make money off every Klan member recruited in Louisiana.[10] While racial hatred and segregation were the deep emotional themes that attracted white men to the Klan, leaders like Davis depended on those deep feelings to fuel their enterprises financially. Davis drew a percentage of Klan money from membership dues as well as the sale of Klan literature, paraphernalia, and robes.

What the FBI needed most were good sources and good informants. The bureau's senior resident agent in Alexandria, Louisiana, located in the center of the state, Paul Lancaster, developed an Original Knights informant who had experienced a change of heart about the Klan and wanted to do something to redeem himself. It was Lancaster, a native of Buffalo, New York, who would rush to Ferriday in the middle of the night in December 1964 to interview Frank Morris, an African American businessman mortally wounded when Klansmen set fire to his shoe shop. From his hospital deathbed, a heavily sedated Morris described his attackers to Lancaster, who recorded Morris's words in a case that failed to result in a single arrest, although a grand jury was convened on the matter in 2011 in Concordia Parish but took no action.[11] In Alexandria in 1963, Lancaster collected a report written by his new informant, who pointed out that Klan leaders were destroying "our faith in the federal government, refusing to entertain constructive ideas on how we can live in harmony with the Negro without keeping him in slavery, and setting ourselves up as judge, jury and executioner. For this reason I went to an FBI agent and agreed to work as an informant rather than get out." The informant said the Klan's theme song should be "We Hate Niggers!" above all things. The way to succeed, the Klan preached, was to use force and violence to discourage Blacks and whites from forcing integration and ultimately a realignment in the balance of power.[12]

Key details were learned about the Original Knights when FBI agents Eugene E. Bjorn and W. J. Danielson Jr. drove to Dry Prong in Grant Parish north of Alexandria. There they found thirty-six-year-old Thomas Fontenot, a pest control operator who had recently quit the Klan in disgust. He provided the bureau an excellent inside look at the operation of the Original Knights and its takeover by men who advocated violence.[13]

In 1962, an acquaintance had asked Fontenot to attend a Klan meeting in a private home in Grant Parish where six or seven others were in attendance. There to recruit him was John Deason Swenson, the grand dragon of the Original Knights appointed by preacher Davis. Swenson painted the Klan as a nonviolent Christian organization made up of only good, clean-living men who had been secretly investigated by Klan leaders and then brought into the fold. One of the Klan's goals was to use economic pressure, including boycotts, against any group, business, or individual that sponsored "integration activities." After taking his oath, Fontenot helped organize the Grant Parish unit of the Original Knights and a unit in Ward 10, which together boasted more than one hundred members. He was elected the Unit 10 exalted cyclops, the Klan term for the leader of a klavern. Soon Fontenot was involved in a cross burning, which he explained was to show the strength of the Klan to local residents or the opening of a new klavern or to symbolize "the destruction of evil in Christ's name." His unit also made harassing phone calls to "straighten people out," such as a call Fontenot made to a local café where Black employees appeared to be having friendly conversations with white patrons.[14]

White politicians came to klavern meetings to seek votes as Klansmen sat in the audience fully robed and hooded. Unbeknownst to the politicians, Klansmen dressed in civilian clothing would later attend public political events to see if the candidate said the same thing there that he had said to them in private. The politician would not recognize the Klansmen in the audience. If he said something different, the Klan would work to defeat him.[15]

But by 1963, the Klan under preacher Davis, Grand Dragon Swenson, and Imperial Wizard Royal Young, a railroad engineer, was breaking apart. The organization had grown from a handful in Shreveport in northwestern Louisiana to hundreds by the time it reached Washington Parish in extreme southeastern Louisiana more than 250 miles distant. By then, others began to crave the power of leadership and the money the leaders were paying themselves. Fontenot said Young was criticized for buying Swenson a new car even though Swenson had "worn out" his old car on Klan business. Additionally, Swenson had a monopoly on robe sales from his business, Barksdale Cleaners, and Klansmen didn't like the fact that Swenson used his Black employees to make their white robes. Young also was criticized for failing to deliver KKK literature to Klan units in a timely manner. In general, Klansmen felt there was inadequate representation statewide: Davis was from Texas, while Young and Swenson were from the Shreveport-Bossier City area. Fontenot thought Young was a "good leader" who opposed violence. Young preached, "Ballots for bullets. Boycotts for Beatings." But he also paid himself thousands of dollars from Klan coffers. During the statewide elections of 1963 during Sheriff's Crowe's bid for a fifth term, a Klan power purge had begun.[16]

By early 1964, Young knew he, Davis, and Swenson were in trouble. Swenson had already begun organizing Original Knights klaverns in Mississippi, but by late 1963 and early 1964 a new group—the White Knights—took over in Mississippi. In Louisiana, Young added new officers to appease the membership. He also held emergency meetings across the state. In Columbia, Young gave an impassioned speech about making the Klan strong politically and avoiding violence, which would result in FBI investigations. He talked about his sacrifices to move the Klan forward. An informant at the meeting told the FBI that the Klansmen there came from northern, central, and southeastern Louisiana, including Washington Parish. Some wanted to burn crosses during the gubernatorial primary in early December, but Young said no. Young dashed to meetings in Vidalia on the Mississippi, crossed the river to Natchez, and raced down to Baton Rouge, but it was too late. Back in Grant Parish, Fontenot sent Young a message that he, Young, was "washed up."[17]

New leadership emerged with the suddenness and surprise of a tornado at night. Fontenot witnessed it firsthand. As Klan membership plummeted in Grant Parish, he made a final effort to reorganize and hold his group together. But at a klavern meeting, Fontenot was shocked when forty-four-year-old Robert "Shotgun" Fuller of Monroe and Murray Martin of Winnsboro, backed up by several armed men, showed up. The forty-one-year-old Martin was a building contractor who also sold insurance out of an office that had two signs on the door—one for his insurance agency and the other as headquarters for the Franklin Parish Citizens' Council. Fontenot took their guns at the door and asked them why they made such a show of force. Martin said he feared Young and Swenson were out to kill him, and he needed a weapon for protection. But Fontenot knew better. Most Klansmen were aware the man with Martin was an intimidating, vicious bully. Fontenot called Shotgun Fuller a "hot head" and "reprobate" who "did not know the meaning of diplomacy."[18]

A short time later, members of the Fishville klavern in Grant Parish began arriving for a meeting, which as a matter of practice for all klaverns was protected by armed Klan guards. Shortly after the meeting began, Fuller walked up to the klavern door, where guards stopped him. He was disarmed and taken inside. Soon another guard dashed toward the building, shouting, "Hey, the woods are full of people lighting cigarettes!" They were there to protect Fuller and show other klaverns that Fuller had a growing armed force to back him up.[19]

Soon Murray Martin, with Fuller's support, was elected head of the Original Knights in Louisiana after Davis, Swenson, and Young were deposed but not before they had appointed Fuller as head of the Klan Bureau of Investigation for the state. It would be Fuller's job to put together wrecking crews for secret missions of arson, attacks, and murders or to investigate and deal with Klansmen who were believed to be informing to the FBI. Violent acts—like the shooting of the two deputies in Washington Parish—were to be approved by the chief Klan investigator on the state level, although these procedures were not always followed. What Klansmen didn't know was that Fuller had a secret. Inducted into the army at age twenty-four in October 1944, Fuller was sent home four months later. He was discharged "by reason of Certificate of Disability for Discharge: Dementia Praecox, simple type," better known today as schizophrenia. Fuller had been suffering mental problems since his late teens. While investigating Fuller's sanity, a military board of officers at Kennedy General Hospital in Memphis measured his mental age at ten years, seven months. Fuller told doctors that he had frequent thoughts of suicide and heard voices, although he no longer bothered "to turn around." He was discharged into the custody of his father, who agreed to put his son into a reputable mental institution for observation and treatment.[20] Whether this was done is unclear.

Robert "Shotgun" Fuller first appeared on the FBI's radar in the 1953 when William Dent arrived as senior resident agent in the New Orleans bureau's Monroe office. Dent was one of many World War II veterans to join the FBI in the late 1940s. He and wife Charlottie married in 1947, the year Dent, a native of Jackson, Mississippi, became an agent. He had served in Europe and Africa during the war and afterward earned a business degree from Mississippi State. Charlottie was an Alabama native who at the time of their marriage was teaching high school in Florida. FBI couples faced many difficulties in the postwar years. Finding an apartment was next to impossible due to housing shortages in the cities. Employers were reluctant to hire FBI wives because agents were often transferred, or the wives would become pregnant. Dent, who started in Cleveland, Ohio, was relocated five times in six years, spending the bulk of the time on the West Coast from Seattle to San Francisco to Stockton. But it was during that period that Dent and Charlottie made lifelong friends with other agents and their wives. If the men worked at night, the wives had "night parties" on the beach, arriving with blankets and dinner. In the state of Washington, Charlottie could see Mt. Rainier in the distance out her front window. In San Francisco she sat on her fire escape and gazed at the bay bridges. In Stockton there was joy when she learned she was pregnant but also sadness when another agent and his wife lost their baby after the child ate aspirins. Then came family tragedy. In 1953, Dent's father and nephew drowned in a pond in Jackson, Mississippi. The bureau granted Dent a hardship transfer to the New Orleans bureau to allow Dent to be nearer his now widowed mother. He was named senior resident agent of the Monroe office, a two-hour drive to Jackson. It was a position he would hold for the next seventeen years. When they arrived Dent was thirty-four and Charlottie was twenty-six.[21]

On April 21, 1954, less than a year after Dent's transfer, Charlottie answered the ringing phone not long before midnight. The anonymous male caller said he intended to come get Charlottie and her child as well as "Robert Fuller and everybody connected with this damn business." Then the caller said, "I'm going to take you for a nice long ride, and don't you forget it."[22] Fuller at the time was a taxi driver and pimp, who often got into fights. Local police considered Fuller Monroe's most dangerous hoodlum. He was also the target of an ongoing federal investigation initiated by Dent for violations of the White Slave Traffic Act (WSTA), which prohibits the interstate transportation of women or girls for prostitution. The anonymous call came to the Dent home eleven days after Fuller had been indicted by the Ouachita Parish grand jury on a charge of receiving stolen goods. A trial scheduled for late May was canceled when a key witness suddenly became unavailable.[23]

At the time the FBI opened the WSTA case against Fuller, the crime rate in Monroe had soared, and local authorities were doing little to stop it. As a result, Charlottie recalled in 2010, Dent soon became Fuller's target and when Dent was in New Orleans on bureau business, the threatening call was made. Charlottie notified another Monroe-based FBI agent, Earl Cox, about the threat. Cox got word to Dent in New Orleans and notified the sheriff's office. Aware of Fuller's background, Cox figured Fuller had made the call. Seconds later the phone rang again. It was Ouachita Parish sheriff Bailey Grant, who asked Charlottie if someone could get her and the child out of the house. Charlottie had already called a friend for help. As she waited, Dent called from New Orleans. "Get out!" he told her just as their friend arrived at the front door. As the friend knocked, he felt a pistol barrel in his back. Petrified, the friend soon learned that the man with a gun was the only police officer on duty in Monroe working that night. He had been dispatched to the scene. Quickly everything was explained, and mother and child safely rescued. Dent arrived home the next day.[24]

"New Orleans was in an uproar," Charlottie recalled years after the trouble. "No other wife and child [of an FBI agent] had been threatened" before. The bureau couldn't prove Fuller made the call, but agents were confident it was him. Dent paid Fuller a visit. If Dent's family were harmed, Fuller would be considered the top suspect, Dent assured Fuller in words more compelling than these.[25] Later in the year, Fuller was booked on state charges for soliciting for prostitution and pandering and was later tried and convicted on the former charge.[26]

For a while Fuller behaved himself, but in 1960 Monroe was shocked when newspapers reported a horrific July 12 shooting that resulted in the death of four Black men and the wounding of another. The *New Orleans States-Item* and *Monroe News-Star* reported that the preceding day Fuller had a run-in with one of his employees, a young man named Charlie Willis. Fuller claimed Willis cursed and threatened him before he, Fuller, struck Willis. The next day Willis and four other Black employees of Fuller arrived at their boss's home south of Monroe before 8:00 a.m., blocking the drive in the rear, where Fuller's truck was parked. The five men were ages nineteen to twenty-four. Two were brothers. They asked Fuller to walk down the road with them and talk. Fuller claimed some of his nine children were outside playing.[27]

Just after he ordered them to go inside the house, Fuller said he turned toward the Black men as one of his children yelled, "Watch out, daddy, there's a knife!" Fuller said one man rushed him with a linoleum hook. Explaining to police that he expected trouble with the men due to the previous day's conflict, Fuller said his loaded double-barrel shotgun was in his pickup, and he had his pockets filled with buckshot.[28]

Fuller fired, blowing the man backward as his stomach exploded with flesh, bone, and intestines. Then, Fuller said, the other four came toward him and he shot them all, reloading the shotgun three times and firing more than eight shells of buckshot while never moving from his truck. Police found the first victim near Fuller's truck. A second body was outside the driver's side of the vehicle they arrived in. His head was blown to bits. The third, shot in the chest, fell dead on the passenger side of the car. The fourth was crumpled on the lawn. The last victim had run past to a neighbor's lawn before he fell. The *News-Star* reported that police said three knives, two with long hunting blades, were found near three of the men. One of the wounded men still had a knife in his hand, police reported.[29]

But the *Louisiana Weekly,* a Black-owned New Orleans newspaper, reported that the "true story behind the wholesale slaughter by a white businessman of three of his Negro employees and wounding of two others may never be known." Friends and relatives of the slain men, however, said, "Fuller was abusive and had slapped one of the men earlier and that the workers were grossly underpaid, and often cheated out of their meager earnings."[30] Fuller had a poor record paying his employees and his bills. He had six judgments against him totaling $3,200.[31] The information about Fuller's abuse provided by families and friends, the paper wrote, "were taken lightly by police." According to authorities, Fuller claimed that Charles Willis, the man he had argued with the day before the shooting, had hit a white man with a shovel during a previous altercation and threatened to do the same to Fuller. He said Willis told him that he had smashed in one white man's teeth and was prepared to do the same to Fuller.[32] However, there were apparently no witnesses to back up Fuller's accusations.

There were multiple problems with Fuller's account of the murders, and it appears police did little questioning, although he was charged with manslaughter and got out of jail on a $25,000 bond. Fuller's claim to have reloaded his shotgun four times and firing it eight times seems impossible. That would take several seconds, more than enough time for some of the men to flee to safety. Was someone else outside with Fuller? In a heavily redacted four-page "Notice to Close File" report by the Department of Justice in 2010, which had briefly reopened the case, a Department of Justice attorney indicated that a relative implicated Fuller's son, William Herbert Fuller, along with Robert "Shotgun Fuller" in the murders and that William Herbert Fuller shot the dying men in the head "to finish them off."[33] But newspaper accounts indicate only one man was shot in the head—obviously by a shotgun blast due to the extent of the injuries. No other contemporary witness quoted in the newspapers placed William Herbert Fuller at the scene.

One of the most chilling events in the aftermath came when Fuller's next-door neighbor Mrs. R. W. Sherman came outside. Newspapers reported that she told police she was still in bed when the shooting occurred. When she went outside, Fuller called her over to him. He stood by Charlie Willis, the man he had previously struck. Willis was barely alive. Fuller claimed he told the young man to tell Mrs. Sherman why he and the others came to his house that morning. Willis reportedly said, "We came down to hurt Mr. Robert." That was a key statement in that it offered Fuller the self-defense route.[34] But it is also obvious that the man would have said anything Fuller would have instructed him to say at that point. With Fuller still holding the shotgun and standing over him, the wounded and helpless Willis had just been shot himself and knew that his four friends were dead or dying. Secondly, it is quite possible Fuller planted knives around each man. Common sense would dictate that the men never intended to provoke Fuller at his own home with his white neighbors around. The five men wanted two things: to be paid what Fuller owed them for their work and to talk with Fuller about why he had hit Willis the day before. Months later, a Ouachita Parish grand jury chose not to indict. Fuller was a free man. But Willis, the lone survivor, was not. He was convicted of the attempted murder of Fuller and was sentenced to five years of probation.

Charlottie Dent was horrified. Fuller, she recalled, killed those men "in cold blood, and it was considered self-defense. That was the justice of the time!"[35] Fuller claimed that after the shooting he received death threats from Blacks. Because of this, he said he decided to join the Klan and asked the organization to protect him.[36] The incident also earned Fuller his nickname: "Shotgun." Three years later, he was among many Klansmen across the state interested in the outcome of the sheriff's race in Washington Parish.

In early September 1963, the sixty-one-year-old Elmer Smith officially announced his plan to challenge Crowe for the third time. He touted his public service, noting his background as the retired Bogalusa fire chief and a former sheriff's deputy and juvenile officer. Smith was thirteen years older than Crowe.[37] In his ads in the *Franklinton Era-Leader,* Smith made the typical candidate statements but hit at Crowe by promising not to squander taxpayer money. Crowe officially announced three weeks after Smith and said in his statement that the sheriff's office "has been taxed to capacity at times to keep pace with the rapidly changing developments in handing criminal matters." He said he would strive to keep Washington Parish "a peace loving community in which to live and rear our children."[38] In October, Wilson Burch, a longtime member of the police jury, the parish's governing authority, announced he was running for sheriff as well. In another advertisement, the sheriff, responding to criticism from Smith, pointed out that he as sheriff investigated crimes and made arrests but the district attorney—not the sheriff—prosecuted the cases. "Certain false rumors in this respect have been widely circulated, and we explain this with the hope you understand our position concerning same."[39]

In another ad in early December, Crowe made twenty-one points on the specific duties and services his office provided, including the acquisition of eight radio equipped police cars, implementation of 24/7 patrols, feeding and housing prisoners in the parish jail, and collecting criminal fines. He also said he had no "dead heads" on the payroll, and not once did he squander a dime of taxpayer money. In another ad, he said there had been no organized crime since he took office fifteen years earlier. He claimed his two opponents were promising services that Crowe already had in place. He found their criticisms petty and meaningless.[40]

On November 22, the *Bogalusa Daily News* lead headline screamed, "Kennedy Dead," communicating the shocking news that President John F. Kennedy had been fatally shot as his motorcade rode through Dallas. As Lyndon Johnson, a Texan, ascended to the presidency, the Klan hoped Johnson, a southerner, would end Kennedy's mission to put before Congress sweeping civil rights legislation. Instead, Johnson followed through with it. During the campaign, Crowe made a promise to the Black community—support him for sheriff and he would hire two Black deputies. The Klan heard about the agreement but didn't worry much because Klansmen were confident Smith would win. Secondly, they thought it was an empty promise made by a politician. They never believed Crowe would in the end hire two Black men. As FBI agents moved across Washington Parish investigating the 1965 ambush of the deputies, they would often hear about the "bitterly-contested" campaign for sheriff in 1963–64.[41]

On December 7, 1963, the clerk of court's office in Franklinton was filled with candidates and their supporters as the primary ballots were counted. Unlike three years earlier when Smith led three candidates by almost four hundred votes, this time Crowe led his two opponents by almost six hundred votes. The incumbent polled 6,414 votes, while Smith followed with 5,854 and Burch garnered 1,727.[42] The election now moved into the runoff stage. It was obvious Crowe was not out of the woods. His two opponents combined had more than a thousand votes more than he did, never a good sign for an incumbent.

In the governor's race, Shelby Jackson, the four-term state superintendent of education and a rabid segregationist much in the Willie Rainach tradition, carried Washington Parish with 4,096 votes.[43] The Original Knights supported Jackson, who finished fifth statewide, and there were unsubstantial rumors that Jackson had provided the Klan with money to support his campaign. Jackson was from the farming community of Monterey in rural Concordia Parish in northeastern Louisiana. One informant told the bureau that Jackson was rumored to have given Swenson as much as $8,000 to be paid to state Klan officers to get the vote out, but this was never substantiated and seems unlikely.[44]

The second-place finisher in Washington Parish was also a North Louisiana resident, John J. McKeithen, who received 3,146 votes.[45] After his election as a state representative, McKeithen served as a legislative floor leader for Governor Earl Long. By the time he sought the governor's post, McKeithen had been serving on the Public Service Commission, which regulates utilities. While he was a segregationist candidate, he became a moderate on race matters during his two terms in office.

On January 11, when the votes were tallied, Crowe had pulled it off again. Four years earlier he had won by 137 votes without Black support due to the purge of the voter rolls. In 1964, he would not have won without Black support, defeating Smith by 136 votes, 7,478 to 7,341. In the governor's race, Washington Parish went with McKeithen, who defeated New Orleans mayor deLesseps Morrison with 52 percent of the almost one million votes cast statewide. In the general election on March 3, McKeithen beat the Republican challenger handily with 60 percent of the 773,390 votes cast. A States' Rights candidate earned almost 2 percent.[46] In the months to come, McKeithen would find the Klan, the racial conflicts in Bogalusa, and resolution of the murder of Oneal Moore among the biggest challenges of facing his governorship.

In 2012, the LSU Manship School of Communication Student Cold Case Project investigating racial murders in the 1960s found in newly released FBI documents from the era that a Klan source for the FBI reported that after the election, McKeithen met with Shotgun Fuller and five other Klan leaders to urge them to tamp down racial violence in the state. The source claimed that up to ten Klan leaders would be paid to achieve this goal and that some were paid. The money, claimed the source, would come through the Fountain Insurance Agency in Baton Rouge, owned by a business associate of John McKinley, chairman of the State Sovereignty Commission.[47] The commission's mission essentially was little more than to preserve the "Southern Way of Life." The FBI could never corroborate the source's information, which seems a fabrication. Fuller often bragged he had McKeithen in his pocket, but Fuller was also a habitual liar, and McKeithen would have had little use for Fuller, especially for political purposes.

Fuller told an agent in early 1964 that by the summer the Klan would have one hundred thousand members in Louisiana,[48] although Klan leader Royal Young reported that Original Knight membership reached three thousand statewide at its peak in 1963.[49] Jack N. Rogers, legal counsel for the Joint Legislative Committee on Un-American Activities in Louisiana, reported in the summer of 1965 that statewide there were up to nineteen thousand Klansmen of which fourteen thousand were Original Knights, figures so inflated that it's obvious Rogers got his numbers from a poor source—Klansmen. Despite men like Martin, who told Washington Parish Klansmen that "tail whippings" were a necessary function of the Klan, and Fuller, who had killed four Black employees with impunity, the state committee's legal counsel felt Original Knights leaders were "composed of persons of some stature and ability."[50] Yet federal judges in New Orleans that same year labeled Washington Parish Klansmen such as Saxon Farmer, Ray McElveen, and Elmer Smith "ignorant bullies" who hid behind the hoods of a clandestine organization notorious for exploiting "the forces of hate, prejudice, and ignorance."[51]

On June 1, 1964, as Crowe began his fifth term in office, Oneal Moore and Creed Rogers were sworn in, becoming the first Black men to serve as deputies in Washington Parish and among the first in the South. By then, new state Klan leaders like Shotgun Fuller were in control and talk of violence at Klan meetings escalated. In every klavern throughout Bogalusa and the rest of the Washington Parish, heated discussions arose over what to do about the Black deputies.

5

SHOTGUN FULLER VISITS THE SHERIFF

One thing Klan leaders despised as much as Dr. Martin Luther King, the national leader of the civil rights movement, was a Klan mole, someone who discussed Klan secrets with non-Klansmen. Worse than that was a present or former Klansmen informing to the FBI. Klan leaders like Shotgun Fuller of Monroe took an active role in warning new recruits that the penalty for telling Klan secrets was death. His travels brought him on several occasions to southeastern Louisiana and Washington Parish, where he listened as local Klan leaders raged about informants and against Sheriff Dorman Crowe, who had hired the two "nigger" deputies. The next thing they knew, they told Fuller, the sheriff's new deputies would be arresting white people and threatening the preservation of segregation and white supremacy. Fuller thought he could help by visiting the sheriff and convincing him to fire them.

For white people not associated with the Klan, Crowe's decision was a surprise if not a shock. Oneal Moore and Creed Rogers, however, were grateful to the sheriff for the historic act, although the price the two men paid for their jobs was more than should have been required. They knew their role as deputies would be heavily scrutinized and criticized by many in the white community, but they were confident of the sheriff's support of them and believed he would back them just as he backed his white deputies as long as they did their jobs. Yet neither Moore and Rogers nor Crowe may have fully appreciated the power the Klan held over white people in the parish and the fear the Klan engendered.

A month after the shooting of the two deputies, FBI agents visited the home of forty-one-year-old James Austin Kennedy near Angie in the northeastern corner of Washington Parish, north of Varnado. For three weeks, Kennedy had been a patient at a hospital in Mandeville for treatment of alcoholism. When FBI agents entered his home, Kennedy was a nervous wreck, drunk and paranoid. The Klan was out to get him, he said. He claimed to have been forced to kill a Black man months earlier.[1] The horrific slaying occurred a few days after Sheriff Dorman Crowe defeated Elmer Smith in the runoff election at a time when the Klan burned crosses in Angie and Varnado. The chilling story occupied the front page of the *Bogalusa Daily News* for several days.

The Black man Kennedy killed was thirty-seven-year-old Willie "Cooter" Weary, who lived in a sharecropper's shack on the farm of a friend of Kennedy's. That friend, Hershell Kennedy, witnessed the mortal shooting. James Austin Kennedy had arrived at Hershell's home at 8:30 Sunday morning, January 19, 1964. Armed with a loaded shotgun, Kennedy said he had come to kill Weary. Kennedy complained that while he was away from home, Weary had attempted to break into his wife's bedroom. Hershell immediately suggested that they run Weary out of the parish, one of the many ways vigilantes took law and order into their own hands. The Klan had adopted frontier justice a hundred years earlier. Hershell never once suggested that Kennedy take his complaint to the sheriff's office. "I thought I could reconcile him by using this approach," Hershell told the newspaper. "When we got to the colored boy's house, he [Weary] denied it."[2]

Next, they took Weary at gunpoint to James Austin Kennedy's home, where two people, including Kennedy's wife, identified Weary as the man who tried to break into the house. Hershell said Weary admitted he tried to break in, but a man with a gun pointed to his head would admit to just about anything if he thought it would keep him alive. Weary also knew that his word would have had no standing against that of a white woman. Hershell told Kennedy that if "he wouldn't shoot him [Weary] I would see to it that he was properly charged or moved away." The men drove back to Weary's tenant house on Hershell's farm where Weary was to gather his clothes before his forced exile from the parish. But as soon as the men got out of the car, Kennedy raised his .20 gauge shotgun and fired once, blowing away the back of Weary's head.[3] Kennedy quickly turned himself in to a deputy and confessed to the shooting. Following a brief investigation by Sheriff Crowe and consultation with district attorney, Kennedy was charged with murder.[4]

A year and half after the Weary murder, FBI agents wanted to know what Kennedy knew about the June 2, 1965, ambush of the deputies. Since Kennedy was in the hospital at the time, it was obvious he didn't physically take part in the shooting. But he would neither confirm nor deny whether he knew anything. He said the only way he would talk would be if he were put on an airplane for a distant locale and that what he knew not be revealed until he was safely miles from Washington Parish. Because of his fear of the Klan, Kennedy refused to divulge who had threatened him or why he had been "forced" to kill Weary.[5] It was apparent that Kennedy was terrified that a Klan wrecking crew might pay him a visit if he talked. If he knew anything about the ambush, he never told the FBI.

While Kennedy's reluctance to talk due to fear was the norm in Washington Parish, in a neighboring parish a former Klansmen had the courage to spill the beans even though it endangered his life. John Hugh Gipson of Slidell, a twenty-seven-year-old logger, who had quit school in the seventh grade, had gotten in over his head with the Klan before realizing he had made a big mistake. He was so disturbed about Klan violence that he went undercover for law enforcement.

Gipson had joined the Original Knights klavern in the town of Pearl River, north of Slidell in St. Tammany Parish, in 1963. St. Tammany Parish is bordered on the south by Lake Pontchartrain and on the north by Washington Parish. The school principal in Pearl River and a preacher were among the men in the community who recruited Gipson. In early July 1964, a month after the deputies were appointed, Gipson and others were tapped by klavern investigator Oscar Anderson to beat Clarence O'Beery, a white man accused by the Klan of drinking too much, staying out too late, and not providing for his family. Wearing black masks, they caught up with O'Beery on a back road a quarter mile from his home, pulled his pants down, and beat him severely with a belt, leaving him hurt and bleeding on the ground. They warned O'Beery to straighten up.[6]

A short time after the beating, Oscar Anderson asked Gipson to come to a meeting along with a handful of klavern members. Two men from northeastern Louisiana were there, although Gipson didn't know their names. FBI records indicate that one of the men was Shotgun Fuller of Monroe, the top Klan investigator statewide for the Original Knights. Gipson paraphrased what Fuller told them. Fuller said something had to be done "to stop all these smart niggers and things, and that laws was made for something, but sometimes they had to be broken and there had to be some good men to do it." Fuller said it "might even become necessary to have to murder somebody."[7]

Fuller made several visits to the Sixth Congressional District, particularly the parishes that border Mississippi north and east of Baton Rouge. Fuller said he wanted seventy-five men in the district for wrecking crews to carry out projects. He announced that local klaverns no longer needed his permission to burn crosses or commit whippings. Among the Klan office holders in the Sixth District were Saxon Farmer, who was second in command with the title of grand titan. At the meeting at Oscar Anderson's, Gipson was asked if he wished to be placed on a permanent wrecking crew. After agreeing, he was given an oath different from the oath given regular Klansmen, who for the most part were unaware of the identities of the men on the hit squads. Gipson and the others were given a stern warning by Fuller that if any of them ever were to "reveal any secrecy, ever talk," that person would get his head "blown" from his shoulders. Gipson also was told by Fuller that if "a fellow ever talked that they would get him, that they might not get him then, it might be five or ten years later, but he would be gotten."[8]

Later, Gipson attended a meeting in Covington with Saxon Farmer and other Klansmen. Anderson, the Klan investigator and hit squad leader for the Pearl River Klan, asked Farmer if they still planned to burn churches. Farmer said yes. Discussion then turned to burning two Black churches located in the vicinity of Slidell because Klansmen believed congregants were using the churches for civil rights meetings. Although Gipson was chosen for the project, he backed out. Shortly after midnight on August 3, 1965, wrecking crews burned the Providence Baptist Church and the recreation building of the Hartzell Methodist Church.[9]

Sickened by what the Klan was doing, Gipson went to St. Tammany sheriff George Broom, confessed his own crime, and revealed all he knew. The sheriff asked Gipson to continue attending Klan meetings and keep him informed on Klan activities. Three months later, Broom arrested the suspects, including Gipson, for the beating of Clarence O'Beery, as well as those involved in the arson of the churches. Gipson soon appeared in court and admitted his participation in the O'Beery beating. He also identified the Klansmen involved in the church arsons. At Broom's request, Gipson was placed in protective custody for a journey to Washington, DC, to speak before the House Un-American Activities Committee, which was investigating the Klan.[10] There he was provided additional protection. Gipson knew that his life was in peril now that he had gone public, and like James Austin Kennedy, he was fully aware the Klan might retaliate.

Two months after the deputies were attacked, word spread through the Klan community in Louisiana and Mississippi about the Klan killing of one of its own. This murder was one of the many reasons so many Klansmen and former Klansmen—like James Austin Kennedy and John Hugh Gipson—lived in fear. A forty-seven-year-old alcoholic from Franklin County, Mississippi, Earl Hodges had left the Klan due to its constant emphasis on violence. Hodges later told friends and acquaintances that he despised Klan leaders and wanted nothing more to do with them. The divorced Hodges also expressed a desire to turn his life around, to go back to work, and to reunite with his two sons. But Klan leaders in Franklin County feared Hodges would reveal Klan secrets, including the murder of two Black teenagers in May 1964. As a result, Hodges was invited to a meeting to discuss their differences. A brawl broke out, and Hodges was viciously beaten and dumped along the roadside near the shotgun house in which he lived with his father. Hodges stumbled home and left a trail of blood from one end of the house to the other before dying in the backyard. The savage murder of Hodges terrified everyone in Franklin County and elsewhere, including those who belonged to the "invisible empire."[11]

In the State Line community of Washington Parish, a seventy-five-year-old Klansman and former justice of the peace who held Klan meetings in a tenant house on his farm explained to two FBI agents why the Klan acted the way it did and why the Klan was right about it. He said there was too much lawlessness, too many married men cheating on their wives, police not doing their jobs, and the federal government trying to ram civil rights down the throats of hardworking, honest white Americans who didn't have the guts to do what the Klan did. Klansmen had to do something, he said, and the FBI was wasting time and taxpayer money on a fruitless probe into the attack on the two deputies. FBI informants, he said, were traitors and cowards, adding that he would prefer a son of his drop dead than "pimp" for the FBI. Even if he knew who shot the deputies, he said he would never tell the bureau.[12]

That attitude was ingrained in many Klan leaders in Washington Parish, recalled FBI agent Milton Graham. As agents investigated the murder and enforced the newly passed civil rights laws, they faced constant verbal assaults from Klansmen and sometimes fought fire with fire. "You had to be aggressive," Graham said. "It was a constant verbal bout." Yet agents were always able to find Klansmen who had come to realize that the Klan was little more than a criminal operation. These were prime informant candidates. "You could turn a lot of them when violence occurred. A lot of them [had]no use for the shooting of Oneal Moore. . . . And you'd get violent acts occurring like the burning of a church," Graham added. Only a certain percentage of Klansmen would commit crimes such as these. As Graham explained, "A lot of them just joined to be like in a club, in a group, and maybe some advantages relative to businesses that they are conducting. And one informant could lead you to another. You'd never go to their house to talk to them. And they couldn't come to our offices so you had to find an out-of-the-way place somewhere on a dirt road some place where we could meet quickly and not have cars come by." But Graham agreed with the old Klansman at State Line who complained about the FBI ramming civil rights down their throats: "We *were* stuffing it down their throats.... We had to do it. I'm glad we did it. It was a just cause."[13]

During the spring of 1964, Sheriff Crowe was sworn in to his fifth term, a record for Washington Parish that still stands. A short time later, on June 1, the day before the Civil Rights Act of 1964 was passed, Oneal Moore and Creed Rogers were given their oaths of office as Washington Parish deputies. The Civil Rights Act outlawed segregation in schools and public facilities and accommodations and established equal employment. It also outlawed race-based voter purges, such as the one led by Ray McElveen and Saxon Farmer in 1959. The new deputies were assigned patrol unit WP-14. In 1994 Rogers shared his memories of the day he was sworn in as a deputy and expressed his appreciation to the Crowes in a tribute published in the newspaper.[14]

"I will always remember the joy and respect I received as others watched me take that oath," he wrote. "I only wish my partner, Oneal Moore, could have been here with me to honor this family who believed in us." Rogers still bore the physical and mental scars of the attack decades earlier but still felt the opportunity to become a deputy was one of the greatest in his life and that it opened doors for other Blacks in Washington Parish. He thanked Crowe for the job and for setting the "right examples" for his deputies to follow. Rogers said the sheriff was a fair man who backed up his employees and celebrated their achievements. "Sir," Rogers wrote, "I love you and wish you and your wife the very best."[15]

When the deputies were appointed, Klan klaverns discussed the appointments at length. Many Klansmen were shocked that Crowe went through with hiring the two Black men. The general talk early on was that the deputies would not last a year because Crowe would either fire them or they would quit their jobs. But many Klansmen vowed vengeance. When the deputies went to work, Crowe assigned them to patrol the predominantly Black communities of the parish. In the racial tension of the era, such a plan seemed the most sensible and safest way to begin. But the sheriff did not forbid the Black deputies from arresting a white person if a crime was committed, a policy the Klan had expected Crowe to implement. In Varnado the hiring was considered an abomination. A source told the FBI that at a klavern meeting there in the summer of 1964, one member commented: "Those niggers won't live long enough to arrest anybody!" Elsewhere in the parish, the question arose among Klan leaders as to what could be done to get the deputies removed short of killing them. At a district Klan meeting on the outskirts of Franklinton during the summer, it was decided to have Klan boss Shotgun Fuller meet with Crowe. Fuller promised he would change Crowe's mind about the deputies.[16]

Approximately a month after the deputies were put on the payroll, Crowe received a call from Fuller, who told the sheriff that it "was rather important" the two have a visit. A couple of days later, Fuller showed up at Crowe's office in Franklinton. Crowe related the early July 1964 encounter a few days later to FBI agent Frank Sass, who had worked in Washington Parish for a decade. Crowe had never met Fuller or two of the three men with him.[17]

Sass believed that the two unknown men may have been Houston Morris, a thirty-year-old native of Rayville and a Klan officer, and Billy Skipper, age thirty-two, a plumber and electrician from Denham Springs who served under Fuller as the Klan investigator for the Sixth Congressional District, which included Washington Parish. Skipper was one of several Klansmen who had purchased weapons from Howard Lee, a bricklayer and self-employed gunsmith who served as exalted cyclops of one of the Klan units in Bogalusa. The FBI learned that Lee, a federally licensed gun dealer, had purchased 684 rifles from an Alabama wholesaler but had no records concerning the disposition of 184 of those weapons, which were 6.5-mm Italian military surplus rifles, many of which were sold to Lee's fellow Klansmen. Lee was later convicted of violating federal gun laws and sentenced to three years in a federal penitentiary.[18]

The third man with Fuller was James "Buster" Ellis, a Bogalusa Klan leader whom Crowe knew. Ellis had been accused of threatening a Black man in town in February 1964 after the man sought service at a white-owned restaurant. Ellis had also purchased four cases of weapons from Lee. Ellis and his employee sold the rifles to Klansmen out of his Bogalusa shop, Ellis Auto Repairs.[19] Ellis served as exalted cyclops of a Klan unit, the biggest in Bogalusa with 160 members. All told, the five Klan units in Bogalusa in the summer of 1964 counted 428 members, likely the biggest concentration of Klansmen in the state.[20] There were smaller but active Klan units throughout the parish in Franklinton, Varnado, Pine, State Line, and Sheridan, with possibly four hundred members combined. Informants told the bureau that Klansmen composed more than half of the twenty-nine-man Bogalusa auxiliary police department. Crowe told agent Sass that Ellis occasionally "piped in" during the conversation with Fuller but did not know what he was talking about.[21]

A short time after arriving, Fuller "launched into a tirade" about how much he despised Black people and implied that "it would be wise to get rid of the colored deputies." Crowe listened for a while as Fuller went on about what a fine organization the Klan was. Fuller could not understand why the sheriff would insult the white residents of the parish by hiring two Black men with authority over whites. Crowe soon had enough. He told Fuller he didn't need his advice or anyone else's on how to run the sheriff's office. Fuller asked if his deputies would be allowed to join the Klan. Crowe answered that he did not interfere with what his deputies did off duty if their personal lives did not adversely affect the sheriff's office or violate the law.[22]

The FBI interviewed Ellis more than a year after Crowe informed the bureau of the meeting with Fuller and only a few weeks after the attack on the deputies. Ellis said the thirty-minute meeting began with Fuller telling a lie by claiming that the Original Knights had three thousand members in Washington Parish in an obvious effort to either impress or intimidate Crowe, which didn't work. Fuller also indicated that Crowe could count on Klansmen for political support if he cooperated and let them assist Crowe in handling the Black population.[23] Obviously, Fuller wasn't aware of how hard the Klan had fought the sheriff during the previous two elections. Crowe showed Fuller the door.

After the meeting, Fuller went to see Russell Magee. While Saxon Farmer was the leader of the Klan in Bogalusa, the head of five units there, Magee was the leader in the town, villages, and rural areas of Washington Parish, including some klaverns outside the parish. Sources told the bureau that no move was made by the Klan without his blessing. A forty-one-year-old dairy farmer and teacher, Magee was a descendant of a pioneering Washington Parish family. His farm and home were in the community of Thomas in the extreme northern end of the parish near the Mississippi line, about fifteen miles southwest of Tylertown, where McElveen was arrested, and only a few miles from McElveen's camp at State Line.[24]

Like sheriff candidate Elmer Smith, Magee was one of several Klansmen who sought public office during the 1963–64 campaign. He urged other Klansmen to "infiltrate" every public body or group that existed, from the highest offices in the land to the school board and PTA.[25] Magee ran against incumbent representative Buster Sheridan, an agriculture teacher in Angie. Sheridan prevailed at the polls in a three-way race, winning in the first round, but Magee made a good showing, finishing in second place after politicking hard for the job.[26] Many knew the six-foot-two Magee as a man with a mean streak who, like his longtime buddy Ray McElveen vilified Black people. During the campaign for representative, Magee leaned hard on people to support him and pressed those in power to appoint him to boards and commissions. Many said he wanted to be a big man and had a voracious appetite for power. These traits apparently worked well. In 1965 before the shooting of Moore and Rogers—the school board on a five-to-four vote, avoiding the superintendent's recommended candidate—appointed Magee to a plum supervisory position known as the "visiting teacher," although other candidates for the job were more qualified and had longer tenure. The new position, which included teacher supervision, counseling to school dropouts, and keeping a school census, was secured by Klan members or sympathizers on the board, and it included a hefty pay raise.[27] Prior to his appointment, parents at Thomas High had complained that Magee allowed students during school hours to make billy clubs filled with lead.[28] Those clubs were handed out to Klansmen and used by them against civil rights pickets and demonstrators on the streets of Bogalusa. One school board member seeking to get men like Magee out of the system introduced a resolution to prevent members of the Klan from serving as teachers. After a long silence, the motion failed for lack of a second. The appointment caused friction on the board for months.[29]

The Klan also targeted Senator B. B. "Sixty" Rayburn of Washington Parish, a longtime member of the Louisiana State Legislature considered by some as a voice for the common citizen. Rayburn emerged the victor—beating two opponents in his reelection bid, including Klansman Frank Cooper of Franklinton. Rayburn died in 2008. He served five decades in the Louisiana State Legislature, half of that time as chairman of the Senate Finance Committee, before being indicted in federal court in 1995 for taking bribes from a video-poker truck stop owner. A populist Democrat, Rayburn was the only one of five defendants not convicted. For the rest of his life Rayburn lamented that the feds broke him financially and beat him politically by falsely charging him with something he didn't do. He often repeated, "I did not sell my vote."[30]

Visited by FBI agents in 1965, Rayburn called his Klan opponent, Frank Cooper, a violence-prone "nut." Cooper was a dedicated follower of Russell Magee and attended Klan meetings throughout the state. He worked as a sawmill operator, farmer, and feed salesman and had sold insurance for the Farm Bureau. Senator Rayburn blamed Magee, Elmer Smith, Ray McElveen, and McElveen's father, Diaz, for putting the thirty-five-year-old Cooper in the race. Interviewed by the bureau a few months after the shooting of Moore and Rogers, Rayburn said he understood the deputies were doing a good job. Concerning politics, he said he was on the "outs" with the Klan.[31]

Two weeks after the shooting, FBI agents visited Magee at his dairy farm in Thomas. Magee admitted being a Klan leader and acknowledged he did not like Crowe, claiming that Crowe promised to support Magee in the state representative election, but instead he voted for the incumbent Sheridan. Magee said Crowe did nothing when Magee complained about intoxicated adults showing up at football games and about Blacks, who he claimed sold moonshine whiskey and involved themselves in illegal activity.[32] Magee said Fuller came to see him after the meeting with Crowe and indicated that the two Black deputies would never arrest a white man and that in the event of an automobile accident Moore and Rogers would not "handle or touch a white woman in any manner." Instead, they were to call for assistance from white deputies.[33]

Magee acknowledged that he and Ray McElveen had known one another all their lives. In fact, Magee said they were the same age, attended school together, joined the marines together, fought in the Pacific together during World War II, and afterward helped lead the Marine Corps League in Bogalusa. Magee said the Bogalusa Klan considered McElveen too radical and beyond control because he always favored "tearing somebody up." He indicated that McElveen had drifted in and out of the Klan during the past months. Like McElveen, Magee took part in wrecking crew missions and was fond of making use of a strap on his victims. He told agents that during the previous few years he and McElveen had had a falling out, but Magee would not state the reason.[34] However, a source told agents that the confrontation came during segregationist Willie Rainach's 1959–60 campaign for governor. Magee and McElveen were deeply involved in the Rainach effort. Magee was the campaign coordinator, while McElveen was charged with handling campaign contributions. During the campaign, the source said, "a large sum of money turned up missing. McElveen could not give an accurate account of what happened to the money and as a result Magee accused McElveen of using the money for his own personal use."[35]

The unpredictable Fuller also told Magee something else—that he thought Crowe was a pretty good sheriff. Magee said nothing about the statement, but inwardly seethed with anger. He told confidants that the sheriff had apparently "pulled the rug" over the Fullers' eyes.[36] Without question, Fuller's comment stunned Klan leaders in Washington Parish. They now had little use for him. How could Fuller compliment the very man who had betrayed the white population of Washington Parish by hiring Black deputies?

CRIME SCENE PHOTOS

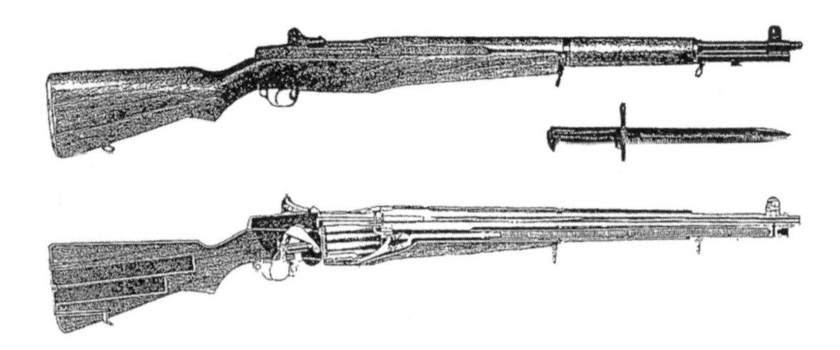

The FBI believed an M-1 Tanker Garand 30.06 semiautomatic military rifle may have been one of the weapons used by Klansmen during their nighttime attack on the two Black deputies. When Klansman Ernest Ray McElveen was arrested, an empty cartridge clip for an M-1 Garand was found on the seat of his pickup but not the weapon. (FBI file photograph)

Ernest Ray McElveen's 1955 Chevrolet pickup truck had two distinguishing characteristics—a white grill and a Confederate flag license plate mounted right of center. The original sideboards on the pickup described by deputy Creed Rogers were never found, but the FBI added sideboards for this photograph for witnesses to view. (FBI file photograph)

The patrol car of Washington Parish Sheriff's Office deputies Oneal Moore and Creed Rogers was heavily damaged during the ambush by Klansmen on the night of June 2, 1965. Moore, the driver, was killed instantly in a volley of gunshots. Rogers survived the attack and provided a detailed description of the pickup carrying the perpetrators. (FBI file photograph)

The railroad crossing where the Klan attacked Oneal Moore and Creed Rogers in 1965 is still there today. Their patrol car crashed into a large oak in the vicinity of the trees on the right side of the highway in the distance. (Photograph by the author)

KLANSMEN

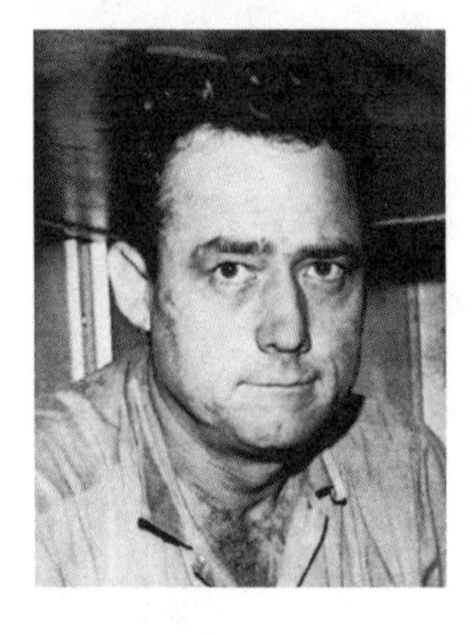

Klansman Ernest Ray McElveen, a decorated World War II veteran who lived in Bogalusa, is shown in his jail cell hours after his arrest in the shooting of Black deputies Oneal Moore and Creed Rogers. McElveen was held for eleven days in jail before his release on $25,000 bond. He refused to make a statement to the FBI and was never indicted in the shooting. (Photograph courtesy Associated Press)

Washington Parish Sheriff's Office deputy Doyle Holliday escorts Klansman Ernest Ray McElveen from the Walthall County jail in Tylertown, Mississippi, for transport to the Washington Parish jail in Franklinton, Louisiana, on June 4, 1965. McElveen was charged but never convicted in the 1965 murder of Black deputy Oneal Moore. (Photograph courtesy Associated Press/Charles Kelly)

Shreveport police fingerprint Original Knights' founder Roy E. Davis (*center*) in 1961 after his arrest in connection with a series of Klan cross burnings. The seventy-year-old white supremacist preacher had a criminal record that spanned four decades. (Noel Memorial Library, Northwest Louisiana Archives, LSU–Shreveport)

Saxon Farmer, head of the Bogalusa, Louisiana, Ku Klux Klan and a suspect in the murder of Black deputy Oneal Moore, is sworn in at the House Un-American Activities Committee hearing in Washington, DC, on January 5, 1966. The FBI learned during its decades-long investigation that Farmer had told another Klansmen before the murder of Moore that the Klan was going "to get" the two Black deputies recently hired by the white sheriff. (Photograph courtesy Associated Press/ Harvey Georges)

Bogalusa city attorney Robert T. Rester appears before the House Un-American Activities Committee on January 7, 1966, in Washington, DC. An Original Knights officer, Rester tipped off Klansmen about city hall's plans concerning civil rights and demonstrations. Years after the June 1965 shooting of the two Black deputies in Washington Parish, he confessed to others that he had been one of the assailants. Acquaintances said Rester was a crack shot with a rifle. (Photograph courtesy Associated Press/John Rous)

In 2007, the FBI excavated this area of the former home of Klansman James Wilford Moore in Bogalusa, Louisiana, where it was alleged he had buried in concrete the guns used in the 1965 shooting of two Black deputies in Washington Parish. Moore's ex-wife, who told the FBI in 1965 that her then husband was not involved in the shooting, changed her story in 2007 and said that immediately after the shooting he had confessed to her his involvement. No weapons were found in the pit. (FBI file photograph)

LAW ENFORCEMENT

Deputy Creed Rogers, pictured years after the shooting, retired from the Washington Parish Sheriff's Office in 1988. His precise description of the pickup that carried the attacking Klansmen led to the quick arrest of the truck's owner, Ernest Ray McElveen. Before his death in 2007, Rogers had come to believe that he would not live to see justice. (FBI file photograph)

FBI agent Ted Garner, pictured here in his Marine uniform shortly before his career with the bureau began in the 1960s, was one of scores of agents who investigated the attack on the two Black deputies. Garner told the author that the Black deputies' arrest of a white man for driving while intoxicated was one of the events that instigated the shooting. (Photograph courtesy Karen Wolf)

Washington Parish Sheriff Dorman Crowe (*center*), pictured here in the mid-1950s, hired the parish's first two Black deputies, Oneal Moore and Creed Rogers, in 1965. The Klan supported its own candidate in the 1960 and 1964 sheriff elections, but failed to unseat Crowe, a man Klansmen despised. After Black voters gave Crowe the winning margin in 1964, the sheriff did what he promised and hired two Black deputies. Enraged, Klansmen vowed revenge. (Photograph courtesy Robert Bobby Crowe)

William "Bill" Dent, the FBI's resident agent in Monroe, Louisiana, in the 1950s and 1960s, spent considerable time during those years investigating Robert "Shotgun" Fuller, who rose through the Klan ranks after shooting five Black men, killing four. Dent investigated Klan crimes throughout the state. (*Concordia Sentinel*)

MOORE FAMILY

Maevella Moore with daughter Tresslar sitting at her side, mourns the murder of her husband, Oneal, during his funeral in Varnado, Louisiana, in 1965. (*Times-Picayune,* June 11, 1965; Capital City Press/ Georges Media Group; Baton Rouge)

Maevella Moore (*seated*) shown with her daughters in 2016. *Left to right:* Sheronda Martin, Veronica Smith, Regenia Moore-Lee, and Tresslar Lewis. (Photograph courtesy the Moore family)

Marvella Moore, holding daughter Tresslar, with daughters Regenia (*left*) and Veronica (*standing*). Not pictured is daughter Sheronda. (Courtesy the Moore family)

Oneal and Maevella Moore on their wedding day in 1954. (Photograph courtesy the Moore family)

Oneal Moore (in his deputy uniform) holding daughter Sheronda. Also shown are daughters Tresslar (*left*) and Veronica (*seated*). Not pictured is daughter Regenia. (Photograph courtesy the Moore family)

POLITICAL ADS FOR GOVERNOR

John J. McKeithen was elected Louisiana governor in 1964 and found himself spending much time in Bogalusa during his first term. Running as a segregationist, McKeithen evolved into a moderate on race and worked to reduce Klan violence in Washington Parish and statewide. He also supported the FBI investigation into the murder of Oneal Moore and often asked the bureau on the progress of the case. During the Democratic primary for governor in 1963, McKeithen finished second in Washington Parish. (*Concordia Sentinel*)

Shelby Jackson served as the state's superintendent of education when he ran as a staunch segregationist in the 1964 Louisiana gubernatorial election. Klansmen in Washington Parish campaigned as forcefully for Jackson as they did against Dorman Crowe, the sheriff. Jackson led the field in the 1963 Democratic primary in Washington Parish with 4,096 votes. John J. McKeithen, the eventual statewide winner in the race, finished almost one thousand votes behind Jackson in the parish primary. (*Concordia Sentinel*)

6

THE ARREST OF A WHITE MAN

Approximately two weeks after Shotgun Fuller demanded Sheriff Crowe fire the two Black deputies, an incident occurred that stoked even greater outrage within the Klan and ultimately led to the attack against them. In 2012, retired FBI agent Ted Gardner recalled with clarity that moment in history.[1] Gardner had arrived at the New Orleans FBI field office a month before the shooting and months later investigated the case directly under the leadership of Stephen Callender, a veteran agent who for a period kept up with the reams of paperwork compiled during the investigation. Gardner said the trigger for the June 2, 1965, assault came after an intoxicated white man bumped into the back of the patrol car as they traveled along a road.[2] The white man was charged, convicted, and sent to the penitentiary. A year later, this incident was the number one topic for Klansmen in a meeting in Bogalusa with Governor John McKeithen only hours before the deputies were ambushed.

The white man's name was Murl "Bill" Rogers (unrelated to Creed Rogers), a fifty-eight-year-old tractor salesman born in Franklinton. Murl Rogers had battled alcohol addiction for years. In June 1963, he had been admitted to the East Louisiana State Hospital for treatment of that disease. Rogers was said to be an unpredictable, mean drunk. Hospital and prison records show that he was well mannered and courteous when sober but unpredictable and unruly when imbibing. There was no telling what he might do, intentionally or otherwise.[3]

Rogers and his wife had four children. For a while they went to church together. Rogers was a Baptist. He liked to read and watch television, but the drinking ruined all of that. Rogers and his wife separated. He told the authorities he believed he had been arrested at least forty times for drunk driving. Maybe he had been pulled over that many times, but his record revealed a charge of disturbing the peace by being drunk on the highway in 1958, two drunk driving arrests in 1959, and a third in the winter of 1962.[4]

On July 27, 1964, Oneal Moore and Creed Rogers, almost two months after they became deputies, observed the headlights of a car moving swiftly toward them from behind. In seconds, the car bumped into the rear of the patrol car. Both vehicles pulled over. The deputies observed that Rogers's speech was slurred. He was wobbly. (Rogers would later argue that he had not been drinking but was high on medicine prescribed when he was treated previously for his alcohol addiction.) They took him into custody and drove him to the parish jail in Franklinton, where a white deputy booked him. Four days after his arrest, Rogers pleaded not guilty to a charge of drunk driving. But on November 4, 1964, when the case came to court for trial, he pled guilty to a third DWI offense and was sentenced to one year in the Louisiana State Penitentiary in Angola.[5]

He was released during the summer of 1965 and returned to his old job of selling tractors at a Franklinton dealership. FBI agents Milton Graham and Alexander Jamieson interviewed Rogers at the tractor dealership. Rogers said he did not blame the deputies for arresting him. They were just doing their job. Rogers denied that he spoke to local Klansmen about the arrest, but he was lying. When pressed, Rogers acknowledged that his sister might have asked Russell Magee to get him out of the penitentiary.[6] Magee bristled about the arrest when the FBI asked him about it. He claimed that when the deputies were hired, the white people were not mad at them but at the sheriff. They were not really police officers, anyway, Magee said, just two Black men "employed by Sheriff Crowe to pay off a political debt." Magee said it would have been "politically expedient" for the sheriff to have released Rogers without charge. If white deputies had arrested Rogers, there would have been no outcry. However, no white man deserved to be arrested by a Black man for any reason, Magee said.[7]

When confronted by agents, Rogers claimed he did not know that one of his sisters was married to a Klansman but added he did not associate with this sister or her husband. Rogers did acknowledge that one of his good friends was Frank Cooper, a follower of Magee who faithfully attended Magee's Klan meetings.[8] Cooper had run as the Klan candidate for state senate against incumbent Sixty Rayburn in 1963. Rayburn and other Klansmen considered Cooper a radical, even by Klan standards. Rogers said he and Cooper had been friends for years and were next-door neighbors.[9] Cooper was among the handful of Klansmen who greeted McElveen to show their support for him when he was released from the parish jail.[10]

The two deputies had performed their duties just as they should have when they removed the intoxicated Rogers from behind the wheel. Although their action might have saved the lives of others, it ultimately endangered their own. The sheriff supported the deputies and presented the case against Murl Rogers to the district attorney for prosecution. Tragically, however, the sheriff and his deputies had sown dragon's teeth.

Entering their sixth month on the job in December 1964, Moore and Rogers had an encounter with yet another white man. The man worked as an enforcement agent for the Louisiana Department of Wildlife and Fisheries while secretly serving as the chief investigator for the Washington Parish Original Knights. Levert Strahan answered directly to Shotgun Fuller, head investigator for the Klan statewide, as well as to Russell Magee and Saxon Farmer. The Klan's investigative department was known as the Klan Bureau of Investigation—or the KBI—a name that amused and disgusted FBI agents. The forty-one-year-old Strahan was a jumpy, nervous man who had joined the Original Knights during the summer of 1963 when asked to attend a "conservative" meeting that turned out to be a Klan recruitment gathering. Top leaders for the Original Knights at the time—John D. Swenson and Royal Young—were recruiting heavily in Bogalusa and Washington Parish during that period.[11]

Strahan had been appointed a game warden in the late 1950s. He told FBI agents that Sheriff Crowe had tried to block his appointment because during the 1959–60 election Strahan supported the sheriff's opponent, Elmer Smith. Strahan said he openly campaigned for Smith during the 1963–64 race. Six months after the deputies were appointed, Strahan claimed he "came upon" Oneal Moore and Creed Rogers hunting rabbits with the aid of a spotlight along a rural road in the vicinity of Varnado. He considered ticketing the two for night hunting but instead gave them a warning. Afterward, he said Crowe tried to get him transferred out of the parish.[12]

Crowe, however, had a different take on what happened. He told agents that Strahan accosted both deputies and accused them of "shining rabbits." The sheriff said Strahan intended to issue a citation but that his superior, Leroy "Slick" Seal, a resident of Varnado and purported Klansman, had advised Strahan against it. Crowe said the deputies were target practicing on the night in question and showed two FBI agents the container the officers were using as a target. Crowe was so furious over Strahan's actions that the next day he sent a letter to the commissioner of the Louisiana Department of Wildlife and Fisheries:

> Last night, my two colored deputies were in the Varnado area. They passed a trash pile and stopped" and were shooting at a can with a pistol. Levert Strahan came by and wanted to arrest them for hunting rabbits at night. Levert called Leroy "Slick" Seal, and he told him to forget about it. Levert has been giving a considerable amount of trouble in this area and I feel you should know about it.
>
> These two colored deputies are doing a good job and after this happened last night they came to my house and told me about it. If these deputies were wrong I would not uphold them.[13]

Once again, just as in the arrest of Murl Rogers, Sheriff Crowe backed up his Black deputies privately and publicly.

During the time Oneal Moore and Creed Rogers were working as deputies, Klan units in Washington Parish were closing ranks. They voted to defect from the Original Knights and operate independently. As coordinator of Klan activities for the Sixth Congressional District, Russell Magee informed Klansmen that Shotgun Fuller and other Klan leaders statewide were fighting again. Magee had little use for Fuller after his unproductive meeting with Sheriff Crowe in July 1964. In proposing the defection, Magee said he wanted the Klan to rename itself with a Christian title. He wanted the new group's structure to be the same as the Klan. By operating as a church group, Magee argued the Klan would gain public support and possibly avoid FBI investigations. He wanted each unit to place a cross above the entrance of the meeting places with a sign proclaiming it to be the "Interdenominational Church Association."[14]

Klansmen agreed to withdraw from the Original Knights but rejected Magee's choice for a new name. Instead, an alternative was chosen—the Anti-Communist Christian Association (ACCA). The new organization was incorporated in a short time before the deputies were hired. It operated with the same purposes the Klan propaganda machine claimed: to promote Americanism and white supremacy and maintain segregation. Magee handpicked the new leaders—Charles Christmas, a balding fifty-eight-year-old employee of a car dealership in Amite in Tangipahoa Parish, and Saxon Farmer. Christmas was the president with the title of grand dragon, while Farmer was vice president, known as the grant titan.[15]

As the subject of the two deputies was a constant topic among Klan leaders,

Magee's paranoia about them and other matters was showing through. He said the military was sending spy planes over various Klan meeting places to listen in on Klan strategy. Magee once physically checked Klansmen for recording devices and had the building examined for the same.[16] At a meeting at the Disabled American Veterans Hall in Bogalusa, units from outside the parish, including Ponchatoula, Hammond, and Amite, were in attendance, approximately seventy-five Klansmen in all. Magee assigned two of McElveen's close associates—Jim Fisher and Dewey Smith—to draw up a constitution for the new organization with the help of Robert T. Rester, the city attorney for Bogalusa. The ACCA constitution was a replica of the Klan's. Magee said a statewide Klan split was reoccurring because Klan money was being misspent by leaders, alleging that Shotgun Fuller spent more than $1,700 of Klan dollars for a new car.[17]

By spring 1965, the Original Knights had undergone a four-way split. At a meeting at the Belmont Motel in Baton Rouge, Klan leaders gathered in Magee's suite to discuss reuniting the factions. Not only did the reunification fail, but two Klansmen, one being Houston Morris, once Fuller's right-hand man, were on the verge of a fistfight and had to be separated. Among the visitors before the meeting began was state district judge John Rarick, the candidate the Klan would support in 1966 when he unseated Congressman Jimmy Morrison in the Sixth Congressional District. Just as legislator Willie Rainach had led the staunch segregation defense in the 1950s, John Rarick, who lived in St. Francisville in the Sixth Congressional District, was its cheerleader in the 1960s. When Congressman Morrison, who supported the Voting Rights Act of 1965, accused Rarick of having Klan ties, Rarick unsuccessfully sued him for a half million dollars. But FBI documents proved Morrison was right. In October 1963, Houston Morris had sworn Rarick into the Original Knights.[18]

The forty-two-year-old judge was a native of Indiana who had moved to Louisiana two decades earlier. During World War II, Rarick was captured during the Battle of the Bulge and spent four months in a Nazi prison camp before escaping. It took him fourteen days to make it safely to an American encampment. In Washington Parish, the Klan went all out for Rarick, distributing literature and putting together a political rally for him in Bogalusa on the Fourth of July. Klan leaflets denounced Morrison and painted him as a fervent supporter of Presidents Kennedy and Johnson. It was true that Morrison was a moderate on race, a stance intolerable to Klansmen. During the campaign, a Klan pamphlet proclaimed, "Jimmy Morrison Fiddled While Bogalusa Burned," referring to the violence and civil unrest in Bogalusa throughout 1965. The Klan took credit for Rarick's victory over Morrison.[19]

Magee's political plans had also included defeating President Lyndon Johnson and others in 1964, but those goals were not realized. As the Klan leaders fought for control and violent members took over statewide, the Washington Parish Klan had lost its momentum when it failed to defeat Crowe earlier in the year. But when the Bogalusa Community Relations Board announced plans to invite former congressman Brooks Hayes to town to help whites and Blacks work through the newly passed civil rights laws, the Klan predicted this integrated meeting would lead to the total integration of the parish, top to bottom. One source told the FBI that the proposed meeting gave the Klan new life and a purpose to which, it believed, most white people would relate. Bogalusa civil rights leader Robert Hicks believed the cause for equal rights was advanced when the Klan blocked Hayes's appearance through the intimidation of local government officials and the white business community. Many whites from throughout the nation wrote letters protesting the lack of free speech in Bogalusa.[20]

For much of 1965, the streets of Bogalusa were arenas in which the Klan and segregationists waved Confederate flags, heckled and targeted Black activists as they marched, picketed, and protested to make the new civil rights laws a reality. On some occasions, police looked the other way or simply made no effort to halt Klan violence. Civil rights groups had stunned the city when they announced they were targeting Bogalusa as a test site in the quest for equality, jobs, and economic opportunities. Mayor Jesse Cutrer urged calm and patience.[21] A Community Affairs Committee was appointed to help ease tensions, and Blacks made a list of several demands of the city, including desegregation of public facilities and accommodations, the appointment of Blacks to local boards, and the employment of Black policemen.[22] Most rights outlined in the new law did not automatically happen. African Americans had to go to the courts to demand these rights, such as school desegregation. In Ferriday, Robert "Buck" Lewis, a civil rights leader, recalled he could walk through the front door of any café or restaurant if he was picking up a meal for his boss, but if he wanted something to eat he had to go to the back door.[23] In Bogalusa, some restaurants admitted Blacks, but others did not. To get service from those who refused Blacks, a lawsuit had to be filed. The same was true for public and private jobs, better pay, equal city services, and so on.

Governor John J. McKeithen had come to believe that the Klan in Washington Parish was the best organized in the state. He feared Klan violence would increase unless he and local officials got them off the streets. At a conference in Baton Rouge with Mayor Jesse Cutrer, Bogalusa commissioner of public safety Arnold Spiers and State Police colonel Thomas Burbank, the governor pondered whether to ask the state's congressional delegation for help. McKeithen believed the fifty-year-old Cutrer was doing the best he could in a hostile situation.[24] Cutrer had been elected mayor in 1962. He operated the Red Bird Ice Cream Company, which he had established in 1937. While the editor of the student newspaper the *Daily Reveille* at LSU in 1934, Cutrer wanted to publish a letter to the editor criticizing Governor Huey Long, who was then a US senator preparing to run for president. Long heard about the letter before it was published and ordered LSU president James Monroe Smith not to run it. Despite the order, the article ran. The next day, Smith told Cutrer that a faculty member would begin supervising publication of the paper. Cutrer and six other students resigned because of these events. When departing the newspaper office, they put a sign on the door that read, "Killed by Suppression." Afterward, they were expelled but soon welcomed at the University of Missouri. Later, the LSU Board of Supervisors expunged the expulsion.[25]

McKeithen told the Bogalusa delegation that federal action was required. Specifically, he wondered if Sixth District congressman Morrison of Hammond, Second District congressman Hale Boggs of New Orleans, and US senators Allen J. Ellender and Russell Long would lend a hand. Could these four officials, McKeithen wondered, pressure federal authorities to use their subpoena powers to investigate the Klan in Louisiana? If the government could prove that the aim of the Klan was to use violence to stop civil rights, then would the public exposure kill the Klan? McKeithen was ahead of the feds in this thinking. By the summer, the Department of Justice would file lawsuits against Bogalusa, the police department, and the Original Knights, some of that legal action based on previous suits filed by Bogalusa civil rights leader Robert Hicks. Cutrer complained that his reputation had been gravely damaged by allegations that he was a Klansman, which he said were not true. FBI documents appear to back up Cutrer's statement. Cutrer suspected, but could not prove, that City Attorney Robert Rester was a Klansman.[26]

In addition to growing Klan violence, the situation was further complicated when McKeithen learned that a Black organization known as the Deacons for Defense and Justice, which had been organized in Jonesboro in northern Louisiana and later formed chapters in Bogalusa, Homer, and Ferriday. The Deacons soon gained a unique place in the civil rights history of Louisiana and the nation. They appeared only for a short time and disbanded once their mission was complete. To protect Black communities and civil rights workers, the Deacons armed themselves. McKeithen feared a fatal bloody street war would result if he and other public officials did not step up and try everything possible, including meeting not only with Black leaders but also with Klan leaders.[27]

Months earlier in Jonesboro, five Black men had been hired, but later let go and allowed to work only as part-time, unpaid police officers during racial demonstrations over the new civil rights laws. Later, a motorcade of hooded Klansmen drove through the Black neighborhoods of Jonesboro led by a police car. In January of 1965, CORE set up offices in Jonesboro. Shortly afterward, three white males threatened CORE workers that 150 Klansmen would enter the Black section of town and wreak havoc. As news of the threat spread, Black men began to arm themselves. African American evangelist Frederick Douglas Kilpatrick told the FBI that the name "Deacons" was taken from the church, while the word "Defense" indicated the group would defend Blacks and whites from the Klan and violent white segregationists.[28]

In late February 1965, six CORE workers visited Bogalusa for a meeting at the Bogalusa labor hall with local Black leaders Robert Hicks, Albert Z. Young, and others. Earnest Thomas, representing the Deacons, said the group would combat violence with violence. While they had no plans to start any trouble, they did not plan to back away. Thomas said Blacks should organize patrols so that if a Black person were being arrested, the patrol would witness the arrest and could defend the person in front of the police. He believed that if the Black patrols composed of armed men confronted police that officers would back away and not make an arrest. Hicks supported the idea. In March, a month after the Washington Parish Klan changed its name to the Anti-Communist Christian Association, the Jonesboro Deacons filed papers of incorporation with the state, citing a dedicated purpose to protect through legal means "those rights guaranteed" to all citizens, particularly minorities. The directors were Percy Lee Bradford (president), Earnest Thomas (vice president), Charlie White (secretary), Cosetta Jackson (treasurer) and Elmo Jacobs. Soon Charlie Sims, an insurance salesman, was named the new president.[29]

By the summer, the Deacons were getting nationwide publicity and, like the Klan, greatly inflated their numbers. In Louisiana, it is unlikely that membership reached more than a few dozen. In 1965, a Deacons chapter was organized in the north Louisiana town of Homer, near the Arkansas line, and a chapter was formed in Ferriday with an estimated membership of twenty-three. The *Wall Street Journal* reported that the Deacons had formed a chapter in Varnado to protect the widow of Oneal Moore. But the FBI determined that "interviews with Moore's widow has not established that any protection is being undertaken by the Deacons and there is no known chapter" in Varnado.[30]

During the volatile spring of racial unrest, Congressman Morrison received a letter from a female constituent in Varnado. He forwarded it to FBI director J. Edgar Hoover. In the handwritten letter, the constituent requested that the Justice Department investigate the Deacons and leader Charles Sims. "They are supposed to have Machine guns, and hand grenades," the woman wrote. "I live seven miles from that arsenal, in the hands of a bunch of idiotic Negroes, and I want that investigated."[31]

A month before the shooting, a Klan and Citizens' Council parade and rally in Bogalusa drew an estimated twenty-five hundred to three thousand attendees.[32] At the same time, McKeithen voiced his support of Mayor Cutrer, who had infuriated the Klan by sitting down with Black activists and considering their demands.[33] Now McKeithen was in the Klan's crosshairs. Speaking before a crowd of three hundred at the Bogalusa Chamber of Commerce during the spring, McKeithen had urged calm and praised efforts to reduce violence. He pleaded that the citizenry give leaders time to work toward a peaceful resolution of the issues at hand.[34] Cutrer held meetings with the Bogalusa Voters and Civic League, the Bogalusa Council Commission, and a group of state mediators appointed by McKeithen, including labor leader Victor Bussie, longtime civil rights activist Camille Gravel, and state senator Michael O'Keefe.[35] Among the speakers at the Klan rally was George Singlemann, the secretary of the white Citizens' Council of Greater New Orleans, which counted Ray McElveen as a member. Singlemann said McKeithen had "turned his back on the white people." Rev. H. L. Thompson of Zachary prayed for McKeithen, claiming the governor "had lost his nerves." At a meeting of the United Conservatives of America, composed and led locally by Klansmen, district judge John Rarick said sixty congressmen "have declared themselves traitors by signing the voters rights bill in Congress," including the man he would defeat in 1966, Congressman Morrison. Other speakers included Saxon Famer, Russell Magee, and Dewey Smith.[36]

But as the Klan took a strong stand against any further talks or progress on race relations, CORE and the Bogalusa Voters and Civic League jointly announced plans to up the pressure, including seeking the integration of Cassidy Park, a place that had never been open to Blacks. Violence escalated. There were fistfights, whites staged sneak attacks on unsuspecting marchers, multiple arrests were made, and charges and countercharges were voiced daily. A newsman was attacked covering the protests, and an FBI agent was punched in the face. On May 23, the mayor stunned the Klan when he agreed to some of the key demands of the Black community, including desegregating public facilities, hiring Blacks to the police force and city administration, and repealing segregation laws. With a major victory now in their hands, activists set their sights on segregated white businesses.[37]

In response, white and Black leaders upped the ante. Saxon Farmer announced that the Citizens' Council was spearheading a recall petition against Cutrer. He claimed that he would get twice the fifteen hundred signatures needed to call for a new mayoral election.[38] McKeithen once again defended the mayor and expressed his hope that the recall petition fail. Cutrer was in a tight spot. Segregationists claimed he was giving up too much to Blacks, while Black leaders said the mayor had not given enough. In expressing his support of the mayor, McKeithen cited a statewide poll of whites and Blacks that said citizens approved of the way he was handling the racial turmoil.[39]

CORE national director James Farmer (no relation to Saxon Farmer) thanked the mayor for his efforts. James Farmer had attended Oneal Moore's funeral with the protection of two state troopers. The FBI received tips that Farmer's life was in danger. A Klansman had attempted to hit Farmer in the head with a blackjack during a march. Farmer also praised Mayor Cutrer for agreeing to some of the demands. In a speech before several hundred at the Ebenezer Baptist Church, Farmer said Cutrer had done more than any other southern mayor, though he also said there was no doubt that the mayor's capitulations were due to the pressure of the movement. Farmer urged Black protesters to conduct themselves "with dignity and your victory will be that much sweeter. The only losers are those who profess segregation and racism." Day after day, Klansmen read the *Daily News* and seethed. Of all the comments by Farmer printed in the paper, one was remembered more than any other. Farmer warned that Klansmen would resist the progress but suggested it did not really matter because "they have become a laughing matter."[40]

On May 30, more violence broke out. More than one hundred state troopers and city police were on the streets. CORE's field secretary for the South, Ronnie Moore, announced a parishwide campaign to recruit Blacks to take part in the movement. He said thousands would come to Bogalusa to push for equal rights. Cutrer vowed that such a march would be stopped.[41]

In Baton Rouge, McKeithen feared losing control of the situation. He knew that the key to stopping the violence was keeping the Klan and segregationists off the streets. The FBI would learn during its investigation that on May 31, 1965, two days before the attack on Oneal Moore and Creed Rogers, McKeithen had slipped unseen into Bogalusa for a secret meeting at the home of the Klansman leading the effort to recall the mayor. At that meeting, Klan leaders would rant about the arrest of a white man by the Black deputies.

7

SECRET MEETINGS, SUSPECTS, AND FROGGING

Governor John J. McKeithen took office as Louisiana's governor on May 12, 1964, twenty days before Oneal Moore and Creed Rogers began their duties as deputies in Washington Parish. By the time he returned to Bogalusa a year later, after several prior visits, he had educated himself somewhat on the Black and white communities that uneasily coexisted there. Meeting with both Black and white leaders, he realized that while race relations were poor in many areas of the state, including the place of his birth in the northeastern section, no place was as volatile as Bogalusa. McKeithen understood white people, and he knew well what they were thinking during this moment when the future of segregation was being tested by the fervent movement for integration. Social harmony for whites, wrote historian Jack E. Davis, existed if white people continued to dominate "political and economic institutions," while totally excluding Blacks from them. To whites, Davis wrote, equality would mean "black culture would contaminate society with a lesser standard of values—lowering moral and ethical norms, diminishing individual initiative and responsibility, disrupting social institutions, and ultimately retarding, if not reversing, the advance of civilization. The southern way of life, the familiar and the predictable, would disappear into chaos." In Louisiana, the future of the old way of life would be determined in Bogalusa.[1]

That city's civil rights movement, wrote historian Adam Fairclough, was "arguably the most militant in the South" and forced the governor and business community to push for the implementation of the new laws aimed at ending segregation. At the same time, Bogalusa also was home to one of the most militant Klan groups in the South. A federal court in New Orleans found that Klansmen in Bogalusa and Washington Parish attempted to intimidate not only Blacks but also federal judges, the governor, a congressman, the mayor, and a host of other public officials. This volatile condition created by two determined opposing sides was years in the making.[2]

Bogalusa had been built in 1906 as the site for a sawmill on land purchased by New York brothers Frank and Charles Goodyear, who also owned the Great Southern Lumber Company. The brothers bought huge tracts of forest in both Louisiana and Mississippi.[3] The railroad followed, connecting communities throughout the region. Washington Parish had been formed in 1819 with Franklinton designated as the seat of government. Before white settlement began, Native Americans occupied the land, the Choctaw being the most predominant tribe. Early white settlers in Washington Parish had survived on small farms along the creeks, where they raised cattle and hogs and grew sweet potatoes, beans, peas, and corn.[4]

By the 1920s, much of the virgin stand of yellow pine was gone, but a reforestation effort begun in the 1920s saved the local lumber industry. Two decades later, Gaylord Container Corporation bought Great Southern, which had not only built the town but also maintained law and order with officers who answered only to the company. The mill was unionized in the 1930s, with whites and Blacks creating separate locals. In 1942, Gaylord opened a pulp and paper mill which merged with Crown-Zellerbach in 1957 and expanded.[5] The bad smell released from the mill's smokestacks did not bother most families in the region, who benefited from the jobs and supporting industries. As in most mill towns of the era, strong wills and stronger knuckles were required to get by.

Historian Fairclough wrote that vigilante justice, especially against Blacks, had been a brutal fact of life in Washington Parish since its beginning. But African Americans still made gains. They owned land in the parish, and many were self-sufficient and independent. Bogalusa's population was 40 percent African American. When the NAACP was all but shut down by state segregationists and judges during the 1950s, Blacks in Bogalusa formed the Bogalusa Voters and Civic League. There was a leadership change in January 1965. Setting a bolder, more militant agenda were forty-two-year-old A. Z. Young, a World War II veteran, and thirty-five-year-old Robert Hicks, a former offensive guard for an all-Black semipro football team who is credited with facilitating organization of the Bogalusa chapter of the Deacons for Defense and Justice. Both were employed at Crown-Zellerbach, where Hicks became a savvy union organizer for Black workers.[6]

Daughter Barbara Hicks Collins said in 2020 that her father believed in the Constitution as the supreme law of the land, but "as a black man, he was profoundly aware that the practices against blacks in America, especially in the south and in Bogalusa, were separate and unequal in all aspects, bar none."

When the Civil Rights Act passed in 1964, Hicks decided there would be no better time to push for full equality, asking those who were reluctant, "What have you got to lose?" Often he would tell them, you have the lowest-paying jobs, you cannot advance, your houses need repair, your children are short-changed in school, you are treated as a second-class citizens, you have no voice in local government, and Black women face even more discrimination than Black men. Barbara feared he would be killed, but after the Deacons for Defense and Justice pledged to protect him with their lives, she was comforted. She said her father "particularly wanted me to understand more about why black people and white people think the way they do and how learned beliefs drove them to do the things they did or would not do."[7] As a team, the leadership of Hicks and Young, merged with the arrival of civil rights groups, became a powerful force that seemed to thrive on any adversity hurled at them by the white Citizens' Council and the Klan.

Day after day in the spring of 1965, activists and Klansmen inched toward all-out war. All the while, many whites not involved with the Klan were growing bitter over the daily tensions, closed streets, confrontations, and rhetoric from both sides. Few whites grasped that Blacks were seizing the moment to see that equal rights become a reality then and not a promise for some time in the future. But fear in the Black and white communities was high. Nobody knew what was going to happen next. As the violence and the war of words heightened, the town became a powder keg that Governor John McKeithen feared would explode without intervention. Two days before the attack on Oneal Moore and Creed Rogers, McKeithen made one last attempt to avert disaster when he quietly arrived at the doorstep of Saxon Farmer, the leader of the Klan in Bogalusa and next-door neighbor of Sheriff Dorman Crowe.

The two leading Klansmen at the May 31, 1965, meeting with the governor—Saxon Farmer and Russell Magee—were close friends of Ray McElveen. McElveen had joined Farmer in leading the Citizens' Council purge of black voters in the parish, an effort also designed to help fellow Klansman Elmer Smith defeat Crowe for sheriff. Magee had been McElveen's friend since childhood and comrade on the battlefields of the Pacific during World War II. Another participant was Klan investigator Levert Strahan, the game warden who had accused the two deputies of night hunting, an accusation that led Crowe to complain to Strahan's boss that his deputies were being harassed.

At the meeting, McKeithen sought a commitment from Klan leaders to stop the violence on the streets of Bogalusa. Klansmen agreed but also had demands. Two conditions were considered of minor importance—that Strahan be given a captain's commission within the Louisiana Department of Wildlife and Fisheries and that Elmer Smith be appointed to the Louisiana State Sovereignty Commission. The main condition, and one on which Klansmen harped was this: that the governor secure the immediate release of Murl Rogers from the state penitentiary. Rogers was the inebriated white man convicted of a third DWI offense as a result of bumping into the back of the black deputies' patrol car.[8]

Magee and Strahan, interviewed by agents in the weeks after the ambush, admitted that they had attended the meeting and had promised to help hold down the violence. Smith did not attend but was fully briefed by those present. McKeithen made no indication that he would meet the conditions imposed by the Klan. Smith told agents that for six months he had been trying to help Mayor Jesse Cutrer by advising violence-prone Klansmen and segregationists to stay off the streets of town.[9]

Three hours before the murder on June 2, Strahan, Magee, City Attorney Robert Rester, and three others met at the mayor's residence to discuss the recall petition against the mayor being circulated by Saxon Farmer. Smith told agents he and the others had been trying for days to get Farmer to drop the recall.[10] McKeithen had explicitly stated his support for Cutrer and his opposition to the recall. By the time the meeting ended, it was approximately 8:30 p.m. The fatal attack was less than two hours away.

These circumstances would cause FBI agents to scratch their heads. Why would the Klan attack the two black deputies after a meeting among its leaders and the governor designed to stop the violence? Agent Ted Gardner said in 2012 that as a result of the meeting and the Klan's belief that McKeithen had no choice but to get Murl Rogers released from the penitentiary, Klansmen may have "figured they owned the store and could do what they wanted" because the governor had come to them. But did a renegade group—tired of the agreements Cutrer made with black leaders and the governor's support of Cutrer—break off on its own at the last minute and shoot the deputies? One of Cutrer's commitments was to hire black police officers. Did this growing momentum for black civil rights in Bogalusa coupled with the sheriff's unforgiveable sin of hiring Moore and Rogers send McElveen and others over the edge? Did McElveen and others act on their own?

Two weeks after the murder, on June 17, Murl Rogers was released from the state penitentiary, not due to an intervention by McKeithen but on Rogers's good behavior during his incarceration. He had served seven months of a twelve-month sentence. Strahan never received a captain's commission as a wildlife officer, and Elmer Smith was not appointed to the sovereignty commission.[11]

McKeithen had disclosed to the news media after the murder that he had made a "secret trip" to Bogalusa on May 31—without providing details—to persuade "some white residents" that the "course they were pursing could lead only to disaster." In the two days between the meeting and the night of the murder, the governor said he had felt "we were on the road to solving the differences and troubles" in Bogalusa and would avoid open warfare between Blacks and whites.

Within an hour or so after the attack, FBI agents digging through the bureau's files found a tantalizing lead, one that on the surface appeared to signal a quick resolution of the case. A confidential informant had told an FBI agent in mid-May that three Bogalusa Klansmen planned to kill the deputies. They were identified as plumbers Virgil Corkern and Edward Burkett as well as Rayford Dunaway. Were any of the three, or all three, in the pickup with McElveen when the deputies were attacked? While a list of possible conspirators was being compiled, the big question would always be, Who was in the pickup?

Virgil "Crowbar" Corkern, a forty-two-year-old father of three who had a sixth-grade education, had been on the FBI's radar since the spring. He had been involved in attacks on Blacks on the streets of Bogalusa and had joined other Klansmen armed with clubs who ordered Blacks to depart a white-owned restaurant where they were attempting to get served. Later, Corkern and others walked into Cassidy Park holding clubs, belts, and brass knuckles with plans to disburse blacks and CORE workers who had entered for the first time ever.[12]

Corkern had joined the Klan around the same time as Burkett. Their wives were in the Klan's Ladies Auxiliary. But the friendship of the two had ended weeks before the murder. Burkett told the bureau that when he and his wife decided to get out of the Klan, they took the auxiliary records compiled in Mrs. Burkett's handwriting to the Corkern's home. Mrs. Burkett wanted Mrs. Corkern, the new recordkeeper, to copy the records in her own handwriting so that Mrs. Burkett could destroy the records in her handwriting. But the Corkerns rejected the idea.[13]

An argument ensued between the two men over the matter, resulting in Corkern pointing a pistol at Burkett's head and threatening to shoot him. "Only a mad man would do that," Burkett told agents, adding that he thought Corkern was mentally unbalanced. The fifty-one-year-old Burkett signed an affidavit charging Corkern with assault with a dangerous weapon. The two men appeared before a judge, but before the case proceeded Burkett dropped the charges.[14]

Burkett and Corkern denied that they were involved in the attack, but Burkett's demeanor troubled agents. One agent noted that he "trembled, perspired heavily and cried but denied his emotions indicated any guilty feelings." However, both men's alibis for their whereabouts the night of the murder partially checked out, but there were gaps in Corkern's timeline.[15]

The third suspect, at age thirty, was a decade or more younger than the other two suspects. Rayford Dunaway, a stocky carpenter with wavy blonde hair, was described by FBI sources as a high-strung notorious liar who physically abused his wife. He also was reportedly so afoul of debtors that his wages were garnished. Dunaway was of special interest to the bureau because he and Ray McElveen had been identified as members of a Klan wrecking crew that beat Jerry Varnado, a white man. Dunaway was also identified as one of the men who attacked journalist Bob Wagner, a correspondent for WDSU, a radio and television outlet in Baton Rouge. Varnado told the bureau that when he was giving his police report about the hooded men who kidnapped and beat him, Dunaway was brought in for questioning as a suspect. Varnado said he had delivered a solid punch to the face of one of his attackers. He said McElveen came to the police station later and was observed to have a black eye.[16] The FBI learned that McElveen was there to see if Dunaway needed to be bailed out of jail. Dunaway acknowledged to agents that he had known McElveen for four or five years and that McElveen became so emotional over the topic of integration that he would ramble and become "almost incoherent." Dunaway claimed he and his wife visited his ill mother-in-law the night of the murder and went straight home afterward.[17]

A fourth suspect from Bogalusa emerged as well. Eleven days after the attack, Eddie Dubuisson spotted FBI agents outside the Del Mar Hotel and pulled over. "I hear you want to talk to me," he said, slamming the door of his vehicle.[18] The forty-four-year-old Klansman had a troubling past. Two years earlier he had committed himself to the state hospital in Mandeville for treatment of depression. In 1964, Bogalusa police arrested him for the aggravated assault of his wife. But Dubuisson claimed his shotgun had accidentally discharged in her direction when he was removing it from his truck. She dropped the charges.[19]

Yes, agents answered, they did want to talk to him. What held their interest were statements he had made to Bogalusa police and to associates. He had walked into the police station proclaiming that he had heard the "niggers" had ordered the police not to enter the Black neighborhoods in town. Dubuisson wanted police to know that in the event they needed someone to go there, he would do it. He had a wife and family, he said, and he would die for them. A police officer said Dubuisson was "very emotional" and seemed "very disturbed."[20] Later, Dubuisson told the informant that the "FBI was after him and they had good reason to be."[21]

What also interested the FBI was Dubuisson's relationship with his best friend, a known Klan radical in Bogalusa named H. A. Goings. Dubuisson operated a Conoco service station that he leased from Goings. Dubuisson had once been active in Unit 2 of the Bogalusa Klan, where he served as an armed guard. But there were reports that he had grown disgruntled and had dropped out. Goings, meanwhile, had been busy on the streets of Bogalusa attacking civil rights demonstrators and pickets. Goings and another Klansman were seen passing out clubs to a group of youths and then stationing them along a parade route planned by civil rights groups. After interviewing a few witnesses, the FBI determined that Dubuisson and Goings appeared to have an alibi: they had been spotted together in Bogalusa at the time the attack was underway in Varnado, seven miles north of town.[22]

Within hours of the attack, the FBI latched onto a new suspect described as a mouthy, blowhard Klansman from Varnado who lived near the murder scene. Just about everybody in Varnado said thirty-five-year-old Robert "Bobby" Lang should be considered a suspect, while one thought he did not "have the guts" to take part in the murder.[23] Jessie Bell Thigpen, who had seen the pickup and the patrol car during the attack, named Lang and failed sheriff's candidate Elmer Smith, among others, as likely suspects. These men were "nigger haters," she said, who opposed the hiring of the two Black deputies.[24] FBI inspector Joe Sullivan interviewed Mrs. Cecil Rester, whose son's mechanic shop and gas station was the focus of a Klan boycott after he stood up to Klansmen over various matters. She said the white community in Varnado was "split into various cliques" in which "people pick on one another and gossip about each other." The only way to survive in the community, she said, was to stay home and not socialize.[25] Her comments rang true in the decades to follow, as just about everyone in town had an opinion on who committed the murder, and many in the community at one time or another was implicated by their own families and friends.

Lang served as exalted cyclops of the Varnado Klan. A short time after the attack, Lang's brother Jimmy, also a Klansman, was surprisingly open with agents about Varnado and the shooting. While Bobby Lang worked for Tidewater Construction, a contractor employed by Crown-Zellerbach, brother Jimmy, a heavy drinker who had had open heart surgery in 1963, was a representative of the mill's painter's union and operated a liquor store outside Bogalusa. Jimmy told FBI agents that he used to like Blacks until the civil rights movement began. Now in general, he said, he did not like "the nigger." Jimmy said he was one of four original members of the Klan in Varnado and that the meetings were held at his house. Klan leaders like Russell Magee were hungry for political power and depended on the Klan vote, particularly in the last sheriff's election. Brother Bobby, he said, supported Elmer Smith. Jimmy also offered the bureau a stunning tidbit—that Bobby, a former constable, was set to be Elmer Smith's chief deputy until Crowe pulled off another miracle at the polls and defeated Smith, the Klan's candidate, for the third straight time. It was a hard pill for Bobby to swallow.[26]

While Jimmy Lang was cooperative during his first interview, he was anything but in interviews to follow. Like brother Bobby, he grew combative, accusing agents of harassment and complaining that the civil rights movement was part of a communist plot supported by traitors and politicians within the federal government. During the second interview, he said agents had misunderstood him during the first visit. He had never been in the Klan but offered to provide his fingerprints. Minutes later he changed his mind and refused. His temperature rising, he told agents that if they wanted additional information from him, they would need a warrant for his arrest. "All this fooling around is a bunch of shit," he said.[27]

Retired FBI agent Milton Graham, among the first agents assigned to investigate the attack on the deputies, had more than his share of confrontations with radical Klansmen. One came when Graham and another agent went to visit Randle Cozell "Jelly" Pounds, a forty-year-old Original Knight. Agents were directed to find out where Klansmen lived and worked, to obtain their military records, and to provide descriptions of the vehicles they drove. Agents spied on Klan meeting places, taking down license plate numbers and descriptions of the vehicles there to find out who was inside. And, most importantly, then interviewed them. Pounds was one of the most violent Klansmen in Bogalusa, having been involved in an assault on a CORE worker and having been arrested for an attack on CORE national director James Farmer. As the agents walked toward Pounds's home, the Klansman unleashed two Doberman pinschers. The agents made it to the safety of their car just in time as the dogs snapped at the door handles. The next morning, Graham was waiting for Pounds at the end of the dirt road leading to his home. When Pounds saw Graham, he was stunned. Graham recalled that Pounds was "extricated from his car, and told never, ever to sic his dogs on agents again." Graham told Pounds that the agents "would never want to hurt his dogs but doing that was a bad idea. . . . We weren't in the habit of physically attacking people and it was more of a case of keeping them off balance and creating a situation that they couldn't function in too well."[28]

Across the Louisiana state line north of Washington Parish along a gravel road in Mississippi not far from Tylertown where Ray McElveen was arrested, two agents pulled into the drive of Glenn Reid, a thirty-six-year-old heavy equipment operator who was nursing numerous wounds. Reid was a big man, weighing 210 pounds, who had black hair streaked with gray and long sideburns. A few days earlier while he was operating a bulldozer, the top of a tree fell on him. He suffered a concussion and other injuries that left him temporarily unable to work and unable to pay his bills. He had just built a new house and was deeply in debt. Reid did not say much, but agents suspected he was holding back. They returned two weeks later and learned that Reid's only income was a monthly stipend of thirty-five dollars a month in workers' compensation plus the rent he received for the lease of his land. Across the road from Reid's house, agents observed Reid's renter loading several cows into a trailer. Reid excused himself briefly, got into his pickup, crossed the road onto his seventy-five-acre pasture, and visited with the man who leased the land. A few minutes later, Reid returned to his home, where agents began to push him harder for answers. He identified the man in the pasture as his close friend, Klan leader Russell Magee. Reid was now nervous and apprehensive. But the agents kept pressing him. Finally, he suggested the agents concentrate on the Varnado Klan. Then Reid admitted he was a member but claimed that due to his accident he had not been to any recent meetings.[29]

The agents listened intently, allowing Reid to talk at his pace. In a bit, Reid said the Varnado Klan was responsible for the attack on the deputies. He claimed that Ray McElveen did not participate in the shooting but was part of the conspiracy. Others had heard that, too, and that McElveen's truck was a decoy. Another story held that McElveen's truck was used in the shooting although McElveen was not in the truck during the attack but waiting nearby in the car belonging to the shooters. After the attack, the rumor went, the men in McElveen's truck exchanged vehicles with McElveen and loaded their weapons back into their car. There also was a rumor that a second truck had followed the deputies but the one McElveen was driving got to the deputies first. Reid said he was approached to take part in the killing but refused. He claimed that several members of the Varnado Klan knew about the shooting and had attempted to give him details, but he walked away because he did not want to know anything about it. He said the one man who would know all the details, whether he participated or not, was Bobby Lang.[30]

Many things other than his Klan background made Lang a prime suspect. Anyone who knew him had heard his tirades against Blacks and civil rights. He had sworn many members into the Klan after threatening some to join. But most everyone recalled that Lang's bullying came when three or four men were standing at his side. One man said Lang and his followers had run him out of Varnado because he supported Dorman Crowe for sheriff. The man said he returned to town later and singled out Lang, challenging him to a fight. Lang refused and walked away.[31] The mayor of Varnado said Lang had tried to recruit him into the Klan. The town marshal said Lang had in the past involved himself in vigilantism.[32]

Many people recalled seeing Lang arrive at the crime scene twenty to forty-five minutes after the shooting and said that he made several eyebrow-raising comments. One witness told the bureau that the first thing Lang had asked upon arrival was whether "both" deputies were dead. Lang also approached Scraps Fornea, who had observed the shooting. Fornea was sitting on a bench in front of a vacant store when Lang walked over. Noticing the wounded Creed Rogers, Lang said, "Look at that—same old hat he had on at the sheriff's office this evening." Lang told Fornea that he had seen Rogers and Oneal Moore there earlier in the evening, but Rogers had no recollection of seeing Lang that night. Lang also volunteered that if Scraps had seen "flashing guns," one of the guns could have been an M-1 rifle because it "throws a flash from the muzzle of a gun 8 to 12 inches."[33] The FBI lab would determine that the rifle used in the killing was most likely an M-1 Garand.

When interviewed by agents, Lang said on the afternoon and night of the murder he was busy cutting bean poles before dark for his garden and frogging afterward. A bean pole is six to eight feet long and cut from a sapling. The pole is leaned over a wire strung a few feet above the ground between two posts. Butter bean or lima bean plants grow up the pole like vines and produce fruit. A Varnado man said he and Lang cut one hundred bean poles in a wooded area near a cemetery beginning at 4:35 p.m. before arriving at Lang's house, where they unloaded Lang's portion around 6:15 p.m.[34] Lang then claimed that between 7:30 and 8:30 p.m. he and his son arrived at a friend's house near Bogalusa and from there went frogging. The friend said they caught numerous frogs and one turtle in a body of water near Bogalusa. When Lang and his son left for home—about a twenty-minute drive—Lang asked what time it was. The friend looked at his wristwatch—it was 10:45 p.m.[35] The timeline presented would mean that Lang was driving home with his son around the time the deputies were attacked.

But there were nagging uncertainties. The next morning after the shooting, Lang, as part of his morning routine, picked up eighteen-year-old Richard Fonda, who like Lang was employed by a contractor at the mill. Fonda observed a frog net in Lang's car. Lang told Fonda that he and his son had been frogging the night before and that if the FBI asked, Fonda should tell the truth. But Lang also told Fonda that if asked, he should tell agents Lang had been frogging on the night of the murder, although Fonda did not know that until the morning after the shooting.[36]

Lang also worried about the details he had given agents during his first interview. He had originally said that he had cleaned the frogs before going to the murder scene but amended that statement by claiming that the frogs were cleaned and dressed afterward. The point is interesting because those who saw Lang at the crime scene said he was wearing clean khaki clothing. Frogging is a muddy experience. Why would Lang put on clean clothes to go to the crime scene and then return home to gut and slice open frogs? Lang also felt a need days later to point out to agents that he had run his finger through a bullet hole in the exterior of the patrol car at the crime scene, perhaps to explain beforehand why his fingerprint might be on the victims' car.[37] No one else made such a statement.

Not long after the initial interview, Lang was feeling the heat and by autumn he hired Baton Rouge lawyer Ossie Brown, who also represented Ray McElveen as well as other Klansmen. Lang also asked a local politician to contact Governor John McKeithen to insist that the FBI leave him alone. The governor refused to help.[38] In Varnado, crime scene witness Scraps Fornea was visited by Brown, who said Lang could name three or four witnesses who saw the suspect's truck before the shooting. Brown additionally disclosed that his defense in McElveen's case would be that Blacks were responsible for the attack.[39]

Various friends and acquaintances said Lang was on pins and needles over the investigation. He told others that the FBI was requesting his guns and tires for inspection but said he would not cooperate. Interviewed two months after the shooting, Lang told agents he had nothing to say. He still refused to allow the bureau to interview his son, who reportedly had accompanied him on the frogging trip. Lang said agents would "twist" what his son might say. He said he would consider being polygraphed if questions were limited to the shooting. Previously, Lang had approached Oneal Moore's father-in-law on the streets of Bogalusa and told him he was not involved in the shooting although, he said, the FBI believed he was. In October, Lang railed against agents for hounding him. He insisted he was innocent. He wanted the FBI off his back and complained that agents were camping "at his doorstep."[40]

Lang seemed to be on the way to clearing himself but then would be implicated on a different front. He did agree to be fingerprinted. His prints were not found on the patrol car or in McElveen's pickup. A short time after the shooting, on June 9, FBI agents learned from sources that Lang had boasted he intended kill James Farmer, CORE's national leader. As agents continued to investigate, they poked holes in Lang's accounts. Agents were obviously suspicious that Lang had created the bean pole and frogging stories to provide a timeline for his activities prior to and during the murder. Interviews of residents living in the vicinity of the woods where the bean poles were allegedly cut and of those living along the body of water where Lang allegedly went frogging contradicted Lang's alibis. No one recalled seeing anyone during the crucial time periods provided by Lang and his companions. At the same time, the FBI learned that Lang had asked others to assist him in creating an alibi.[41]

More intriguing information would be discovered. Creed Rogers, still recovering in October from injuries suffered in the attack four months earlier, recalled that the car that passed the patrol cruiser and the dark pickup at a high rate of spend on the outskirts of Varnado the night of the ambush was a well-tended dark 1954 Chevrolet. When agents interviewed Lang in October, they observed that his well-tended dark blue 1954 Chevrolet sedan had been repainted grey. Lang denied he had repainted the vehicle to disguise it. Agents also learned that Lang had "converted his FM automobile radio into a radio capable of receiving police calls and transferrable from his grey Corvette to his repainted grey 1954 Chevrolet." Backed into a corner, Lang told agents the FBI was making his life difficult and he feared that the Black community would become aware that he was a suspect in the shooting. He pointed out that he was the last white resident living on the same road as Oneal Moore's widow.[42]

STUTTERERS, LEAKERS, AND A JAILHOUSE MOLE

Within a few weeks of the shooting of the two deputies, FBI agents developed a handful of good Klan informants but were hard pressed in getting ordinary citizens to open up about what they saw, heard, or knew. At the same time, those who did talk demanded anonymity, and none wanted to testify in court. This required agents to conduct numerous reinterviews. "The basis for the recontacts here and in other areas in this case," FBI case inspector Joe Sullivan informed FBI director J. Edgar Hoover in July 1965, "lies in reluctance of the residents of these rural Louisiana communities to confide immediately to strangers in a case where the Klan has taken a strong position against the Government."[1] As the Klan pushed back against civil rights and integration on the streets of Bogalusa, it also sought to instill fear in anyone who talked to agents.

In Varnado, Velma Seals, a middle-aged woman employed at the local lumber mill, exemplified the concern. She had confided a secret to three town residents but refused to acknowledge it to the FBI. The basic story she told one friend was this: A few hours before the attack on the deputies, Seals had returned home from work at approximately 6:30 p.m., ate a light supper, and then began painting her living room. While painting, she heard the sound of a pickup and the voices of men having a loud discussion across the street at the Esso service station. A while later, around 9:30 or 10:00 p.m., she saw the idling truck parked once more at the Esso. Again she heard the voices of men talking loudly. This time they were using profanity and arguing. This unnerved her. After a few minutes had passed—about the time of the attack on the deputies—she heard several gunshots, one after the other. So disturbed by the sights and sounds of the evening, she could not go back to sleep all night. She told a neighbor that the next day or so she saw a picture of Ray McElveen's pickup in the newspaper. Seals believed it was the same truck she had seen parked at the Esso station the night of shooting. A handful of men were putting something into the back of the pickup, possibly furniture, possibly sideboards. She confided that she intended to remain silent on the matter and did not want to get involved.[2] The man operating the Esso station that night later told agents that he closed for the night around 6:00 or 6:30 p.m. but saw nothing unusual. However, he said Velma Seals had told him that she had heard a pickup idling at the station after it closed.[3]

When interviewed by agents the first time, Seals said she was painting her dining room (not her living room as she reportedly told one friend). While painting, she said she had the television on and the window air conditioning unit operating. The noise of both, she insisted, would have prevented her from hearing any sounds from the outside. She claimed not to have heard or seen anything out of the ordinary but did mention that her curtains had been removed from her dining room window while she painted. This gave her an open view of the station across the street. When told during the second interview that agents had witnesses who said that Seals had told them she saw or heard a pickup, she was adamant that she had seen or heard nothing, adding that if she were forced to testify in court her story would remain the same.[4]

Agents were so struck by her demeanor that they wrote a separate report specifically on that, noting that during conversion on general topics Velma Seals was relaxed, logical, lucid, and clear about her activities the day of the murder. But when confronted about the allegation that she saw and heard something that night, she "abruptly began to stutter, exhibited nervousness in facial muscles and control of hands." At times she "stuttered so badly she could hardly utter a syllable."[5] It was obvious to the FBI that she was terrified.

Another female resident of town told agents that when she saw a dark-colored pickup parked near her house shortly after 10:00 p.m. she heard what sounded like four shotgun blasts from the general direction of the truck. Several fox hunters were in the woods on the night of the attack, and it was possible these shots came from them, although the FBI never determined that. Then the witness watched as the truck traveled through town and disappeared. Ten minutes later—about the time the deputies were attacked—the woman heard several shots fired in succession, maybe six or seven blasts, and then watched as the same truck passed her house again. She saw a driver and a passenger inside but not well enough to identify either. She did not see anyone in the rear of the pickup, which had "natural wood sideboards."[6]

While exploring every possible motive for the attack, the FBI early on determined this was a Klan project and that the principle motives were political and racial in nature. "The facts of this case clearly point at this time to a Klan escapade," Inspector Sullivan wrote to FBI director J. Edgar Hoover. "The Klan was the only local group we found who had any objection to the employment of the Negro deputy sheriffs. The Klan was the only source of continuing complaint concerning the employment of these men. The Klan felt that the only reason Sheriff Dorman Crowe was reelected was because of his commitment to employ Negro deputies. They are interested in discouraging political dealings with the Negroes as opposed to blocking white voting to secure political victory."[7] Of all the Klansmen in Washington Parish, none were more vocal in their opposition to Sheriff Crowe and the hiring of the deputies than McElveen and Saxon Farmer as well as Russell Magee, who could count on several Klansmen to carry out his orders.

After the shooting, the FBI found a handful of witnesses who saw McElveen's truck racing along the gravel roads through the countryside between Varnado and Tylertown. Like the witnesses in Varnado, they also feared the Klan. Rumors had circulated through Varnado that two vehicles had been involved in the shooting—a pickup and a car. And yet another rumor indicated that there were two trucks. There were also rumors that McElveen's truck was used in the crime but he was not driving it. Stories also circulated that McElveen and the shooters had switched vehicles before and after the shooting and that both vehicles traveled together out of town. Along the escape route, three men described seeing a black truck racing down the maze of interconnected gravel roads they lived on. They said the truck was followed by an early to mid-1960s two-tone Ford car that had extra-large taillights.

Wilbert Hodge, pastor of the Central Missionary Baptist Church, said he had gone to sit up with a sick friend at a house on a gravel road located more than six miles from Varnado. As he placed his pocket watch on a bedside table, he observed it was 10:40 p.m., a short time after the shooting. At that moment, he heard "the loud noise of vehicles" speeding down the road. He wasn't sure either would make the curve near the house because they were going so fast. The car he saw was a 1962 or 1964 Ford with large rear taillights. It appeared to be in excellent condition. Three people were in the front seat. He said a heavyset man appeared to be driving the dark-colored early 1950s pickup. The truck was going so fast it almost turned over. It had sideboards. Interestingly, Hodges said that thirty-five minutes later he saw the car again but not the truck. This time the car was heading back toward Varnado around the time Ray McElveen was being arrested by Tylertown police.[8]

Delos Singley, a farmer, saw the dark-colored pickup as well and described the car as similar to his own 1962 Ford, which had large round taillights. Singley was perplexed as to how the driver of the car could see to navigate because he was following so closely behind the pickup as both vehicles kicked up dust and gravel, enshrouding both in a cloud.[9]

Fielding Crain, whose home was located fourteen miles northwest of the crime scene, said he was outside somewhere around 10:30 p.m. A gate to his livestock pen had been left open and a calf had wandered out. After putting the calf back in the pen, he heard a vehicle traveling excessively fast along the road. He quickly recognized the truck as belonging to Ray McElveen, whose camp was located not far from Crain's home. McElveen often passed by—at least two or three times a week—as he traveled to and from the camp and Bogalusa. Crain further stated that in addition to having seen McElveen in the truck multiple times, two months earlier a wheel had dislodged from the pickup one night near Crain's house. It sat along the roadside until the next morning. Crain walked over as McElveen and two of his sons repaired the damage. "I know that truck," Crain said. There was yet another key identifier—the sound of the truck: it had "a distinct noise to the exhaust that was louder than ordinary." Twenty-five to thirty yards behind the pickup was a two-toned car that, judging from the big taillights—each was six to eight inches in diameter—was similar to a 1960 Ford. Agents asked Crain, by far the best witness, if he would testify in court. No, Crain answered, explaining that he had previously had a run-in with the Klan—a cross was torched in his yard eight months earlier. He also refused to sign a statement. With a wife and a house full of children, he figured it was too risky for him to do anything other than mind his own business.[10]

Thomas Alvin Kemp lived close to Crain. He too heard a vehicle that sounded like a pickup pass by his house. While he didn't see the vehicle, he said the exhaust was exceptionally loud, the same thing Crain had told agents. Kemp heard the pickup turn onto a gravel road that led to Tylertown, where McElveen was arrested.[11] Living nearby was Glenn Reid, the heavyset out-of-work heavy equipment operator who agents learned was leasing pastureland to Klan leader Russell Magee. After acknowledging to agents that he was a member of the Varnado Klan, Reid had listed Bobby Lang as a logical suspect in the shooting. But now Reid too was on the suspect list.[12]

In the meantime, Louisiana State Police superintendent Thomas Burbank reported to the FBI that there were thousands of trucks in Louisiana and Mississippi like McElveen's. In Washington Parish alone, there were 170 such vehicles, 200 in adjourning parishes and counties. All were manufactured in the mid-1950s. The FBI visually checked each registered truck and compared it to McElveen's. Of all the dark-colored pickups checked, some were black, some were blue, some were green. A few had white grills on the front. A handful had a Confederate flag decal or license plate.[13]

Only one truck—that of McElveen's—had the Confederate flag license plate mounted to the right of center as Creed Rogers had vividly described.

In Franklinton, veterinarian Bob Rollins learned from his clients during the early summer of 1964 that the Klan would soon become a force to be reckoned with in Washington Parish. On several occasions, Klansmen had tried to recruit him. One told Rollins that the Klan had investigated him, approved him for membership, and invited him to the next meeting to join. Out of curiosity, Rollins asked if the Klansmen would be dressed in hoods and robes. He was told they would be. Rollins declined. A month after the shooting, FBI agents visited Rollins. He told them that his refusal to join the Klan had irritated Russell Magee, who often tried to bully him into joining. Once Magee told Rollins he had "better" join. A day or two after the murder of Oneal Moore, Magee barged into Rollins's office with a copy of the *Bogalusa Daily News* in his hands. On the front page was a photograph of Moore's widow and their children. An enraged Magee threw the paper at Rollins. "Here are *your* friends," Magee seethed.[14]

Rollins was asked by agents if he knew any Klansmen capable of shooting the deputies. In addition to Magee, he named thirty-eight-year-old Sidney Brock, a neatly dressed rancher and farmer who held racially segregated rodeos at his own arena in the community of Warnerton near the Mississippi line.[15] Brock had been one of the Klansmen in the Franklinton area outraged over the drunk driving arrest of the white man, Murl Rogers, by the two Black deputies. In 1965, Brock served as the exalted cyclops of the Franklinton unit of the Original Knights, although he denied to agents at the time that he was even in the Klan. But Brock's activities on the night of the murder and two nights later keenly interested the bureau.

Washington Parish Sheriff's Office deputy Percy Thomas arrived at the courthouse in Franklinton hours after the shooting, around 1:15 to 1:30 a.m. After parking in the rear of the courthouse near the jail, Sidney Brock pulled up and walked over to Thomas's car. Brock asked about the "shooting of the nigger deputies." Thomas told him that one deputy was dead and the other wounded. Brock explained that he had been in bed when he received a phone call about the attack. To find out what happened, he decided to drive to the courthouse. Many Klansmen like Brock had criticized Sheriff Crowe for hiring the two Black deputies, but to Thomas's cynical amazement Brock said that he now believed the sheriff "had done the right thing by hiring them."[16]

Deputy Thomas was suspicious of Brock's keen interest in what happened, telling agents that Brock was "just too inquisitive about the shooting" and "was more interested in knowing the results of the shooting and if anyone had been arrested as a result." Additionally, the deputy told agents that he "could not visualize a man getting out of bed in the middle of the night, getting fully dressed, and going downtown to find out about something that did not concern him." Thomas had no doubt that Brock was somehow involved.[17]

When agents approached Brock about his visit to the courthouse, they found him at the feed mill in Franklinton. He said he had received a call about the shooting around midnight but claimed the caller did not identify himself. That's why he decided to go to the courthouse. Brock called the shooting deplorable and said he had no idea who did it. As for his activities prior to the shooting, Brock said he had visitors arriving in two vehicles at his home that night, the last guest leaving no later than 11:00 p.m.[18] But Franklinton police chief Carruth Miller said he was heading home around 8:00 p.m. and drove by Brock's house, where he saw eight to nine automobiles parked outside, indicating that a meeting was in progress. This was not unusual, Miller said, because Brock often had Klan meetings there. The police chief said that when the deputies were hired, he was approached several times by Franklinton residents who asked whether he intended to work with the two Black deputies and if he planned to ride in the same car with them. It was Miller's opinion that the killing was politically and racially motivated because the Klan's nemesis, Sheriff Crowe, had hired two Black men as deputies, which some in the white community found passionately objectionable.[19]

Equally interesting to agents, however, was Brock's activities two nights after McElveen had been transported from the Tylertown jail to the one in Franklinton. Retired FBI agent Ted Gardner, looking back on the case in 2012, said he and other agents knew in the 1960s that Brock had planted a mole in the jail that night to monitor McElveen's comments and actions: "The Klan arranged for a member of the Franklinton PD to arrest a Klansman and put him in a cell directly across from McElveen so he would know who McElveen met with while he was in jail."[20] But Brock would admit to nothing in the 1960s. Decades would pass before he would own up to what he did.

In 1991, he finally admitted he was the exalted cyclops of the Franklinton Klan in 1965 and that he did indeed plant the mole.[21] FBI records indicated that the mole was Henon Carrier of Wilmer in rural Tangipahoa Parish. He was brought to the parish jail at 10:30 p.m. by Franklinton police officer Farrell Simmons on the night of June 4 on a charge of drunkenness and released the following day,[22] leaving behind a fingernail clipper and a pocketknife in the storage locker. The jailer recalled that Carrier did not appear intoxicated.[23]

McElveen, who made a few initial remarks at the time of his arrest, clammed up at the Tylertown jail and said nothing to police or anyone else after being transported to Franklinton and remained silent for the rest of his life. While the assumption was that the Klan planted the mole to make sure McElveen did not talk, there was another possibility. Was Brock, on behalf of himself and Magee, simply trying to find out what happened because Klan leaders did not know? If McElveen had recruited his own wrecking crew without their authorization or knowledge, these Klan leaders would have wanted to know who was involved because the crime would have been committed without their blessings and because they had failed to deliver on a promise to the governor two days before the shooting to tamp down Klan violence.

On the night of August 17, the FBI prepared to reenact the shooting of the deputies under the same conditions as the event had occurred. Surviving deputy Creed Rogers was physically able to be at the scene although doctors had told him not to be hopeful that the sight in his right eye would return. His hands, which he used to brace himself before impact with the windshield, were numb and weak. Doctors believed repair to the nerve damage would restore feelings in his hands. With help from the sheriff's office, McElveen's pickup was driven from evidence storage in Bogalusa to Varnado. Once everything was in place, agents checked the scene as Rogers got into a patrol car to re-create his actions and observations.

Just as on the night of the shooting, the street was abandoned. The only witnesses who admitted to seeing the crime—Scraps Fornea and Jesse Bell Thigpen—were on the scene as requested by agents. In preparing for this reenactment, the FBI needed the clearance of District Attorney Woodrow Erwin. Additionally, Sheriff Crowe provided representatives of his office to arrange for the truck to be at the scene as well as the two eyewitnesses. But just before the re-creation began, several vehicles pulled in and parked. Among the individuals arriving was McElveen's attorney, Ossie Brown. Immediately, the test run was canceled. The big question for the FBI was who tipped off Brown?[24]

Brown had been born in Winnfield, the hometown of Huey P. Long, a year before Long began his first term as governor in 1928. Reared outside Baton Rouge in Baker, Brown became one of the most popular students in high school. He composed the school song and became president of Boys State. At LSU, he was a drum major for the Golden Band from Tiger Land, played basketball and tennis, and was elected president of Sigma Chi. In 1944, the freckled eighteen-year-old lived at the Sigma Chi house and registered for the draft. After serving in the navy during World War II, he got his law degree from LSU and in time became a nationally known defense attorney, having successfully defended one of the US soldiers tried following the 1970 My Lai massacre in Vietnam. His client was the only serviceman acquitted on all charges. Two years after the massacre, he was elected district attorney of East Baton Rouge Parish.[25]

During the 1960s, Brown defended not only McElveen but other Klansmen as well. He also defended a host of Klansmen before a federal court in New Orleans in 1965 following the Bogalusa civil rights clashes. Other Klan leaders in southeastern Louisiana who became targets of the FBI investigations either hired or were prepared to hire Brown if need be. A segregationist during that period of his life, Brown was well known by Klansmen and had numerous connections in the Klan.

Immediately, the bureau went to work searching for the source of the leak. Headquarters informed the New Orleans office that it "is apparent that the local prosecuting attorney and sheriff cannot be trusted as there was an obvious leak which disclosed the plans of your investigative activity or no one would have been there.... You should be most circumspect in your dealings with the Sheriff and tell him nothing in regards to your investigative activity."[26]

Quickly, however, the FBI learned that the DA was out of town before plans were finalized for the test run and no one in his office was aware of the details, thereby elevating suspicions that the sheriff's office was the source of the leak. Crowe, too, was out of town and delegated authority to his chief deputy and brother-in-law, Doyle Holliday, to work with the FBI on the reenactment.

Two deputies were used to assist in making arrangements in Varnado but neither man discussed the project with anyone, the FBI learned. But Holliday, a close friend of Bogalusa police chief Claxton Knight, had disclosed the plans to Knight and asked him to drive Holliday's personal car to Varnado on the night of the test. When questioned by the FBI whether he had any knowledge concerning the scheduled test run, Knight lied and said no. Holliday told agents that Knight "must have in some fashion disclosed the planned course of action to a third person and thus caused the information to leak to defense counsel." Knight, the FBI concluded, was the source of the leak. All bureau personnel were told to always be "circumspect in dealing with Knight." They never trusted him again and neither did Holliday on matters concerning the murder investigation.[27]

Retired FBI agent Milton Graham felt Knight and other leaders in the Bogalusa Police Department might not "do bad things themselves, but had sympathy for the troublemaker."[28] *Los Angeles Times* reporter Jack Nelson, in his book *Scoop: The Evolution of a Southern Reporter,* said that in 1965 Knight's face was "twisted in rage" when the two ran into each other outside the federal courthouse in New Orleans during the hearings on Bogalusa. Nelson had written a story for the *Times* "about Bogalusa's meanness." Someone had sent a clipping to Knight and others in Bogalusa. Nelson wrote that Knight "waved the clipping back and forth before thrusting it into my face," questioning Nelson as to whether he had written article, to which the reporter answered yes. "Well, I'll tell you one goddamn thing," Knight growled. "People in Bogalusa have seen it, too, and they don't like it a goddam bit! You better keep your ass out of Bogalusa."[29]

Once the FBI identified Knight as the person who told Ossie Brown about the reenactment of the attack on the deputies, agents then moved on to another task—identifying the man in Brown's company in Varnado on the night of the planned test run. It turned out to be Dewey Bernard Smith, one of several Klansmen from Washington Parish called to testify before the House committee investigating the Klan in 1966. Smith also was one of McElveen's best friends. A conspiracy theorist who often railed against the federal government, Smith once expressed his allegiance to the Klan over the United States. Several individuals reported seeing Smith and McElveen together often, and after the shooting Smith was among the men who helped post McElveen's $15,000 bond. Smith put up almost $2,000 to that end and was at the courthouse when McElveen was released, joining attorney Brown in immediately going to McElveen's camp for purposes unclear to this day.[30]

Unlike most Klansmen, Smith was well educated and seemingly secure financially. Born in the parish seat of Franklinton in 1920, he served five years in the military and went on to study at three universities before obtaining a degree in horticulture. Smith served as leader of two different Klan units (at different times) in Bogalusa. In February 1965 while exalted cyclops of Unit 1 he told his followers that if any Klansman were arrested, he would use his own money to bail them out of jail. He attempted to disrupt the integration of a school in Bogalusa and once said that he owed no loyalty to the United States because the last two presidents—John F. Kennedy and Lyndon B. Johnson—were both traitors. On another occasion, he proclaimed that the only way to prevent communism from spreading was to kill some of the country's politicians. In federal court, Smith admitted to assaulting and threatening Blacks seeking their civil rights in Bogalusa and taking part in the economic boycott against Blacks and against white public officials and businessmen who appeared sympathetic to civil rights. The FBI also discovered that he had authored at least five Klan leaflets circulated in Bogalusa.[31]

In the summer of 1965, agents observed Smith in his Dodge station wagon parked in front of an old church building in Bogalusa. He agreed to be questioned but first stated that everyone in town was upset "over the invasion of about 100 FBI agents" to investigate matters in which the federal government had no authority. He said the bureau was simply a tool of politicians. Smith railed against Sheriff Crowe. He charged that numerous murders and crimes in the parish were unsolved because the sheriff would do nothing that would hurt his chances for reelection. That's why Dewey Smith said he tried to run as a write-in candidate in the general election in 1964 after Crowe defeated challenger Elmer Smith (no relation) in the Democratic primary. But "because of trickery," Dewey Smith claimed he was disqualified, adding that the clerk of court failed to advise him that he had to furnish an affidavit stating that he was not affiliated with communists.[32]

Dewey Smith launched his campaign immediately after Elmer Smith was eliminated from the race. In early February 1964, the Washington Parish Board of Election Supervisors voted by a majority of two to certify Smith as a write-in candidate opposing Crowe, the nominee on the Democratic ticket. Dewey Smith's political ad in the February 20, 1964, issue of the *Franklinton Era-Leader* outlined his case against Crowe:

> Our present Sheriff, as anyone can see by looking at the returns in the last two primaries, received the support of the Negro bloc vote and is therefore obligated to the NAACP which delivered the vote. The responsible people of the parish cannot sit idly by and allow this to continue. It is time that we took our parish back from the hands of machine politicians working hand-in-hand with the NAACP and put responsible people in control. I believe in justice and fairness for all people regardless of color, however, to solicit a bloc vote in itself is admitting that special privileges go along with that vote.[33]

When Smith was disqualified as a write-in candidate he appealed, but in late February a state appeals court refused to intervene because Smith had failed to sign the necessary affidavits certifying that he was not a communist or a member of a subversive organization such as the Ku Klux Klan. In 1966 when appearing before a congressional committee investigating the Klan, Chief Investigator Donald Appell questioned the Klansman. "Mr. Smith," Appell asked, "having taken a Klan oath in which you promised to keep secret to yourself the secret of a Klansman, except treason against the United States, rape, and malicious murder, how could you in good conscience, having taken that oath, appear on a ballot as a candidate for the office of sheriff?"[34]

Smith refused to answer. Appell then asked, "If you had been elected sheriff, under your oath, wouldn't you have had to give protection to your fellow Klansman?" Again, Smith refused to answer.[35]

While being interviewed by agents in Bogalusa, Smith said he first met McElveen in 1959 when Smith moved to Bogalusa. He said the two men developed a business and social affiliation. This close relationship began during the time McElveen challenged hundreds of Black voters, resulting in their names being removed from the voter rolls. Smith claimed that Crowe orchestrated McElveen's arrest in part to settle that political score. He said there was no way McElveen was involved in the shooting but that he could have been provoked to do so due to the "communistic policies of the government."[36]

Those who attacked the deputies had done the community a disservice, Smith said, because it was "like killing a snake; they merely cut off the tail, not the head." He felt white people had been pushed to the limit by the federal government, which had been penetrated by the communists who ultimately killed Kennedy when he shifted from his communist platform. Smith also opined that maybe McElveen had a personal reason for not confiding to authorities what he was doing on the night of the murder when racing in his pickup through Tylertown. Maybe it involved "extramarital relations," Smith said but added that he did not know if that was true.[37]

By July 1965, Smith's name was added to a growing list of suspects, including Bogalusa Klan leader Saxon Farmer, Washington Parish Klan leader Russell Magee, Varnado Klan leader Bobby Lang, game warden and chief Klan investigator Levert Strahan, and Klansman Glenn Reid.

"A LOT OF THINGS CHANGE . . . IN FRONT OF THREE FEDERAL JUDGES"

In the Atlantic in late August of 1965, the National Weather Service took notice of a tropical disturbance that would soon grow into a monster hurricane. It would be named Betsy. The storm was located 690 miles south of Miami on September 2. That same day in New Orleans, a federal three-judge panel prepared to hear a lawsuit filed by the US Government against the Original Knights of the Ku Klux Klan over its longtime pattern of violence and intimidation against Blacks, civil rights activists, businesses, and public officials in Bogalusa.

As late summer turned to autumn, one of the Klan's attorneys, Ossie Brown, pushed for and then withdrew a request for a preliminary hearing for his client, Ray McElveen, while members of a Washington Parish grand jury, packed with McElveen supporters, hatched a plan to forever free the Klansman from future prosecution by the district attorney. In Baton Rouge, Governor John McKeithen's every effort to calm the situation in Bogalusa by reaching out to Black leaders and working to end Klan violence had once appeared headed for a positive resolution. But the attack on the two Black deputies on June 2 put everything in jeopardy. Bogalusa exploded. McKeithen grew frustrated as the street violence and protests paralyzed the town during the summer, and at one point he seemed to throw up his hands in defeat. But the governor would announce a new plan by early September just before Betsy ripped through Louisiana.

In July President Johnson had sent John Doar to Bogalusa to assess the situation along with FBI inspector Joseph Sullivan. Doar met with Bogalusa's top officials and Black leaders as well as the governor. A. Z. Young and Robert Hicks of the Bogalusa Voters and Civic League had rejected a proposal by McKeithen for a thirty-day "cooling off" period that included a moratorium on marches. The governor was seeking a brief period of peace after six months of turmoil. While Doar and Sullivan refused to say much to the press, White House press secretary Bill Moyers said Bogalusa's problem was a local one that would have to be solved locally. That seemed impossible. African American author and television journalist Louis Lomax, among the national activists visiting Bogalusa following the murder of Oneal Moore, told one assembly, "You can't save Vietnam without first saving Bogalusa." Hicks, speaking at the Ebenezer Baptist Church in Bogalusa, said it was obvious that neither the city nor the state had the power to do anything. "We will see if the federal government is powerless."[1]

As chief of the Justice Department's Civil Rights Division, Doar quickly set up an office at the Bogalusa Post Office. Not long after his arrival, he witnessed the July 17 failure of police officers to protect pickets at the Pine Tree Shopping Center from marauding white men. An injunction previously ordered by Judge Herbert Christenberry, referred to as "Judge Crystal Ball"[2] by Klansmen, required demonstrators be provided police protection. A lawsuit filed previously by some of those demonstrators sought $425,000 in damages on claims that not only did police officers refuse to provide protection but that they were also involved in the harassment. One man claimed he was brought to the police station, where five hooded men threatened him. Nine witnesses claimed they were struck by white bystanders or cursed by them while the lawmen stood by. When public officials claimed that they had not witnessed many of the attacks alleged by victims, the judge found it hard to believe. Public officials, he said in court, "should know what's going on in their own city."[3]

Christenberry had issued injunctions against the Bogalusa Police Department and Washington Parish Sheriff's Office on July 10 ordering them to protect demonstrators and marchers. Seven days later, several bloody incidents occurred during two days of demonstrations at Cassidy Park. "I was there on the 17th and saw it all," recalled Doar. "So did Joe Sullivan. I will never forget Inspector Sullivan moving in, dressing down local police authorities for their failure to do their duty and in effect, keeping the peace."[4]

On July 19, the Justice Department went to court, filing an action for civil contempt alleging local authorities had violated the injunction. The injunctive relief requested was designed to prevent dozens of local and area white men, most of them Klansmen, "from interfering with persons seeking to exercise their constitutional rights." By the time the civil case went to trial in the fall of 1965, the investigation into the murder of deputy Moore, according to Doar, included "25 volume-size FBI reports averaging in excess of 100 pages each. The information contained in these reports . . . was used by us to prove our civil case in Federal Court."[5]

In all, the federal government filed five suits—one seeking an injunction against the Klan involving violence and intimidation against Blacks, one against Commissioner of Public Safety Arnold Spiers; one against Police Chief Claxton Knight; one against Thomas Sisters Café, Virginia Inn, Landry's Fine Foods, and John Sumrall's Service Station for failing to serve Blacks; and a fifth against Vertrees Adams, a Washington Parish deputy sheriff accused of beating and harassing civil rights workers.[6]

With tensions peaking, Mayor Cutrer publicly urged whites not to harm civil rights demonstrators as the United Klans of America staged a huge rally at Crossroads, Mississippi, across the Pearl River from Bogalusa on July 22. All the while, whites continued to throw rocks, cracked ice, and tomatoes at marchers in Bogalusa. There were cases, too, where Blacks attacked whites, some of the attacks resulting in serious injuries. Young said the Black community would work to hold down the violence but "if blood is going to be shed, we are going to let it rain down on Columbia Street—all kinds, both black and white. We are not going to send Negro blood down Columbia Street by itself, that's for sure."[7]

For FBI agents like Milton Graham, a northerner who had begun his career with the bureau only months earlier, the murder investigation and the task of establishing peace in Bogalusa were enormous undertakings. "We would watch these things and observe," he said. Inflamed passions "created situations where somebody was going to get something thrown at them or punched or something and we had to be on top of all of that. . . . We had to deal with those things while we were working around this murder case. Every day it was working something to do with the Klan. . . . They would verbally attack you and call you some kind of lover and everything else. And then you had to kind of respond. You had to be aggressive."[8]

One day he ran into McElveen and some of his relatives and friends weeks after McElveen had been charged with murder and posted bond. "I was by myself. They were kind of looking at me and laughing. . . . I went over to them and said, 'Is there something funny, you know, if you got something to say, don't mumble it, say it to me, and, at least be man enough to tell me to my face.'" To Graham's surprise, McElveen knew the agent's name and said there was no problem. "There was a guy behind us," Graham said, who "kept hitting his fist with his hand . . . walking back and forth behind me, in a kind of threatening sort of gesture you might say. . . . The next day, I went to the post office and waited for the fist banger and he came out and he left in his car. I was behind him and he knew it. He stopped his car in front of his house and I got out, started to get out, and he ran to his house and ran right through the screen door!"[9]

On July 22, the day of the United Klans of America rally, whites paraded about Bogalusa in cars with Confederate flags waving before heading to the rolling hills of the Crossroads community near Poplarville, where African American Mack Charles Walker, accused of the rape of a white woman, was kidnapped and later killed by a lynch mob six years earlier. Cars were bumper to bumper on Highway 26 leading to the event. Speakers and a microphone were assembled on the back of a flatbed trailer. A front-page story about the event in the *Bogalusa Daily News* noted that most of the attendees came from Bogalusa, Washington Parish, and southeastern Louisiana and that "Confederate stars and bars were everywhere—shirts, dresses, hats, sticks." The event was billed as a family affair. A four-month-old child was dressed in full Klan regalia. Vendors sold rebel flags, Klan literature, and records, while a four-piece "hillbilly band" played "Dixie," "The Old Rugged Cross," and "Cotton Fields."[10]

The temperature peaked at ninety-six degrees, but an afternoon shower cooled the rally grounds. E. L. McDaniel of Natchez, the grand dragon of the Mississippi Realm of the United Klans of America, introduced the guest speaker, Robert Shelton. As head of the fastest-growing Klan organization in the United States in the 1960s, the well-dressed Shelton stepped up to the microphone, a big diamond ring on his left hand. Shelton characterized civil rights workers, like those in Bogalusa, particularly the white ones, as "tennis-shoe-wearing sex-perverted beatniks." He called Justice Department officials such as Doar and Sullivan "pimps."[11]

In Baton Rouge, McKeithen read about the rally and saw the comments. Only nineteen months into his first term as governor, he had grown increasingly frustrated with how to handle the racial matters. The attack on the two deputies was a hard blow, especially after he had drawn assurances from Klan leaders two days prior to the murder of Moore that they would instruct their members to stay home. He had promised a quick resolution of the murder, but now he realized that nothing was a sure thing. "There is nothing more I can do," he told the press, but that would prove to be only a passing sentiment.[12]

Two big stories caught the eye of *Bogalusa Daily News* readers on September 2. One announced a hurricane was brewing in the Atlantic,[13] and another centered on the first meeting of a state biracial committee known as the State Commission on Race Relations. McKeithen created the committee at the suggestion of the Council for a Better Louisiana, which was concerned by racial conflicts, especially in Bogalusa, that caused an economic boycott by out-of-state companies. Jointly heading the commission were LSU president emeritus Troy H. Middleton, a segregationist who had served with distinction as a general in World War II, and Dr. Albert W. Dent, president of Dillard University, a historically Black institution of high learning. The forty-two-member body held its first meeting on September 1 and immediately initiated a search for an executive director. McKeithen told the press, "There is no reason why we cannot live in peace and harmony, work together and help our state and live in it without frustration." He said he was trying to position Louisiana to get a handle on the state's racial problems and to lead the nation by finding solutions. He admitted his own naivete in trying to handle the situation over the preceding months. "I realized I had to have help."[14]

On September 5, another story made headlines across the state and nation. More than one hundred Bogalusa and Washington Parish residents were subpoenaed for a hearing on the federal government's injunction suit against the Original Knights. All three judges hearing the case were residents of New Orleans. In addition to Judge Christenberry, who was well familiar with the Bogalusa and Washington Parish issues, the panel also included judges John Minor Wisdom, who presided, and Robert A. Ainsworth.[15]

Born in the late nineteenth century, the sixty-five-year-old Christenberry was a graduate of Loyola Law School. After Christenberry had spent several years in private practice and later as a prosecutor, President Harry Truman appointed him to the US District Court of the Eastern District of Louisiana, where he served as chief judge from 1949 until 1967. Known for his unfaltering memory, long work hours, fearlessness against threats, and intensity in the courtroom, Christenberry often questioned witnesses himself, a trait that did not always please the attorneys in his courtroom.[16]

Wisdom was sixty years old and had earned a law degree from Tulane, finishing first in his class. President Dwight D. Eisenhower named him to the US Fifth Circuit of Appeals in 1957.[17] Ainsworth was a fifty-five-year-old Mississippi native who had served from 1952 to 1961 in the Louisiana state senate, seven of those years as president pro tempore. President John F. Kennedy named him a federal judge in the eastern district in 1961.[18]

Baton Rouge attorneys Michael S. Ingram and Gerald McKernan and McElveen's attorney, Ossie Brown, represented the Klan defendants. Justice Department lawyers included D. Robert Owen of Dallas, director of the southwest division of the civil rights division, and assistants Kenneth G. McIntyre and Martin Glick.[19]

Even as Wisdom gaveled court into session on September 6 in New Orleans, more violence was reported in Bogalusa between Black pickets and white bystanders. The next day, seventy-one witnesses were sworn in. The Klan was charged with using terror and intimidation to prevent Blacks from exercising their civil rights and for harassment and intimidation of public officials—ranging from the mayor to the governor—for supporting integration. Bogalusa city officials, policemen, a number of African Americans, FBI agents, and four white members of CORE were sworn in as well. At the same time, ninety-five miles away in Bogalusa, a rally by an organization known as the Minute Men was held. The event was sponsored by the Anti-Communist Christian Association, the new Klan organization in Washington Parish that fronted for the Original Knights and counted as members the very Klansmen on trial in New Orleans. The Minute Men claimed as its major goal the protection of the country from a communist takeover. Among the two thousand segregationists waving Confederate flags while attending the event was District Judge John Rarick of St. Francisville, who would soon defeat Congressman Jimmy Morris for the Sixth Congressional District post, a position he would hold for four terms.[20] In 1980, Rarick was the presidential candidate for the American Independent Party, which had been founded by former Alabama governor George Wallace more than decade earlier.

On September 8, Betsy slammed the Florida Keys with 140-mile-per-hour winds before heading into the gulf. It tore up southern Florida. Water rose six feet in the lobbies of Miami Beach hotels.[21] In New Orleans, the judges and attorneys met in chambers to work out a plan to bring the trial to a recess as the threat for a Louisiana landing increased. Two Klan leaders, Saxon Farmer and Charles Christmas, were ordered to produce Klan records, and FBI agent Frank Sass described attacks by whites on civil rights workers and on an FBI agent. When one Klansman refused to name members or officers of the ACCA, the judges sent him outside and told him to think about it. When the man returned, he named the financial officers and said Saxon Farmer controlled the organization's money.[22]

Charles Christmas finally admitted that the ACCA and Klan memberships were the same and that the ACCA had been formed "to improve the public image of the KKK to that of a more law-abiding organization." This admission was a key component to the prosecution's case in showing that the ACCA and the Klan were one and the same. On the other hand, Farmer continued to be evasive, so Judge Wisdom proposed that he sit on the witness stand "until the hurricane breaks over our heads" and "testif[y] truthfully." Judge Christenberry suggested that "it might be better to let the hurricane hit over Parish Prison with Mr. Farmer in it until he decides to tell the truth." Yet Farmer remained defiant, avowing, "I will just have to go to prison because I have no lists. I have sworn to tell the truth."[23]

Christmas later presented a partial membership list of the Klan and ACCA, and Farmer reluctantly admitted that the two Klansmen had prepared the membership lists from memory. Farmer also admitted that all Klan units were ordered to destroy their records and terminate the practice. He said records and lists were kept until "we were harassed by the FBI."[24]

Clayton Hines of Bogalusa testified that he had served as secretary of Klan Unit 2 in Bogalusa and discussed a list containing 151 members from Washington Parish, including the name of Bogalusa city attorney Robert Rester. Hines said that a month earlier he was sworn out of Unit 2 at a meeting where the destruction of records was discussed as the court case loomed. He said he had seen a list of Unit 2 members that was compiled in Rester's office. After Christmas and Farmer began to transfer Klan operations from the Original Knights to the ACCA, Klansmen turned in their Klan membership numbers and were issued membership cards to the ACCA.[25]

On September 9, court dismissed mere hours before Betsy hit the Louisiana coast at 10:00 p.m. with gusts of 150 miles per hour and sustained winds of 110 miles per hour. Grand Isle was destroyed. The eye passed the southwest side of New Orleans and west of Baton Rouge with winds as high as one hundred miles per hour. Gusts at Bogalusa reached eighty-five miles per hour. Betsy slowly pushed through northern Louisiana, leaving much of state without power. Phones were out; crops were ruined. Red Cross shelters quickly filled.[26] Betsy left behind eighty-one dead, the bulk in Louisiana, and $1.43 billion in damage, the most ever recorded at that time. FBI agents like Milton Graham were among the survivors. "There was water up to the eaves on a lot of houses" in New Orleans, he recalled. "Dogs on roofs. Snakes in houses. . . . The yards were full of furniture." Everything was "a mess" and "smelled bad."[27]

A week after Betsy ripped through Louisiana, a new storm appeared to be brewing in the Washington Parish county seat of Franklinton, where McElveen's attorney, Ossie Brown, withdrew his request for a preliminary hearing. The

Bogalusa newspaper called the announcement a "surprise action." McElveen had been attempting to have the charges dismissed and to recover his client's pickup, guns, and other personal possessions that had been seized as evidence. District Judge Steve Ellis had postponed the hearing a week before Betsy hit, and weeks prior to that the first scheduled hearing had been canceled because the key witness, Deputy Creed Rogers, was unable to testify in court due to his injuries. But throughout the parish, there were rumors that something was afoot.[28]

In early November, the venue became more concrete when the *Bogalusa Daily News* reported that members of the parish grand jury were taking matters into their own hands. Albert Laveige of Varnado, a grand jury member who identified himself as a spokesman for the panel, said jurors had twice tried to get a hearing. The first was set for October 21, at which time Erwin said he did not have enough evidence to bring a case. Laveige said a second hearing was slated for October 28 with the judge, district attorney, and sheriff each given notice in writing. But Laveige said only Sheriff Dorman Crowe appeared and gave jurors what evidence he had. He said the DA failed to show up and failed to summon witnesses. Because of this, Laveige decided to go public. He complained that the grand jury process could "drag on and on," adding that the DA apparently did not know enough about the law to know that the grand jury "can just take the charges on which the sheriff arrested the man [McElveen] and give a true bill [indictment]." But he said jurors "want to hear the evidence," claiming that ten of the twelve jurors had already agreed to a hearing, adding, "We think we ought to do something."[29]

Because of this, Laveige said, Louisiana attorney general Jack Gremillion was asked to intervene and had opined that a majority of the grand jurors could call a hearing without the permission of either Judge Ellis or DA Erwin. Contacted by the newspaper, Gremillion said he had rendered no such opinion but had been contacted by clerk of court Dewaine Seal, and later the clerk's brother, Leroy "Slick" Seal, came to Baton Rouge and asked that an opinion be withheld. (Nobody in Washington Parish knew it at the time, but Slick Seal had become a person of interest to the FBI in the murder of Moore.) The attorney general said he did not want to get involved in Washington Parish's business but did point to a Louisiana statue that stated a majority of the grand jury could call the panel into session. Gremillion said this could only be done by petitioning the judge.[30]

In response to Laveige's contention that Erwin was not cooperating with the grand jury, the DA issued a statement to the *Bogalusa Daily News.* He said that at the request of another grand juror, he met with Judge Ellis when the grand jury convened on October 21 and advised jurors that the case had not been solved and shared what evidence he had. After hearing from the sheriff, the grand jury adjourned. "The next thing I know," Erwin said, "a 'so-called' petition was brought to my office by the office of Clerk of Court, requesting another meeting of the Grand Jury." He said that seven members signed the petition and a meeting was requested on the same day the petition was delivered. Because the DA was in New Orleans that day concerning the federal injunction trial, he could not attend, but Judge Jim Richardson and Sheriff Crowe did.[31]

"There is a persistent rumor throughout the parish," Erwin said, "that pressure is brought upon the present Grand Jury to indict Mr. McElveen; that he would then obtain a speedy trial and be acquitted, thereby forever barring any future prosecution upon the same charge. I will not be a party to such action and have so informed the Grand Jury. Fortunately, I believe there are enough good men on the present Grand Jury to see this does not happen. This case has not been solved and is not ready, in my opinion, for a Grand Jury."[32]

The DA said McElveen had a "legal remedy" to get the charges dismissed by seeking a preliminary hearing in order to determine probable cause. If the judge found the evidence insufficient to support the charge of murder, he could drop the charges. The question then was why did McElveen's attorney withdraw the motion for a preliminary hearing? Ossie Brown commented that he had "abandoned" the preliminary hearing because he feared it would delay grand jury action. On November 5, only eight jurors, all acting on their own, showed up in court. But they were one short of a quorum. As a result, nothing happened.[33] Behind the scenes, Crowe told the FBI that when he met with the grand jury in October one juror said McElveen "shouldn't have a finger pointing at him all his life." Crowe said it was obvious this juror did not think McElveen was guilty. Erwin told agents that if the grand jury did reach a quorum and return a true bill against McElveen, he would dismiss the charges. Friends, Klansmen, and other supporters of McElveen were apparently tampering with the grand jury, Erwin said, although he was not sure if attorney Brown was involved. The grand jury did not convene again on the McElveen matter.[34]

In early December in the case of *United States v. Original Knights of the Ku Klux Klan,* Judge Wisdom issued the court's ruling. His first sentence read:

"This is an action by the Nation against a klan." In summary, the three-judge federal panel ruled that the Klan defendants admitted and federal prosecutors proved in court that Klansmen did everything they could through intimidation, harassment, and interference to prevent Blacks from being treated as equals under the eyes of the law; to prevent civil rights organizations from encouraging Blacks to "assert their rights"; and to keep public officials, police, and businesses from treating Blacks equally. The purpose was to keep Washington Parish segregated from "cradle to coffin," just as it always had been.[35]

"A Negro who is clubbed in a public park may fear to order coffee in a segregated sandwich shop or he may decide that it is the better part of valor not to exercise voting rights," Wisdom wrote, continuing,

> The owner of the sandwich shop who receives threatening calls for having served Negro patrons may conclude that taking care of his family comes ahead of hiring Negro employees. The intimidation or violence may be effective not only as to the particular individual against whom it is directed but also as to others who may be less courageous than the Negroes brave enough to parade in Bogalusa or register to vote in Franklinton. The acts of terror and intimidation admitted or proved in this case, acts characteristic of a masked, secret conspiracy, can be halted only by a broad injunction enjoining the defendants from unlawfully interfering with the exercise of civil rights by Negro citizens.[36]

The court cited the case of Ralph Blumberg, the radio station owner in Bogalusa who editorialized against the Klan and supported integrated meetings to resolve racial issues. The Klan quickly initiated an economic boycott again him. Blumberg, despite his efforts to continue operations, watched his list of advertisers dwindle to a handful and eventually lost his business. The judges also alluded to the cancellation of the integrated meeting featuring former congressman Brooks Hayes to discuss how Blacks and whites could work together to improve race relations. That meeting was called off due to Klan threats of violence. The court alluded to an Original Knights leaflet distributed in Bogalusa that suggested Mayor Jesse Cutrer, state representative Buster Sheridan, state senator B. B. "Sixty" Rayburn, Sheriff Dorman Crowe, Congressman Jimmy Morris, Governor John McKeithen, and Senator Russell Long should be "tarred and feathered" for opposing the Klan and supporting rights for Blacks. The flier ended with this threat concerning the

Brooks Hayes meeting before it was canceled: "Those who do attend this meeting will be tagged as integrationists and will be dealt with accordingly by the Knights of the Ku Klux Klan."[37]

Additionally, the judges did not accept the Klan's legal position that it was a private organization made up of private persons and "beyond reach" of the civil rights acts authorizing the attorney general to sue for an injunction. An "unusual feature of this litigation is the defendants damning admissions," Judge Wisdom wrote. The major admission was that the Klan took numerous actions to prevent Washington Parish Blacks from exercising their civil rights. Klansmen and the ACCA, Wisdom wrote, were "a fearful conspiracy against society" that held men "silent by the terror" of their actions and their "power for evil." Perhaps the most damning insult felt by Klansmen was this statement by the judges: "None of the defendant klansmen is a leader in his community. As a group, they do not appear to be representative of a cross-section of the community. Instead they appear to be ignorant bullies, callous of the harm they know they are doing and lacking in sufficient understanding to comprehend the chasm" between their hateful beliefs and "the noble charter of liberties under law that is the American constitution."[38]

The court enjoined "the Original Knights of the Ku Klux Klan, its dummy front, the Anti-Communist Christian Association, and the individual defendants from interfering with orders of this Court and from interfering with the civil rights of Negro citizens of Washington Parish."[39] Klan lawyer Jerry McKernan, reported the *Bogalusa Daily News,* stated that he would appeal the ruling to the US Supreme Court if Klansmen so desired, claiming that the federal government "was trying to limit activities of private individuals" and calling the issue a matter of individual freemen. The court's injunction required that the Klan and ACCA issue monthly reports on their activities and cease all their hateful practices.[40]

This was a major victory for the civil rights movement, the federal government, and the rule of law, affirming that in this case, at least, the court intended to see that federal law was enforced and civil rights delivered. The naming of dozens of Klansmen as a result of the suit chilled many Original Knights in Washington Parish who had previously enjoyed practicing their evil work behind a hood. When the injunction hearing was under way in September, the FBI had discovered that attorney Ossie Brown had told Saxon Farmer and Russell Magee that they should submit a list of Klansmen to keep Farmer from going to jail.[41] When Farmer and Charles Christmas released those names to the court, Klansmen were incensed and felt betrayed. They even began to believe that Russell Magee was not called to testify because he was an FBI informant. When the FBI had first arrived in Bogalusa, Farmer had berated Klansmen and warned them that if they were interviewed they should give agents only their name, age, and address, nothing more. When Farmer returned to Bogalusa after giving up the names in court, he was asked why he betrayed his membership. "A lot of things change when you get in front of three federal judges," Farmer replied.[42]

In a report to J. Edgar Hoover the News Orleans FBI office indicated that the court ruling was a stunning success for many reasons, including the fact that "the principle officers of the Klan have been forced to disclose substantial information which was available previously only through our confidential informants." The act of disclosing a list of the names of Klansmen to protect Klan leaders gave the bureau "tremendous new leverage in dealing with individual Klansmen and affords us the most benign circumstances that we have had since this investigation was undertaken for pursuing our target and penetrating the Klan for information" concerning the attack on deputies Moore and Rogers. "The conspiratorial shell of the organization has been pierced. Individual members have no security in a tight-lipped attitude when their officers failed to protect them. Meaningfulness to their oath to secrecy becomes naught."[43]

10

RACIAL CASES MOVE TO COURT

McElveen's Family Secret

A month after the drive-by shooting of the two deputies, Louisiana game warden Leroy "Slick" Seal of Varnado visited the office of Ray McElveen's lawyer in Baton Rouge. There, Seal told Ossie Brown that the Washington Parish Sheriff's Office had issued radio dispatches describing the pickup in which the shooters were riding as being the color green and later as being the color blue. McElveen's truck being black, Brown planned to use this as part of his defense of McElveen if the case went to trial. He was also building a defense based on rumors that Black men had committed the murder of Oneal Moore. Seal told FBI agents that the deputies had recently arrested several Black men in robbery cases, as well as a Black bootlegger.[1] Maybe they had a motive. The FBI traced the source of the rumors to the Klan propaganda machine. Although various descriptions of the color of the pickup went over police radios initially, a fact generally known, the question that interested the FBI was, Why did Slick Seal, a wildlife enforcement officer employed by the state, feel the need to provide investigative information to attorney Brown much like Bogalusa police chief Claxton Knight had done on an earlier occasion?

By 1966, Brown had become the go-to man for Klansmen in Washington Parish. As the FBI and Justice Department blanketed the area with agents and attorneys, Brown found himself inundated with calls from Klansmen worried they might be targeted. Radical white segregationists so favored the preservation of white rule that they rejected the thought of assisting the federal government and decided they would help not only the Klansmen who were in trouble but also the lawyer who was defending them. But in 1966 and 1967 state and federal prosecutors brought several racial violence cases to court. Just as importantly, it now rested upon white jurors to return guilty verdicts when warranted in cases where Blacks were the victims.

Many whites knew at least one white person who had been the victim of

Klan violence. Throughout Louisiana and Mississippi during the mid-1960s, the Klan showed how a terrorist organization could hold an entire populace in fear. Klansmen raped, tortured, torched, and killed. Countless homes and businesses, even churches, were destroyed by fire. Men and women were beaten so severely that some could not work for days and lost their jobs and income. Fear of the Klan caused lifelong nightmares for many. The Klan's economic boycott in Bogalusa diminished businesses and disrupted the economies of the targeted communities. In Washington Parish, Klansmen were embedded in every form of government and in places of leadership. Even Russell Magee, who headed the Klan in the parish, had managed to gain power within the school system and by 1966 was seeking an appointment to the local draft board so he could send Blacks to the military and perhaps to places like Vietnam.

Looking back on his work in Washington Parish after a half century, FBI agent Milton Graham recalled local police as a mixture of unqualified lawmen, Klansmen, and Klan sympathizers. While Sheriff Dorman Crowe personally worked cooperatively with the FBI, other lawmen, such as Claxton Knight and some members of the Bogalusa Police Department could not be trusted. He recalled Slick Seal as someone who cooperated reluctantly but on some occasions the nickname "said it all." For Graham, 1966 would be a busy and dangerous year.[2] For many FBI agents, the investigation into McElveen and the shooting of the two deputies, along with related cases, would lead each to a lifetime of experiences within the confines of twelve to eighteen months.

Additionally, 1966 was a year of momentum for the FBI as some white people in Washington Parish began to take a stand for what was right. But no one profited more from Klansmen and white men accused in racial cases than attorney Ossie Brown, whose advice was sought by many of the suspects in the attack on the deputies, including client Bobby Lang of Varnado, who claimed as his alibi that he was frogging on the night of the shooting.

Many residents interviewed by the FBI in the community felt that if anyone knew who attacked the two deputies it would be Slick Seal, who spent his adult life in law enforcement in Washington Parish. Upon his death at the age of ninety-five in 2016, he had served as a game warden for twenty-seven years before his retirement as a major in 1979. Years after that, he worked as chief deputy for the Washington Parish Sheriff's Office. His first job in law enforcement came when Governor Earl Long appointed him as town marshal of Varnado. Later he was elected the town's police chief. Seal also had operated a service station and worked at the papermill and in 1965, when FBI agents first interviewed him, operated a grocery store in a building connected to his house in Varnado.[3] In 2019, his son, Randy "Country" Seal, was reelected to his third term as Washington Parish sheriff. He had first been elected in 2011, when he defeated Robert "Bobby" Crowe, the son of the late sheriff Dorman Crowe.

Several residents in Varnado told agents in 1965 that Seal was a Klansman. Some thought he could have masterminded the attack on the deputies. Others said that Seal, who was fifty-two at the time, would know who the killers were because everybody knew him: many confided in him and most everybody liked him. A few said he was physically involved in the shooting but offered no proof. In his account given to agents, Seal said he had been asleep on the night of the attack when awakened by his wife as she came to bed. At that time, he heard what he thought were firecrackers going off nearby. His wife looked outside and observed a patrol car had crashed into an oak tree down the street. Seal got up and dressed in his street clothes and with his wife, who was wearing a housecoat, walked over to the crime scene. They saw the two deputies in the car, thinking at first that both were dead. They saw and spoke with Scraps Fornea and Jessie Bell Thigpen, who had each witnessed the shooting.[4] Others at the scene saw Seal and his wife. There seemed no way that Seal could have been in the pickup and a minute or two later at the crime scene.

The FBI had information that Seal had been in the Klan in 1964 and had been seen at a Klan meeting in Bogalusa. He would neither confirm nor deny Klan membership, nor would he identify other suspected Klansmen. He did, however, acknowledge that he was a member of the white Citizens' Council.[5] Years later, in 1987, the FBI received an anonymous letter that identified four men as having been the murderers. Slick Seal's name was on the list, as was Earl Stringer's, a Klansman from Angie, and Bobby Lang's. The fourth name on the list was Varnado resident Vexter Rester, a member of the white Citizens' Council who died a month after the shooting. Not a bit of proof—only rumors and speculation—placed these men in the pickup.[6] Seal told the bureau in 1965 that both he and Rester as part of a white Citizens' Council project had placed a billboard in Varnado depicting civil rights leader Rev. Martin Luther King attending a communist training school. Two months after the shooting, when repairing the sign, which had been damaged, Rester fell dead of a heart attack. His guns were reported stolen that night and rumors flew that Rester had used one of the guns to shoot the deputies.[7]

An enormous problem for agents working in Varnado was keeping up with the names and multiple family connections. There were many similar surnames, such as "Seal," "Seals," and "Seale," for example. Family feuds were born over accusations of involvement in the shooting. An uncle, for instance, secretly might tell the FBI his nephew was involved the shooting based on a hunch, not fact. Often, the testimonies given agents indicated that a particular person was capable of the murder due to his racial beliefs and temperament but provided no proof of involvement in the crime. FBI agents learned that there were three kinds of people in town: members of the Ku Klux Klan, those who were not members but were sympathetic to the Klan's goals, and those who despised the Klan but were too afraid to speak out for fear of reprisal.

In 1989, another witness implicated Bobby Lang and pointed to the involvement of Lang's brothers-in-law Archie Roy Seals and Shellie Seals. The accuser was Donald Ray Seal, who at the time was incarcerated at the Washington Parish jail with an axe to grind. He told agents he had been jailed on trumped-up charges by Slick Seal, then a deputy. A teenager in 1965, Donald Ray told agents two and a half decades later that he had been sitting under an oak tree on Main Street drinking his first beer in Varnado when he watched the two deputies drive by in their patrol car followed by a pickup driven by Archie Roy Seals. Donald Ray said Bobby Lang and Shellie Seals were in the back of the truck and did the shooting. Donald Ray also claimed Archie Roy's son showed him the guns used in the shooting.[8] Years later, in 2011, Donald Ray added to the story in a television program about the shooting aired on Investigation Discovery. Donald Ray said that when Moore and Rogers passed by in the patrol car, a pickup, unseen before and occupied by Lang and his brothers-in-law, Archie Roy and Shellie, cut on its lights, pulled in behind the patrol car and opened fire as it crossed the railroad tracks.[9]

But these stories conflict with Donald Ray's own words. A few weeks after the attack in 1965, when the FBI interviewed him and his father, the teenager claimed he knew nothing about the murder. In 1989, he told agents that Archie Roy's son had shown him the two weapons used in the attack—an old Bayard Arms double-barreled shotgun and a Remington .30.06 pump rifle. But the FBI had determined that the rifle used in the commission of the crime was a semi-automatic, most probably an M-1 Garand. Additionally, deputy Creed Rogers told agents he and Oneal Moore had watched the truck follow them into Varnado, which deflated Donald Ray's contention that the pickup used by the killers was lying in wait near the railroad tracks. Nothing Donald Ray told agents was supported by the facts.[10]

Agents had interviewed brothers Archie Roy and Shellie Seals in 1965. There was no evidence—other than Donald Ray's allegations years later—that Shellie or Archie Roy had anything to do with the physical attack. But the twenty-nine-year-old Archie Roy drew the FBI's suspicion because he lied to agents. A barber who also worked as an inspector of barber shops for the state, some in Varnado considered Archie Roy a viable suspect because of his friendship with his brother-in-law Bobby Lang, who was married to Archie Roy and Shellie Seals's sister. Both Archie Roy and Lang were considered hotheads and fiery segregationists. One witness said Archie Roy was one of the Klan's leading bullies. He told agents that he had gone to bed after watching the 10:00 p.m. news. Around midnight Bobby Lang had called him with news that the two deputies had been attacked and one was dead. He said he hung up the phone and went back to sleep.[11]

Archie Roy told agents he had known McElveen for fifteen years and that McElveen had sold him the insurance covering his barber business in Bogalusa. During a later interview, agents pressed Archie Roy on his activities the night of the attack. Archie Roy sensed they knew he had lied. He quickly confessed that he had been on the Pearl River, not at home in bed, at the time of the attack. What was he doing on the Pearl River? All Archie Roy would say was that he and others had been "outlawing" (breaking game laws). He would not identify the other men.[12]

Another tip came to the FBI's attention. An anonymous caller claimed that Archie Roy had buried the weapons used in the murder beneath the slab of the new house he constructed in 1965. At the time, Archie Roy refused to let agents dig into the foundation. Years later, he relented. Agents looked but found nothing.[13]

Yet another man, thirty-year-old Willie J. "Dick" Williams, was identified by FBI sources as a Varnado Klan leader, which Williams denied when agents interviewed him. Williams did not mince words, however, on his stance on vigilantism. He said he had nothing to do with the murder of Oneal Moore but that if offered the opportunity, he would have participated in the 1959 mob lynching of Mack Charles Walker, the Black inmate kidnapped from his jail cell in Poplarville after being accused of raping a white woman.[14] Concerning the attack on the deputies, however, Williams had a solid alibi. His time card and a supervisor verified that he was working at the papermill in Bogalusa at the time of the attack in Varnado.[15] But one by one the accusations continued to fly and the FBI followed every single lead until the end.

By early 1966, the bureau was benefiting with more reliable Klan informants following the ruling in December against the Klan in federal court in New Orleans. While a long list identifying Klansmen during the trial caused great dissention in the Klan world, problems escalated when multiple Washington Parish Klansmen were called before a committee in the US House of Representatives investigating the Klan in January. Coverage of hearings by United Press International was printed throughout the month on the front pages of the *Bogalusa Daily News,* and one of the biggest stories was on Russell Magee, who had not been the focus of press coverage during the New Orleans federal trial against the Klan. Ossie Brown's Baton Rouge law firm—Brown, McKernan, and Ingram—represented fourteen Washington Parish Klansmen at the House hearing. While Magee was not called to testify during the New Orleans trial, he was singled out as a Klan leader during national coverage of the House hearings in Washington, DC. He was described as a school system supervisor who was on the Klan payroll and served as a Klan leader, organizer, and participant at Klan rallies. On each question, Magee refused to answer, citing the right guaranteed by the Fifth Amendment to refuse to answer questions that might incriminate him.[16]

Saxon Farmer, the Klan leader in Bogalusa, and the other Klansmen called also took the Fifth. Congressman Charles Weltner of Georgia reminded the Washington Parish Klansmen, some observing the proceedings with smirks on their faces, "Congress will not be trifled with." Those called to testify included a Bogalusa bank employee and government workers like Magee as well as a city electrician and a school bus driver. A committee investigator revealed that eighteen Klansmen had been sworn out of the Klan in Bogalusa so they could join the city's auxiliary police force. Part of the police oath required that the applicant swear he was not a Klansman.[17]

Many were questioned about purchasing multiple surplus army rifles in 1964, a fact not generally known by the populace. One man identified as a Klansmen by the House committee told the Bogalusa newspaper that he planned to go court: "People have been harassing me, intimidating me, and causing me problems I shouldn't have." These stories in the paper opened the eyes of many in Washington Parish. Once thought of as a last line of defense against desegregation, the Klan was now being seen for what it was—a terrorist cell that would destroy anyone who got in its way.[18]

At the same time, hard feelings against Sheriff Crowe, a man McElveen and other Klansmen had passionately campaigned against in recent elections, surfaced in a significant way. Also laid bare were hard feelings expressed against the man charged with prosecuting McElveen, District Attorney Woodrow Erwin. Expressing these sentiments was McElveen's mother, Lena, who paid for an ad in the Bogalusa newspaper titled "Why? Why? Why? An Open Letter to the District Attorney and Sheriff of Washington Parish." In early January 1966 when the ad ran, the murder charge still hung over her son's head even though the district attorney had said the previous fall that the case was unsolved and not ready for a grand jury. She suggested that if Erwin had any evidence against her son, he should present it or drop the charges. But her wrath was firmly aimed at the sheriff.[19]

"No one . . . knows the heartache and pain which comes to a mother when her most priceless possession, her children, are falsely accused of wrong," Lena wrote of her forty-two-year-old son. "I have tried to hold back any statements concerning the malicious accusation which you have made against my son . . . however, as a mother I must now speak out." She claimed that Crowe had denied McElveen bail until he got an attorney, refused to let family members see him, denied him the opportunity to talk to his family or attorney unless it was in the presence of deputies, and referenced the fact that it was Crowe who had signed the affidavit accusing McElveen of murder.[20] She continued: "We have all been threatened, harassed and we shall never get over the hurt done by these elected officials who have worked hand in hand with the Federal Agents in their attempt to ruin and destroy my son—Why? . . . I hope and pray that . . . I shall live to see the day my son will be cleared of this terrible charge."[21]

Due to the heavy workload for agents investigating civil rights cases in Bogalusa and the murder of Oneal Moore, the FBI in late 1965 opened a bureau office in Covington to serve Washington, St. Tammany, and Tangipahoa parishes. Frank Sass, the face of the FBI in the region for twelve years, was transferred to Cleveland, Ohio, while four other agents were assigned to the new office in Covington. In 1966, several civil and criminal cases involving Bogalusa were processed through federal and state courts.[22] One case involved twenty-three-year-old Jimmy Dane Burke who, during a period of violence on the streets of Bogalusa in 1965, attacked an FBI agent. In a crowd of other white men, Burke raced onto the street and assaulted Black marchers. Restrained briefly by officers, Burke broke away and punched Robert L. Wertman, an FBI agent who was photographing the violence. A mistrial was declared in the first proceeding after the jury declared it was hopelessly deadlocked following four hours of deliberations. But the government did not let it die. The case was retried months later, and this time the jurors found Burke guilty.[23]

In early 1966, the FBI's six-foot-six Milton Graham, along with agent David Rarity, had for days been trying to interview the seventeen-year-old daughter of Reggie Adams, a decorated World War II veteran who lived in Bogalusa. The FBI had received information from a Klan informant that the teenager had told others that she had information on the attack on the two deputies. Adams, who completed his service in the army with the rank of corporal, had enlisted at age fifteen and by the time he was seventeen had earned the Distinguished Service Cross for "extraordinary heroism in action against a hostile force" and for "unquestionable valor in close combat" during the allied invasion of northern Africa in November 1942.[24] At age forty in 1965, Adams was determined that his daughter, who suffered from mental illness, would not be interviewed. His wife told the *Bogalusa Daily News* that the two agents arrived at their home in late February to question the teen. Mrs. Adams said agents had approached her husband four or five times about interviewing their daughter, but each time he refused. Adams had been visiting with a neighbor and upon returning to his house immediately told Graham and Rarity to quit "pestering" his family. When they refused to leave without questioning the daughter, Adams went inside and retrieved a weapon. When he returned, he fired one shot from a .410 shotgun at the feet of the agents.[25]

Looking back at the event in 2018, Graham, who had been taunted by Klansmen and attacked by their dogs, said this was the first time he had failed to carry a firearm with him. He and Rarity had locked their guns in the trunk of the bureau car. The agents slowly retreated to their vehicles. Adams's wife told the newspaper that agents cursed and hurled insults at her husband before leaving. Graham said Adams never pointed the gun at the agents, but they retrieved their weapons and tried to get Adams to come to them.[26] Graham acknowledged that the agents yelled at Adams and called him names. "We tried to create a situation where he would come over and we could grab him and arrest him," but Adams stayed put. That night, assistant special agent in charge of the New Orleans FBI field office, Joe Sylvester, arrived in Bogalusa with a warrant for Adams's arrest. Adams turned himself in to Sylvester at the Bogalusa police station and was taken to New Orleans, where he was booked and later arraigned. Adams's daughter was committed to a mental hospital a week after the incident. Later, Graham was at the same facility conducting another interview unaware that the seventeen-year-old was being treated there. While walking across the lawn, Graham looked up and saw the enraged teen running toward him. Attendants caught up with and restrained her.[27]

A New Orleans federal judge later dismissed the assault charge against Adams, a decision that Graham thought was right. "We had great respect for his service," Graham said. "All we wanted was to interview his daughter because it was our duty as agents. She had told others that she had knowledge about the shooting." Some agents thought Graham and Rarity should have used force and disarmed Adams at the scene. "I never agreed with that," Graham said. "I'm glad we didn't have our guns when we approached the house. This man was a war hero who felt his mentally ill daughter needed protection. He had an aggressive demeanor, which probably contributed to the fact that he was good in combat. He went too far but he didn't point the gun at us; he pointed to the ground near our feet."[28]

Two decades later, after he had retired from the FBI, Graham drove through Bogalusa and past Adams's house. He saw Adams out on the lawn. Rather than stop, Graham decided to phone Adams later. "He [Adams] said he respected the FBI and the jobs that the agents had to do. He said everyone was fortunate that no one had gotten hurt that day." Graham agreed.[29]

While Reggie Adams refused to cooperate with the FBI concerning the questioning of his daughter, he did reveal to agents a dark secret he said was long held by the McElveen family involving McElveen's mother, who had published the open letter chastising the sheriff and district attorney over the murder charge filed against her son. Adams had known McElveen for years. Both attended meetings of a veteran's organization in Bogalusa. Adams did not believe McElveen guilty of the attack on the deputies, but he provided the likely origin of McElveen's bitter hatred of Black people and his embedded belief in vigilante justice. In an urgent message sent directly to FBI director J. Edgar Hoover in 1965, the News Orleans field office reported: "Adams related McElveen had to live with knowledge that his mother was assaulted by [a] Negro male when she was sixteen years old. Negro male captured promptly and shot and killed by friends of the family after her father hesitated to personally carry out execution."[30]

Eleven days after Reggie Adams fired a shot at the feet of the FBI two agents, a Black army captain, twenty-nine-year-old Donald Sims, dressed in civilian clothes, left his father's home in Sun, Louisiana, before midnight and drove his used Mercedes-Benz fourteen miles to the Billups service station in Bogalusa. Sims and his wife had been visiting family before Sims headed to Panama to train for an upcoming tour of duty in Vietnam. There were no cell phones in the 1960s, and many people in rural areas had no telephone service. But there was a pay phone at the Billups, and Captain Sims used it to call his brother in Los Angeles. While he was talking to his brother, three gunshots rang out at 1:20 a.m. Sims fell to the ground. One shot hit his shoulder and lodged in his neck. The wound was not life threatening. Sims drove himself to the hospital. Although he did not see his assailant, Bogalusa police found cartridges from a .22 caliber pistol and surmised that the shooter was three to five feet from Sims when firing. The attendant working at the station that night said he was at the other end of the building and did not observe the shooting or the shooter.[31]

The FBI was quickly notified. Secretary of Defense Robert McNamara requested a Justice Department investigation. The Bogalusa Voters and Civic League demanded justice and warned that demonstrations would begin if the culprit was not arrested soon. Once again, Bogalusa was in the national spotlight. City and state officials immediately condemned the shooting. A group of white citizens gathered at the chamber of commerce building and raised $2,500 for a reward for information leading to the arrest of the shooter.[32]

Agent Graham was one of two agents who immediately went to work on the case. He drove to Sun to ask Sims's parents if they knew of anyone who might want to harm the captain. They did not. From there, Graham went to the Billups station to interview the attendant, who claimed to have heard nothing and seen nothing. Graham did not believe him. A short time later, Graham and another agent returned to the station with a plan to trick the attendant. A car parked near the location where the cartridges from the shooter's pistol had been found was covered in dew. The agents scattered fingerprint powder all over the car as the attendant watched. Then they told the man that the fingerprints belonged to the shooter and "we are . . . going to make a case against him and we're going to do our best to get that guy to acknowledge the fact that you saw him do it. You know exactly who did it. And then you're going to be arrested and you're going to jail." There were in fact no fingerprints, Graham said.[33]

He drove the attendant home but despite his best efforts could not get the man to open up. When the attendant learned there was a $2,500 reward, however, he notified Chief of Police Claxton Knight, who called Graham with news that the man wanted to talk. The attendant told Graham the shooter wanted to use the phone. After initially observing Sims on the phone, the man left and returned later, and was apparently angered that Sims still occupied the phone booth. The shooter told the attendant he was going home to get his "squirrel gun" and come back to teach the Black man a lesson. The suspect was forty-three-year-old Thomas Bennett, a sheet metal worker who had also been employed as a taxi driver and service station attendant. Bennett and his wife's blended family included eleven children. He had been drinking that night. The pistol used in the shooting was found in Bennett's home. Within twenty-four hours of the act, Bennett confessed. He was charged with attempted murder and placed under a $10,000 bond, which was signed by two well-known Klansmen—Ray McElveen, himself out of jail on bond for murder of Oneal Moore, and Saxon Farmer.[34]

Bennett's trial was held in Franklinton in 1968. Graham, who had been transferred to New York, returned to Washington Parish to testify. Captain Sims, who had served a tour of duty in Vietnam prior to the trial, was twice the recipient of a Silver Star. Graham said Bogalusa police did not like Sims, who refused to cooperate with them. At the courthouse, one officer was sarcastic to Sims, prompting a brief argument between Graham and the officer. Graham pointed out that Sims did not appreciate, nor would anyone, the attitude of Bogalusa police.[35] *Jet* had reported that Police Chief Claxton Knight had initially told the media after the shooting that Sims was heading to Panama for training but failed to mention that the training was for a tour of duty in Vietnam.[36] From the beginning, Bogalusa police were suspicious of Sims, who drove a Mercedes and was said to have a sizable amount of cash on him while making a phone call in the middle of the night. Graham berated the policeman at the Franklinton courthouse and said Sims had good reason to feel contempt for Bogalusa police, who believed Sims had been having an affair with someone's wife and a jealous husband had shot him. "What do you expect him to act like?" Graham asked. "You think he should cooperate with you people when that's your immediate assumption?"[37]

The all-male, all-white jury took less than an hour to convict Bennett, who was sentenced to twenty years in prison. After the verdict was rendered, Sims's father was so astonished that the shooter was convicted he was "at a loss for words," Graham recalled, adding it was the first time in Washington Parish that a white jury had convicted a white man for violence upon a Black man.[38]

In the months ahead, the FBI grew more curious at the efforts Bogalusa police chief Claxton Knight, who assisted McElveen's attorney, Ossie Brown, in defending not only McElveen but other white defendants charged with racial attacks. In one case, Knight provided Ossie Brown an enormous favor that resulted in a court victory. On July 30, 1966—four months after Captain Sims was shot—the body of twenty-four-year-old African American bricklayer Clarence Triggs was found beside a wrecked car that rested against a fireplug on Louisiana Avenue in Bogalusa. Triggs had been shot once in the back of the head, a bullet having entered the lower left base of his skull before exiting just under his right eye. There were powder burns around the back of his head, indicating a shot was fired from close range. Triggs died on the ground near the car. His clothing was wet, his left arm was coated with blood, and more blood collected around his nose and mouth.[39]

Inside the car, police found blood on the driver's side door, on the floor in front of the driver's seat, down the back of the driver's seat, and in small splatters on the driver's door and elsewhere inside the car. Officers also found a highball glass, broken glass, a full box of .38 caliber Wesson shells, and a broken half-pint scotch bottle. An empty scotch bottle was found lying near the car. A spent .38 caliber Wesson automatic shell was located on the ground thirty-three feet from the car.[40]

Triggs had reportedly been involved in civil rights activities in Bogalusa, and it was suspected that this was a Klan shooting. But during the trial in 1967, the circumstances seemed to indicate that Triggs may have been in the wrong place at the wrong time and that perhaps he was killed trying to perform a good deed by checking on whether the occupants of the car had been injured as a result of an accident.[41]

Bogalusa police chief L. C. Terrell, appointed following the retirement of Claxton Knight earlier in 1966, discovered the car was registered to the wife of Homer R. "Kingfish" Seale. A lifelong friend of Ray McElveen, Seale had been seen before and on the day of the murder in the company of a friend, John W. Copling Jr. Both men were charged with murder.[42]

The chief witness for the prosecution was twenty-year-old Bernadette Crain, described in court as a chronic mental patient. Bernadette testified that she and a girlfriend, both white, were in the Thomas Bar in Bogalusa when Seale offered her a drink. She said she and her girlfriend later agreed to get into a car with Seale and Copling, who had shown her a police badge in his wallet. From there they went to the Rendezvous Lounge. When they departed to go to another bar—without Bernadette's girlfriend—Copling and Seale were arguing. While traveling down the street with Copling driving, the argument escalated into a scuffle, resulting in the accident.[43]

Copling had been in trouble with the law before for preying on young women, particularly for luring them into prostitution. He and another man were convicted in 1961 for transporting two teens—one nineteen and the other seventeen—from Covington to Bogalusa to work as prostitutes. Copling was sentenced to three years in the state pen.[44]

In the Triggs murder, Copling was tried first. Bernadette testified that after the car accident, Triggs had walked over to the car and asked if she was hurt. Almost immediately, Copling pulled out a pistol and shot Triggs through the opened driver's door window. Seale responded immediately, saying, "I ain't having a damned thing to do with it." Bernadette exited the car, looked at Triggs's body, and ran. A fingerprint identified as Copling's was found on the steering wheel horn rim, and Seale's fingerprint was found on the scotch bottle inside the car.[45]

The defense attorney, Ossie Brown, was well familiar with the police and many of the characters living about Washington Parish. Brown tore into the police department in what the *Bogalusa Daily News* called an "evangelical tirade." Brown said he was embarrassed by the lack of evidence obtained by the state. But his theatrics were not all that electrified the court. More shock came when Brown called recently retired Bogalusa police chief Claxton Knight to the stand. The former chief, who had announced a few weeks earlier that he was running against Dorman Crowe for sheriff in the 1967 election, testified that Bernadette was his distant cousin and that months earlier she had given him a letter concerning the shooting. The district attorney, who was made aware of the letter only minutes before it was introduced into evidence, objected to its admission. After an argument between the attorneys, the judge overruled the prosecution's objection.[46]

Knight testified that because of Bernadette's mental state, he did not think the letter was important and simply put it away and forgot about it. Dated

October 5, 1966—three months after the murder of Triggs and nine months before the trial—Bernadette wrote that she had lost her pills and needed to go into the hospital for treatment. The letter continued with a confession: "I done something wrong. . . . I have got to talk to you about something. It's about me and that nigger. I killed that nigger. He wanted me to go to a hotel with him and then he tried to kiss me. But I wouldn't let him, so he got mad and started to slap me. That's when I shot him. I'm not kidding." Bernadette later took a pistol to the hospital and threatened employees. And yet Knight had done nothing and had not alerted the district attorney of the existence of the letter.[47] For the most part, no one believed that Bernadette committed the murder, and it appeared possible that the letter was an effort to get medical and mental help.

There was no evidence to support her words in the letter. Brown nevertheless claimed that someone "with a vile, rotten mind" manipulated "the little girl" to say what she said in court identifying his client, Copling, as the murderer. Brown said he knew the identity of the manipulator but failed to provide a name. He also joked that if he ever left Baton Rouge, he might move to Washington Parish, to which the district attorney replied, "If we don't put a stop to this wanton killing of human beings, whether they be colored or white, I don't think Mr. Brown or any logical human being would want to move here."[48] In addition to Bernadette's mental condition, the introduction of the letter created more than enough doubt for the jury to reach a not guilty verdict. Seale was never tried.

While on the witness stand, Knight said that on the night before he testified in court, defense attorney Brown arrived at Knight's home and requested the letter under the threat of subpoena.[49] How Brown knew about the letter was never explained. But the FBI thought the whole thing smelled. Agents had previously determined Knight had tipped Brown off about the bureau's investigative attempt to re-create the final ride of deputies Oneal Moore and Creed Rogers a few days after the two deputies were attacked in Varnado. When Brown unexpectedly had appeared at the reenactment, the FBI called it off. And two years later—in the trial for the murder of Clarence Triggs—it was Knight who handed Brown a stunning victory in court to the detriment of the very police department Knight had once led.

In August 1966, another notorious case moved to resolution in a Franklinton courtroom. James Austin Kennedy, a forty-three-year-old white man, had abducted and murdered a Black man in 1964. The victim, thirty-seven-year-old Willie "Cooter" Weary, had been killed execution style when Kennedy fired one shot with a .410 into the back of Weary's head. Kennedy claimed that while he was away from home Weary had attempted to break into his house, apparently to rape or harm his wife. The FBI had interviewed Kennedy in 1965, finding him intoxicated and suicidal, and claiming that the Klan had threatened to kill him. Although he had confessed to killing Weary and was promptly charged by the sheriff, he had initially entered a not guilty plea to manslaughter. When the first pool of potential jurors was depleted with only a handful chosen to hear the case in 1966, the district attorney prepared to summon more potential jurors, a sign the DA was determined to try the case. Kennedy apparently felt he would not come out on top. He changed his plea to guilty and got a five-year sentence.[50]

11

"A PACK OF NO-GOOD DEVILS"

As multiple cases involving racial violence wound through the Washington Parish judicial system in 1966 and 1967, FBI agents continued to follow leads on the drive-by shooting of the two deputies. In February of 1966, the bureau's attention focused on two things: the possible involvement of a friend of Ray McElveen's in the shooting and the eyewitness account of a Florida salesman driving through Varnado at the time of the attack. The salesman heard the gunshots fired at the deputies while he was stopped on a bridge on the outskirts by an armed man whose car had a whip antenna on the back. The man told the salesman he had best move on. Agent Ted Gardner, who worked the case during the 1960s, recalled before his death in 2015 that the Klan had apparently set up a military-type patrol on certain roads to monitor cars coming and exiting Varnado at the time of the attack. For the bureau, there were also other things to sort out.

Was there a conspiracy to kill the deputies?

Who was involved directly or indirectly in the shooting?

Who were the shooters in the pickup?

Obviously, McElveen could not drive the truck and fire a shotgun and rifle simultaneously.

No lead was more electrifying in early 1966 than that involving a Bogalusa Klansman who happened to be a good friend of McElveen's and who, like McElveen, was standoffish, moody, and known to make inflammatory comments promoting racial violence. Both were unpredictable and difficult to handle. Both would take secrets to the grave.

James Wilford Moore at age thirty-nine was just two years younger than McElveen. Moore lived on Van Buren Avenue with his thirty-three-year-old wife, Mary, and their five children in a six-room house that Moore had built himself. During the previous years, the couple's marriage had experienced troubles. On occasion, Mary would leave her husband—and the children—only to return a few days later. Moore depended on neighbors and relatives to help him through these challenging times, but neighbors also knew that one of the reasons Mary often left was because Wilford was hard to live with. For more than a decade he had been employed by a construction company in the position of shipping clerk. Wilford grew up in the area around Tylertown, Mississippi, and northern Washington Parish, where he had family and friends. When he was fifteen, he moved to Bogalusa. As the years passed, Moore grew evasive, had little to do with his brothers and sisters, and became known, like McElveen, as too radical even for Klansmen.

Unlike Ray McElveen, who never granted an interview to the FBI, Wilford Moore made himself available multiple times in 1965 and 1966. Moore stated that on the night of the shooting he arrived home at 5:30 p.m. and spent time in the backyard with his wife and children. They had visitors that evening, and later he and his wife watched a Spencer Tracey movie, *Bad Day at Black Rock,* on television.[1] A relative visited that day and found Mary shelling peas while the children played. Moore was in the backyard talking to an insurance salesman.[2] Mary Moore told the FBI that once her husband came home from work on the afternoon of the shooting, he did not leave the house that evening.[3]

On Friday, June 4, two days after the shooting, Moore returned home at noon to find his wife and kids were gone. Mary had picked up his weekly check at his jobsite. They did not return that night. On Saturday, Moore went to his mother-in-law's home in Crossroads, Mississippi, but she did not know Mary's whereabouts. That weekend Moore also went to the neighbor's home and reported that his wife had left him, this time with the children. Mary had taken the family's 1958 blue Chevrolet and had placed some belongings on a trailer. Moore was broke, could not pay his bills, and was looking for a new job, claiming without explanation that he could no longer work at his present job. He mentioned to his neighbor that his friend, Ray McElveen, had been arrested in the shooting of the Black deputies, commenting that McElveen helped arrange Moore's bond when he had been arrested for aggravated assault in 1964.[4]

Moore went to the Bogalusa home of his best friend, John Pope, on June 6. The same age as Moore, Pope worked in Texas during the week and returned home on the weekend. Moore found Pope's father—not his wife and children—at the son's house. Pope arrived a short time later. Although agents had interviewed Wilford and Mary after the shooting, the couple intrigued the bureau more when they later learned that Mary had left Wilford along with one of her friends, Florine Pope, the wife of John Pope. The Popes had two children.[5]

Interviewed by the bureau in 1966, Pope, who told agents he considered

Moore a brother, said he arrived home from his construction job in Texas to find Moore at Pope's house with news that their wives had left them and were heading for Oklahoma, where Moore also hoped to find a job. He said Moore convinced him to join him the next day on a journey.[6]

On the morning of Monday, June 7, Moore's bosses at the Russell Company noted that he had not shown up for work. Moore had good work and attendance records. A company representative told agents that everyone knew about Moore's domestic problems but that his failure to return to work was a mystery. The company was also aware that Moore had been arrested in 1964, but this incident had not affected his job performance. A company worker recalled that the day after the shooting of the deputies Moore had called the attack a "good thing."[7]

Also on June 7, Moore visited neighbor Claude Riles and asked him if he wanted to rent Moore's house. Moore explained that he was leaving Bogalusa for good but would not explain the reason for his hasty departure. Riles moved in, but two weeks later Mary Moore showed up and reoccupied the house.[8]

On the first day of the trip, the two wife searchers traveled to Baton Rouge, where Pope's mother-in-law lived. She had not seen the women or the children. Thirty-four-year-old Florine Pope, later interviewed by the FBI, said she and Mary had made plans the day before their departure to leave their husbands the day after the shooting. She said Mary was upset, claiming that Moore often beat their children severely. And then Mary alleged that John Pope had attempted to be intimate with her. Both women were unhappy with their husbands. Florine told FBI agents that the women had planned to go to Oklahoma, but their car broke down in Baton Rouge.[9]

Interviewed months after their departure from Bogalusa, Florine said she had not seen Wilford or Mary since the week of their departure. She now regarded Mary as "an undesirable woman and a bad influence on her family."[10] Mary was interviewed again in 1966 and said her husband, Wilford, had few friends and confided in no one. She recalled that the day after the shooting her husband came home for lunch and remarked that he was glad he stayed home the night before because the deputies had been shot.[11]

Mary was Wilford's only alibi witness.

While Pope looked for his wife in Bogalusa and later Baton Rouge, he claimed Moore did not look for his wife at all. Instead, Moore acted as if it were urgent that he get out of town. From Baton Rouge, they drove to Texarkana, Texas.

Moore drove most of the way, expressing fear that they were being followed. On several occasions, Pope watched as Moore pulled to the side of the road to vomit, just as McElveen had done three times after being arrested in Tylertown.[12]

The next day they arrived at a motel in Broken Bow, Oklahoma. Moore was so on edge that he insisted Pope go inside to secure a room while Moore waited in the car. He obsessed that they were being followed. After checking in at 6:00 p.m., Moore immediately left and did not return until midnight, at which time he awakened Pope to tell him that the police were outside looking at his car. Pope responded, "So what?"[13]

By now, Pope was more suspicious than ever. What was Moore running from? Pope had observed that in recent years Moore had displayed more and more signs of violence as he became active in the Klan. In Oklahoma, Pope grew afraid for himself and his family. He quizzed Moore about the shooting of the two deputies. Pope, who had also been a Klansman, was surprised at Moore's response: "You have been sworn out of the Klan. . . . You'll just have to decide for yourself if I had anything to do with it."[14]

Moore insisted that they continue to Alaska and get jobs there, but Pope had had enough. He was heading home. Pope told agents that since Moore did not have the funds to buy a car, he had no choice but to return to Louisiana. But Moore made it clear that he was not going back to Bogalusa. Once in the state, Moore demanded that Pope take him to Harvey, where Moore worked for a short time before settling in Mississippi. Pope dropped him off.[15]

When contacted by the bureau in February of 1966, Pope and Florine had reunited, but the two families had not been in contact with one another since the summer of 1965. Pope now believed Mary Moore had tried to break up his marriage. A few years later, the Popes' marriage ended.[16]

Moore eventually told the FBI he had originally been a member of Klan Unit 1 in Bogalusa along with McElveen, a friend he had known for some time. He had worked with McElveen to defeat Sheriff Dorman Crowe, a man Moore acknowledged he despised. He called Crowe crooked and "on the take from bootleggers."[17]

Moore had later helped organize Bogalusa Unit 4, but his radical ways troubled Klan leaders. Moore and McElveen epitomized one of the many problems of Klan organizations: leaders cannot control the actions of their more violent members. In Concordia Parish in the spring of 1964, violence-prone Klansmen, disgruntled with the inaction of their leaders, went underground and formed wrecking crews to deliver violence whenever they wished. They called themselves the Silver Dollar Group, identified as an "action group" by the FBI. Members felt Klan leadership was too timid. When Moore continually urged violent attacks, especially as the Klan early on attempted to remain off the FBI radar, he was booted out of his Klan unit. The same thing had happened to Ray McElveen. Even McElveen's longtime friend and war comrade Russell Magee, head of the parish Klan, said McElveen was too volatile to handle, that he always wanted to hurt somebody.

It took several interviews with Moore by agents before he provided much information about his Klan background. He acknowledged that he had been sworn into the Klan a few years earlier on the farm of Saxon Farmer. He said he had been active in the white Citizens' Council and once served on the ruling board. McElveen had served as president of the council. Moore said he had never been sworn out of the Klan.[18]

For a long time, Moore, like McElveen, advocated alignment with the murderous White Knights, which became the dominant Mississippi Klan in 1964. After being kicked out, Moore recruited several Klansmen and formed the Mitch unit, named after a small community on the outskirts of Bogalusa. Moore later identified some of the members of the Mitch unit, including Howard Lee, who had ousted Moore as exalted cyclops, a fact that informants said angered him. Lee, who had a federal license to deal in the interstate sale of firearms and ammunition, was arrested in 1965 on federal charges of failing to keep adequate records on the rifles he obtained from wholesalers and distributed to Klansmen in Bogalusa. He was convicted and sent to federal prison in Texarkana, Texas. Before his conviction, federal authorities discovered he had sold almost seven hundred military rifles. His rifles were purchased in bulk by Klan leaders, who then sold them to Klan members.[19]

John Pope acknowledged to agents that he, too, had become a member of the Mitch unit and that Moore ruled as a dictator. Moore had designed an emblem especially for the Mitch unit, and wife Mary had made the Klan robes. Pope said that while he was a member of the unit, he heard discussions of violence but never heard talk of action against the two Black deputies.[20] Another member of the Mitch unit said Moore had a violent hatred of Black people. A coworker of Moore's who also was a member of the Mitch unit said Moore was constantly instigating wrecking crew projects and that he could be "crude and stupid." At meetings on many occasions, Moore proposed an attack on a local white man—James Spears—alleging he often associated with

Blacks socially, apparently living in an integrated world that Klansmen would not tolerate. But the Mitch group had consistently voted against the project.[21] So Moore did what he had always done—broke out on his and handpicked his own crew, some from the Mitch unit.

The FBI investigation found that McElveen had done similar things in Bogalusa Unit 1 before he was booted out. Despite that, he kept up with Klan business through his friend Saxon Farmer and occasionally burst into tirades against integration until other Klansmen would walk away. They knew him as being hardheaded and unyielding in his opinions. McElveen and Moore were becoming much like Silver Dollar Group Klansmen—suspicious of Klan leaders, dissatisfied that violence was not being committed on those promoting integration, and certain the Klan should use belts and clubs to beat morality into the poor white men who failed to provide for their families or drank too much. Other Klansmen labeled these unruly members as outcasts and rejects. They had nowhere else to go—unless they formed their own Klan.

In Adams County, Mississippi, one renegade Klansman who had been booted out of the White Knights due his uncontrollable violence, chose another ousted White Knight and one other to help him kill a Black man. The leader, Claude Fuller, told his recruits that such an act might draw Martin Luther King to Natchez in protest. When that happened, Fuller planned to assassinate King. But the 1966 brutal murder of elderly Ben Chester White by Fuller's wrecking crew failed to draw King to Natchez. Instead, the Klansmen, two of them intoxicated, left behind a trail of evidence for authorities to follow and soon the three were arrested. Two of Fuller's recruits were tried locally but not convicted in Adams County, while Fuller never went to trial. Decades later, Fuller and one other member of the wrecking crew were dead. The lone survivor, Ernest Avants, was convicted of the murder in federal court in 2003 after it was discovered the murder had occurred on federal land, opening Avants up to federal charges. But after the murder, the renegade Fuller, who called his group the Cottonmouth Moccasin Gang, caught the attention of the Silver Dollar Group, which appreciated his murderous actions and decided to take him in.[22] This ousted White Knight now had a new Klan home, something neither McElveen nor Wilford Moore could claim in the summer of 1965 when the deputies were attacked.

The incident that permanently damaged Wilford Moore's reputation within the Klan came in the late summer of 1964 after he had formed the Mitch unit.

On August 10, the *Bogalusa Daily News* banner headline read: "Hooded Men Beat Father, Threaten Son." The paper reported that a knock was heard on the front door of the home of James Spears and his family in the community of Mitch. A young man told Spears that he needed help starting his car. Spears, the young man, and Spears's twelve-year-old son drove a short distance down along the road to the railroad tracks, where they found a Ford car with a pink bottom and white top parked on the side of the road. Spears parked behind the car and planned to push it with his vehicle when the young man told him that would not help—that there was a problem under the hood. Spears said he did not know much about motors but would take a look. He quickly observed the coil wires had been detached and at that moment two hooded men, each holding .38 revolvers, jumped from the weeds on the side of the road. Spears later told the FBI that both men were wearing black hoods.[23]

The abductors tied the hands of Spears and his son behind their backs with a rope and ordered them into the pink and white car. Spears pleaded with the men to let his son go, which they did after traveling a short distance. Spears's son ran home and informed his mother of what had occurred. She grabbed a .410 shotgun and went down the road in the dark.[24]

"When I got to where the truck was parked," she said, "I could see the form of a man off the side of the road with a hood on his head. I only weigh 110 pounds and am only five feet tall but I'd stand up to a thousand of them. He ran off in the woods like a snake. They're nothing but a pack of yellow dogs.... Doesn't that show just how brave they are to hide behind hoods and run into the woods when I showed up with a shotgun?"[25]

Spears told the bureau that he and his son had been placed in a car—the pink and white 1955 Ford—before his son was released three hundred yards north on a gravel road. Spears was then transported an estimated three miles northeast to a gravel pit where three men wearing white hoods joined his abductors. He was bound and placed into a 1964 white Ford or Chevrolet. From there, he was taken about four miles to the LSU summer forestry camp off the Bogalusa-Franklinton highway. Spears was yanked from the car, his pants were removed, and he was forced to lie over the hood of the car. He was beaten with a two-inch belt, receiving thirty lashes, and abandoned by his assailants. He hitchhiked home and contacted the Washington Parish Sheriff's Office.[26]

Mrs. Spears told the newspaper, "I used to think maybe there was some good to the Ku Klux Klan, but they're nothing but a pack of no-good devils." A friend of Spears said, "I do not believe that this is the work of the Ku Klux as it is and always has been a decent organization made up of God-fearing men. But, I believe it is the duty of the Klan to step up and help catch these yellow thugs, who are reducing the Klan's name and reputation and endangering the lives of our law abiding citizens." These comments outraged Klan leaders, who realized this wrecking crew attack had not been sanctioned, but the Klan was getting blamed for it.[27]

On August 12, the newspaper reported that the young man believed to have been used as a decoy for the Klan had been arrested by the sheriff's office. The license plate on the car he was driving was traced to the wife of one of the participants. The young man named Wilfred Moore as one of the men carrying a .38 revolver. The man said he did not know all the participants.[28]

Two days later, the newspaper announced that four more men had been arrested. They ranged in age from nineteen to the oldest, thirty-seven-year-old Moore. Each was charged with aggravated assault and battery and violating a state statute making it unlawful for any person or persons to wear a hood or mask in a public place, thereby trying to conceal their identity. The twenty-one-year-old who acted as the decoy was also charged.[29]

Each suspect was placed under $3,000 bond although Moore told the FBI he was the only one to be put in jail. Deputy Doyle Holliday told the FBI that he had obtained confessions from some of the men. He said Moore refused to identify the sixth man, believed from Mississippi, who was also involved in the attack on Spears.[30] Moore refused to discuss the case with the FBI or with anyone else. He kept his mouth shut.

Among the four men who posted Moore's bond was Ray McElveen, who was considered the go-to man for any Klansman arrested for a racial crime. Mary Moore acknowledged to the FBI that she contacted McElveen to get her husband out of jail.[31]

On Monday, June 7, 1965, at Pope's house on Adams Street, Moore sold some personal belongings to raise money for the trip to Oklahoma. One source told agents he had bought some tools and two hunting dogs from Moore for twenty-five dollars each but soon learned one of the dogs did not belong to Moore. The man said Moore appeared desperate to sell whatever he could, adding that the price was "ridiculously" low.[32]

Among the items Moore sold was the .38 special that had a six-inch barrel and an M-1 Garand, according to Pope. Agents located the man who had purchased the .38 special for forty-five dollars, including ten dollars for the holster. But the M-1 that Pope claimed he saw in Moore's possession was of particular interest because it was believed to be the type of weapon used in the shooting of the deputies. Pope had served in the military and told agents he knew what such a gun looked like. But he had not witnessed the actual sale of the weapon. He only recalled looking through a window and seeing the gun leaning on a tree in Pope's front yard shortly before they departed for Oklahoma. When he looked out again, the gun was gone, and Moore did not bring it with them on the trip. Pope had seen the rifle hanging on a wall in Moore's home, along with a giant Confederate flag. Pope said the gun fired .30.06 cartridges (the same type found at the scene of the shooting) and that a clip containing the cartridges was attached underneath.[33]

In fact, Pope said Moore had stored ammunition in a pit located below a concrete slab on the patio of his home. The slab of concrete above the pit took at least two or three men to open. Pope believed Moore buried the M-1 in his backyard or stored it in the pit.[34]

Initially, Moore lied to agents about owning the guns. He had once owned a .303 British Army Enfield rifle, a weapon also considered by the bureau as possibly being the murder weapon. He had bought the gun from a Bogalusa gun collector but sold it, he claimed, without ever having fired it. He said he could not remember the name of the buyer. In a later interview, Moore claimed he had owned a .31 caliber bolt-action Japanese weapon ten years earlier that had been converted to shoot .30.06 cartridges. The gun had been rechambered by a local gunsmith. And, with great hesitation, Moore admitted that he had once owned a sawed-off shotgun that had been cut down to twenty-six inches in length, a violation of federal gun statutes. However, he adamantly denied ever owning an M-1 Garand.[35]

Agents apprised Moore of some of the things Pope had told them about the journey to Oklahoma and their suspicions about Moore's hasty departure. But Moore ignored it, claiming that his supposed close friend John Pope was "nothing more than an alcoholic and what he said could not be relied on."[36] Pope told the bureau he did not want to testify in court against Moore, fearing he would have to leave Bogalusa if he did so.[37]

In mid-February 1966, Moore allowed agents to search his home and the pit he had built into his patio that was covered with a four-foot-long, two-and-a-half-foot-wide concrete slab with metal lifting rings at each end. It was so heavy that agents had to call a wrecker to raise the four-inch-thick lid. They found nothing. Moore said he had built the pit in the spring of 1964. It was around the time Moore and McElveen were pushing for formation of a White Knights unit in Bogalusa and becoming more and more disillusioned with Klan leadership. Others had seen the pit as well, but none had looked inside.[38]

During the spring of 1965, McElveen was on leave from work recovering from ulcer surgery. He drove his pickup to the civil rights demonstrations, watched and stewed at the sight of Black and white activists marching through town. He thought the Klan should do much more to stop it. That spring, Moore visited McElveen at his home, and McElveen visited Moore at his home. McElveen had time on his hands to plot and plan. Moore was grateful to McElveen for getting him out of jail in 1964 after Moore spearheaded the attack on James Spears. Months earlier, a hooded McElveen had suffered a black eye on a wrecking attack when the white victim hit him in the face. Neither McElveen nor Moore bowed to pressure by police to make a statement. They were men who would never implicate themselves or anyone else in anything. They did not intend to be caught.

By early 1966, McElveen was losing weight. One source told the FBI that he looked ill. McElveen feared that a lengthy investigation would uncover damaging information against him. He was right. The FBI picked up one valuable piece of news from a source that reported McElveen had attempted to recruit Varnado Klansman Bobby Lang in the attack on the deputies.[39] Lang had repeatedly told the FBI he had been frogging that night. This was the first indication that McElveen had spearheaded the attack and not Klan higher-ups.

Two days before the shooting, Louisiana governor John J. McKeithen had visited Bogalusa Klan leader Saxon Farmer's home demanding a moratorium on violence. Some of the Klansmen, including Washington Parish Klan leader Russell Magee, indicated they would rein in their men from the streets of Bogalusa. The FBI initially believed that Magee knew all about the attack, but Magee was adamant that he had not ordered it and did not know how it came about. McElveen was so close to Saxon Farmer that there can be no doubt McElveen was told that Klan leaders had promised the governor they would back off and leave the streets to the activists. This would have enraged McElveen and possibly so inflamed his renegade tendencies that it would spark him to form his own wrecking crew and target Oneal Moore and Creed Rogers. At the same time, McElveen would be throwing the middle finger to Sheriff Crowe who had beaten the Klan in three straight elections before committing an unforgivable insult by hiring two Black men with police powers over whites.

A source told the bureau that when McElveen approached Lang about attacking the deputies, Lang responded, "Are you crazy?" While Lang was continuing to talk to agents, he was becoming increasingly paranoid. He claimed Saxon Farmer had been badmouthing him and accusing him of snitching to authorities. Lang was also concerned about his attorney, Ossie Brown, who also represented McElveen.[40] The FBI learned that Brown had remarked that McElveen would never be convicted, partly because he was so introverted and secretive that he refused to talk. "What do you think of a man who would not even tell his attorney what happened?" Brown had lamented.[41]

Later, the FBI asked Lang if he had been approached by anyone to take part in the shooting. He refused to answer, telling agents, "You notice I did not answer your question." Lang appeared at the end of his rope, but he told agents that if he got called before a grand jury he would tell the same story. If he went to jail for that, then so be it. He said he had heard two groups had planned to kill the deputies, but one had beaten the other to it. He added: "I'm sure you have the right man," speaking of McElveen.[42]

Yet another big lead came in early 1966 when the FBI learned that a salesman from Gulf Breeze, Florida, who had been passing through Varnado at the time of the shooting, had been stopped on a bridge by an armed man. The salesman had spent part of his day running his route in northeastern Louisiana before crossing the Mississippi River into Natchez. From there, he made his way southeast traveling through McComb, Tylertown, and Sandy Hook, Mississippi, then southward through Angie, Varnado, and Bogalusa en route to Gulfport, Mississippi. By the time he told the FBI his story, almost seven months had passed. On some things his memory was cloudy, but on others it was clear. As he traveled south on Highway 21, he observed what he thought was a police car turn left off the highway onto the Main Street of Varnado where a short distance away the deputies would be shot. He did not see any other vehicles.[43] If he had seen the deputies' patrol car, then where was the black truck that followed the deputies into town? The FBI wondered if another police car had been behind the deputies and the truck occupied by the killers.

Because the salesman reported seeing a police car turning onto Main Street, FBI agents recalled that Leroy "Slick" Seal, a game warden, drove a car similar to that of the deputies. Seal and his wife had previously told the FBI that they were home at the time of the shooting. Seal said his wife had awakened him after hearing the gunshots. He dressed and the two went to the scene. When contacted by agents in April 1966, Seal said he was recovering from a minor injuries sustained in an automobile accident. He was asked to visit with agents in Bogalusa for a confidential interview at his convenience. Seal reminded agents that he had been cooperative with the bureau and would continue to be but said he had told all he knew and he did not feel well. He declined the request, claiming it would be a waste of time.[44]

As the salesman passed the Main Street turn and traveled southward on Highway 21 toward Bogalusa, he soon came to the bridge that crossed Pushepatapa Creek a mile down the road. On the north side of the bridge, he saw a directional turn signal flashing on a car parked in the right lane. At that moment, he heard a rapid succession of gunfire, apparently the sound of the deputies being shot. As he approached the bridge and slowed down, the salesman saw an individual step from the front of the vehicle waving one arm and waving a flashlight in the other signaling the traveler to stop. The person walked in front of the salesman's headlights to the driver's door window, which was rolled down. Never facing the salesman eye to eye, the man asked the salesman where he was going. When the man talked, he cocked his head to one side. The salesman asked if anything was wrong. The man answered that someone had been shot. He advised the salesman to move on.[45] How did the man know that someone had been shot?

The salesman told the FBI that the vehicle parked on the bridge facing south toward Bogalusa appeared to be a 1960 or 1961 tan, beige, or off-white Plymouth. It also had a whip antenna on the back. These factors suggested to the bureau that the man was possibly part of the wrecking crew in the shooting and used the car radio to communicate with others. His job was apparently to stop any traffic that might interfere with the attack.[46]

The salesman said the man was slovenly in appearance and dress, about forty years of age, six feet tall, and appeared to weigh about two hundred pounds with a potbelly. He was wearing brown trousers and an Eisenhower jacket. He wore a hat similar to the kind worn by bus drivers or service station attendants with a short bill on front. The man was wearing a sidearm in a holster—a .38 special—just like the one Wilford Moore sold five days after the shooting. But other Klansmen had .38 specials. Agents realized the physical description of the man matched that of plumber Virgil Corkern, a Bogalusa Klansman who was among the first three suspects to emerge in the shooting. An informant had told the bureau that Corkern and two others had plotted to kill the deputies a month before the attack. However, Corkern could account for most of his time on the night of the shooting. Agents drove the salesman to Corkern's home, concealing him in the back seat. The salesman watched as FBI agent James L. Theisen interviewed Corkern, who was standing fifteen feet away in his front yard. Afterward, the salesman told agents that Corkern bore a "striking resemblance" to the man he saw at the bridge. He said he would have picked this man out of a photo lineup. Corkern was later asked to visit the FBI office in Bogalusa. The grilling upset him. Corkern said he had a heart condition, high blood pressure, and diabetes and could not stand up to pressure. He was advised of his rights but vehemently denied any involvement.[47] In the end, the bureau could never prove Corkern was the man on the bridge because the salesman could not positively identify him.

But the salesman provided agents one other fascinating bit of information. He was so rattled over the interaction with the armed man on the bridge that he sped up to seventy miles per hour before quickly observing an intersection another mile down the road. The location where Highway 21 and Highway 436 crossed was also known as the Pine-Varnado road. On the northeast side of the intersection, he saw four or five vehicles where four or five men were milling around in front of a house. The headlights on one of the cars were on. He observed one man cross in front of the headlights.[48]

An elderly man and his wife lived on the opposite corner of the intersection. He told agents he and his wife were usually in bed by 10:00 p.m. He recalled seeing no cars parked in front of his house or on the opposite corner of the intersection, where a house was under construction.[49]

Later, the FBI showed the salesman photos of more than two dozen men. He said he recognized the faces of three men—Ray McElveen, Bobby Lang, and Virgil Corkern. It is possible the salesman had previously seen a photo of McElveen following his arrest in the shooting. But there is no other explanation for his recognizing Lang and Corkern. He had passed through Varnado and Bogalusa only twice previously. But this information seemed to give credence to two rumors circulating through Varnado after the shooting—that two vehicles were directly involved in the attack, maybe more. One story was that the three men in the truck who committed the shooting got into a car parked at a house on the outskirts of town located near a bridge and that the guns used in the shooting were thrown into the water. A source told the bureau that he had seen Klan crosses below the bridge. The FBI searched Pushepatapa Creek but came up empty-handed.[50]

On April 2, 1966, Creed Rogers returned to work for the Washington Parish Sheriff's Office, ten months after the shooting. A month later, the FBI closed its temporary office located in room 23 of the Choctaw Motel and had the private phone line disconnected. The investigation would continue but with fewer agents, who would work out of the bureau's new office in Covington. In the June 2 issue of the *Bogalusa Daily News,* this ad appeared in the classified ad section: "It has been one lonely year today, since the death of Deputy Sheriff Oneal Moore, my beloved and devoted husband. He is sadly missed by wife, children, family and friends."

Fifteen years would pass after the shooting before the New Orleans FBI field office opened a letter dated July 2, 1980. It was from Washington Parish Sheriff's Office investigator Dewey Norsworthy, a former Bogalusa police officer. Norsworthy advised that Mary Moore might have information concerning the killing of Deputy Oneal Moore. Mary was located in Phoenix, Arizona, but she had nothing to say to agents. She said James Wilford Moore, her former husband, had never discussed the shooting with her.[51]

Decades passed before in January 2007 a source told the bureau he had been told in 1979 or 1980 that John Pope had been involved in a murder and had buried some guns in a concrete slab. That led agents back to the door of Mary Moore, who was then seventy-five and living again in Bogalusa. This time Mary told a different story. The Department of Justice reported when it closed the Oneal Moore murder investigation in 2016 that a few days after the shooting, according to Mary's final interview with the bureau, she had watched John Pope "place two guns on the patio while her husband mixed cement. Her husband then poured the cement over the guns. When her husband saw her, he ordered her to leave. She asked him about it a few hours later, and he told her that he and Pope had shot the black deputies." Although FBI agents had looked into the pit in 1965 and found nothing, the bureau decided to send new agents back to the Moores' former home forty-two years later. They again found nothing.[52]

But Mary also said in 2007 that on the night of the shooting her husband "came home around 11:00 p.m., and told her to tell the FBI that he was at home watching television the entire night." Mary told the FBI that in 1965 her husband had not left home that night.[53] It is interesting to note that Moore had twice mentioned to the FBI that he and Mary had watched the Spencer Tracey movie that aired from 8:00 p.m. to 10:00 p.m. He even mentioned that he had watched it once before. That suggests that if the FBI had asked him what the movie was about, he would have been able to tell them.

So agents asked Mary, Why didn't you report this information in the 1960s? Because, she said, she "was afraid of her husband and the KKK."[54]

Mary died in 2009.

Wilford Moore and John Pope had each been dead for more than a decade.

What possible motive—other than to finally get the truth off her chest without fear of reprisal—would Mary have had in finally reporting this information to the FBI?

12

"WE'RE GOING TO GET THEM!"

Through the years after the shooting of the two deputies, the list of suspects grew longer and longer. One might have been high on the list in the 1960s before being moved down a few notches during the 1970s, only to rise back to the top again in the following decade based on new information. In the late 1980s, the widow of one Klansman told agents her husband had confessed to the crime. In the 1990s, a convicted murderer told Creed Rogers that he knew who shot up the deputies. Rogers told FBI agents, who later learned that this new suspect had told coworkers of his involvement. Federal grand juries centered on other suspects in the 1990s. The main persons of interest, however, had one thing in common: they could be linked to Ray McElveen.

Early on, the accumulation of evidence indicated the timing of the attack had been hatched hours before the shooting and ultimately involved at least two trucks and one car occupied by Klansmen. At the same time, on the eve of the shooting, an alliance of Klansmen between those in Bogalusa led by Saxon Farmer and a group of dairy farmers and ranchers led by Russell Magee in the vicinity of Franklinton shifted to a partnership between Klansmen in Bogalusa and Varnado, located only six miles apart. In all, five major suspects would arise in the 1980s and 1990s. One of the most fascinating suspects was revealed too late for prosecution, while suspicion on another man resulted in the FBI once again knocking on doors throughout Washington Parish as well as parts of North Carolina.

In 1985 at the courthouse in Franklinton, James E. Burch, a fifty-one-year-old carpenter from Varnado, was found not guilty by a district judge on a charge of aggravated battery. Burch and his wife, forty-nine-year-old Irene, had been married for more than two decades, were the parents of five children, and for the most part had enjoyed a happy life. But there were problems in the marriage. Sometimes Burch, who stood an inch over six feet tall, drank too much. When doing so, he occasionally hit Irene, who stood only a fraction higher than five and a half feet. During that summer, following a night of drinking and an argument with his wife, Burch knocked Irene to the floor with a barstool. It was the last straw for Irene. She filed a complaint with the sheriff's office, and Burch was arrested for aggravated battery.[1]

Daughter Dianne Burch Bass, nine years old at the time of the murder, recalled in March of 2020 that her father's violence was often unleashed when he was drinking. Despite that, Dianne and her siblings loved their parents, faults and all. "Daddy raised us to the best of his ability," Dianne said. "He taught us morals and standards. I loved and respected him. I loved my mother, too. They were good people. Hardworking. They raised us with love and care." Dianne remembers her parents dancing in the kitchen, laughing and talking. "They wanted to do for the kids," Dianne said, "and Dad was the kind of man that if somebody needed something, he would take the shirt off his back." But Diane and her siblings heard the arguments, too, and knew their dad's temper flared when he drank. They knew, too, that their mother held great resentment for the way she was sometimes treated.[2]

In the courtroom, Irene watched and listened in disbelief when the judge found her husband not guilty. She walked out of the courtroom and went outside to her car, where she retrieved a fully loaded .38 caliber pistol. A short time later, Burch emerged from the courtroom into the courthouse lobby. Irene walked to a small concession booth, and as Burch's lawyer walked into the clerk of court's office, Irene stepped out, raised the pistol, and fired five shots, one hitting her husband in the back. A deputy fired two warning shots at Irene. She dropped the gun and surrendered. Thirty minutes after her husband had departed the courtroom, Irene was read her rights and later charged with first-degree murder, illegally carrying a weapon, and discharging a firearm in a public place. James Burch was transported to the hospital where he underwent four and a half hours of surgery and received nineteen pints of blood, twice the amount typically flowing through an adult. The bullet had struck Burch to the right of his spine and fragmented before penetrating his right lung and the right side of his heart. He was pronounced dead seven and a half hours after the shooting.[3]

"Mother just lost it," daughter Diane said, adding that things were different for women back then and domestic abuse cases were not taken as seriously as they are today. But the lives of the Burch children were forever changed. Diane was twenty-nine in 1985 when she and her siblings had to bury their father and watch as her mother pled guilty to his murder and was sent off to prison.[4]

Before she was incarcerated at the Louisiana Correctional Facility for Women in St. Gabriel, Irene saw deputy Creed Rogers and asked for a minute of his time. She had shocking news: her late husband had been involved "in the ambush shooting" of Rogers and Oneal Moore. In 1989, Rogers told the FBI. Agents went to see Irene. According to the Department of Justice closure letter on the Oneal Moore murder case, Irene said that on the night of the murder Burch ordered her

> not to leave the house for any reason. He then left on foot and returned two hours later. He told her if anyone asked, she was to report that he spent the evening at home, and that if she did not, she would not live to testify about it. He also commented that the two black deputies would no longer be able to arrest white people. Later that night, he got up from bed and burned his KKK robe and hood in the furnace. The next morning, he removed the white sideboards from his blue Chevrolet pick-up truck and burned them in the backyard.

Irene said that Burch had bought a .303 rifle—which could have been one of the murder weapons—a month or two before the shooting and that the gun had been damaged in a fire at their home several years afterward.[5]

Years earlier, in 1965, the FBI had identified Burch as a member of the Varnado Klan and listed him as a suspect.[6] He was then employed with the Bogalusa Streets and Parks Department. Burch told agents in their first interview of him that he was home the entire evening on the night of the murder and did not hear about the shooting until the next day. He claimed he was neither in the Klan nor a member of the white Citizens' Council and "tend[ed] to his own business and expect[ed] everyone else to do the same."[7] But the FBI was getting different information. A source told the bureau that Burch had volunteered to assist in any action deemed necessary "to get rid of" the two Black deputies.[8] When the FBI went for a second interview of Burch in the fall of 1965, he denied the accusation and denied knowing McElveen.[9] Yet daughter Dianne said in 2020 that her father did know McElveen.[10] Interviewed for a third time in October 1965, Burch said he was tired of talking. He told agents not to come to his house again without a warrant for his arrest.[11]

In 2020, daughter Dianne says there's no doubt her dad was in the Klan and that he did burn the sideboards from his truck and later bought new ones. "I think Dad may have known who did it," she said of the murder. "I asked him one time if he was involved, and he said he did not do it." Irene Burch told the FBI that her husband had told her on many occasions that McElveen's truck was a decoy, a rumor that circulated after the shooting. Dianne said she had heard that two trucks were involved in the shooting, and later her father told her that he "was in the one [truck] that did not do it."[12]

In 1989, after Irene Burch told Creed Rogers that her husband was involved in the shooting, a state convict offered the deputy yet another tip. The prisoner, who had been convicted of killing four people over three decades, said Elmo Breland, a commercial painter in Varnado, was one of the men who shot the two deputies in 1965.[13] A troubled man who grew up in a poor household in Bogalusa in the 1930s, Breland had held a position of power in the Varnado unit of the Original Knights. Known for his menacing persona, he was quick to fight and was constantly in trouble. During World War II, he served in Guam, but the marine faced two deck courts and a court-martial for bad conduct. During psychological testing, doctors found he had a low IQ and suffered from a mental disability. He was dishonorably discharged in 1950.[14]

Over the next ten years, Breland was in and out of jail, arrested for disturbing the peace in Bogalusa and sentenced to the Arkansas penitentiary for forgery and later to the North Carolina pen for false pretenses.[15] After serving his time, he returned to Louisiana, and in 1964 he joined the Original Knights unit in Varnado along with Bobby Lang and James Burch. According to FBI informants, Breland, then thirty-five, was named special investigator, appointed by Lang and Lang's brother-in-law Archie Roy Seals, both suspects in the attack on the deputies.[16] Lang had claimed as an alibi that he was frogging on the night of the shooting of the deputies. Seals, who initially lied to the FBI as to his whereabouts that night, later claimed he and his outlaw friends had been harvesting wildlife illegally. Seals would not identify where or with whom he had been but stuck to his alibi for the rest of his life. Original Knights leader Robert Fuller of Monroe, who at the time oversaw all wrecking crew projects in the state, approved the appointment of Breland as special investigator for the Varnado Klan, according to informants. Fuller had visited Sheriff Crowe in 1964 in an unsuccessful attempt to persuade him to fire his newly hired Black deputies. One FBI source said James Burch had attended that meeting.[17] As far as Breland's other Klan activities during this period, the FBI files from the era reveal nothing, and he seemed to curtail his criminal activity for the rest of the 1960s.

But that all changed in 1970 when Breland was arrested for the murder of twenty-four-year-old Shelton Tynes at Breland's Little Bourbon Lounge in Bogalusa. Breland claimed Tynes was causing trouble, and when Breland "rapped" Tynes on the side of his head with a gun, the weapon accidentally went off and killed the victim. In 1972, Breland pled guilty to manslaughter and was sentenced to twenty years, his time later reduced to fifteen years.[18] In the late 1970s, Breland was returned from Angola to Washington Parish at the request of Sheriff Willie Blair, who had unseated Dorman Crowe in 1968. Blair placed Breland in protective custody, informing the Department of Corrections that Breland had provided crucial information used "to solve a double murder here involving inmates on work release from police barracks. . . . It is and has been my intention to provide Mr. Breland with protection from those persons against whom he gave evidence, and his return to the state penitentiary system could very well result in serious injury or death for Mr. Breland."[19]

The case Breland helped Sheriff Blair crack dated back to 1974 in Washington Parish. Ellsworth and Dolly Verberne were murdered at their residence, and $90,000 in cash and personal property was taken from a safe inside the home. For two years, the case went unsolved, until 1976, when Frank Scianna was indicted for the murders. Scianna had killed twice before.[20] According to Sheriff Blair, it was Elmo Breland who provided information that cracked open the Verberne case, but because of that, Breland's life was now in danger. The sheriff kept Breland under protective custody until 1979, when Governor Edwin Edwards commuted Breland's sentence to fifteen years. In early 1980, Breland was released.[21] Nine years later, Scianna, convicted on Breland's information, told Deputy Creed Rogers that Breland was a participant in the attack on the deputies.

By no means was Frank Scianna a credible witness. For one thing, he obviously had a grudge against Breland for ratting him out. But in the early 1990s, the FBI found another source that heard Breland brag about shooting the deputies. Breland claimed he planned the attack and led the wrecking crew that committed it. The FBI knew from its 1964 files that Breland had been named special investigator for the Klan in Varnado. Breland told the FBI source that he and Archie Roy Seals were the shooters in the back of Seals's pickup and that another man, Klansman Jimmy Lang, brother of suspect Bobby Lang, was the driver. Jimmy Lang died in the 1960s. Breland also claimed that the weapons used in the shooting were destroyed in a sulfuric acid vat at the Crown-Zellerbach plant in Bogalusa, where many Klansmen worked. That rumor first floated through the Varnado community only days after the shooting. Although an intensive investigation by the FBI indicated that was possible, the bureau found no proof that this had happened. The vats had been removed in the early 1970s.[22] According to Breland, the motive in the attack was simple—white people did not want Black deputies telling them what they could do. He also described Oneal Moore as a "smart ass fuckin' nigger."[23]

In 1994, the FBI found others who had heard Breland talk about the shooting. The Charlotte Paint Company in North Carolina had employed him in 1990. One employee remembered that Breland made "weird" and "off the wall" comments. Breland said that he had been in the Klan in Louisiana and asked his coworker if he had ever been "cut deep and wide." A second employee recalled that Breland hated Black people and frequently made derogatory remarks about them. Breland was described as dirty, lacking in personal hygiene, and always armed with a knife. Another remembered Breland discussing the shooting of two Black deputies in Louisiana and "appeared to know a lot about it." This coworker said he did not really believe Breland until he saw the television show *Unsolved Mysteries* in 1990 that featured the case. But the man recalled Breland often used the words "we" or "they" when discussing the shooting and never used the personal pronoun "I."[24]

In Washington Parish in the early 1990s, agents surveilled Breland, Archie Roy Seals, Ray McElveen, and others. They also used pen registers, a means to see who they were calling on their telephones. In December 1994, the New Orleans FBI reported to headquarters that in recorded conversations between Breland and an informant, Breland seemed to want people to think he was responsible for the shooting but that his comments were of a general nature, adding that he "is not the most intelligent person." Breland lived "in a very disgusting environment in the rural area of Varnado, Louisiana. He presently lives . . . in a house trailer with no running water or electricity" or telephone. The agent opined: "In my four and one-half years as being assigned to this case, Breland has come forth as the leading candidate of one who could have definitely committed this crime. I still have some reservations that Breland might be blowing steam and attempting to gain notoriety by wanting everyone to believe that he was responsible for such a heinous act." The agent also noted that the violence-prone Breland laid out a clear motive for the shooting and indicated that McElveen used his truck as a decoy while the real killers did the dirty work. One agent who investigated the case for years thought that in the decades after the shooting Breland as a suspect "has come forth as the strongest candidate of all."[25]

In 1995, agents discussed Breland with the bureau's Behavioral Science Investigative Support Unit (BSIU) in Quantico, Virginia. After reviewing files and listening to Breland's recorded confessions to a confidential informant, experts felt there "were some accuracies in describing the 1965 shooting, but most were already public information." BSIU suggested that agents confront Breland with the recordings and requested that he be polygraphed.[26] On July 14, 1996, Breland was contacted at his home. He agreed to go to a hotel in Bogalusa for an interview. Breland admitted to being in the Klan and said that Jimmy Lang, the man he told others was the driver of the pickup, had inducted him into the Varnado Klan. He denied being involved in the shooting of the deputies. Confronted with the tapes, Breland brushed it off, saying he was "just bullshitting," just running his "old crazy fucking mouth."[27]

Breland agreed to be polygraphed but told agents he would probably flunk the test. He did. Agents surmised that Breland had bragged to a couple of people in Washington Parish that he was a shooter, but he offered no specific evidence to support his claims. A psychological test administered by the bureau determined that Breland "was boasting about his participating in the incident and that his statements lacked credibility."[28]

Not necessarily eliminated as a suspect, Breland did offer two pieces of information critical to the overall investigation into the attack on the two deputies. He claimed that McElveen was one of three or four decoys "driving black Chevrolet trucks that night." And Breland added that Saxon Farmer, the leader of the Bogalusa Klan, had told him prior to the shooting, "We're going to get them damn niggers!"[29]

In addition to James Burch and Elmo Breland, three more suspects would become the focus of the FBI investigation in the 1990s—Saxon Farmer, Robert Rester, and Jim Fisher. Informants told agents the fifty-eight-year-old Farmer was "too intelligent and too shrewd" to have been physically involved in the shooting, but he would know the details. Parents throughout Bogalusa knew his taste for violence. One man told the FBI he was concerned about his teenage son who had gone to Farmer's house with other teens Farmer was recruiting to take part in the street violence in Bogalusa. After Farmer provided a list of names of dozens of Klansmen in Washington Parish during the federal trial in New Orleans in 1965 because one of the judges threatened him with jail, he lost many followers.[30] Soon afterward, Farmer saw the violent White Knights as his future. For months, McElveen and Wilford Moore had urged such a move.

In December 1965, ACCA grand dragon Charles Christmas abolished Farmer's title as grant titan, second in command. The next month, January 1966, Farmer organized a White Knights chapter in Bogalusa. The White Knights had morphed in Mississippi from the Louisiana Original Knights. Among the Bogalusa chapter's projects was the formation of a boycott committee to take action against a local tire company for firing an employee who was a Klansman, Sears and Roebuck for having Blacks model clothing in their catalog, a handful of cafes and restaurants for serving Blacks, Mobil gas stations because one was operated by a Black man, and a Shell station for having integrated restrooms.[31]

Among the visitors to a chapter meeting, which usually included approximately a dozen members, was Sam Bowers, head of the White Knights who had ordered the murders of the three civil rights workers in Neshoba County, Mississippi, in 1964 and of Black activist Vernon Dahmer in Hattiesburg, Mississippi, in 1966. Bowers gave a rambling talk, pushing members to concentrate on politics, advocating "political warfare," and establishing private segregated schools for whites. He also discussed securing explosive material, burning crosses, and obtaining electronic equipment.[32] The man given the role of investigating possible wrecking projects for the Bogalusa White Knights chapter was Jim Fisher.

The forty-four-year-old Fisher and McElveen had been friends for years. A married father of two school-age children, Fisher was seen accompanying McElveen around town in the days after the FBI's lead suspect was released from jail. Fisher's car had a Confederate license plate on the front bumper. A US Army veteran and a big man at six-foot-three, 201 pounds, Fisher worked as a turbine repair helper at the Crown-Zellerbach plant and repaired automobiles and outboard motors in his spare time to earn extra money. A source told a Bogalusa police sergeant that Fisher was one of several men invited to a meeting at McElveen's home on June 1, the day before the shooting. Even though he was a Klansman, Fisher also served on the Bogalusa auxiliary police force.[33]

Because of his "strong feelings against blacks," his Klan membership, and his close relationships with McElveen and Saxon Farmer, the bureau early on looked at Fisher as a suspect. Fisher's siblings told agents they believed he was in the Klan, but when they brought up the subject, he would not discuss it. His sister drove by a Klan rally at Farmer's house once to see if she could see her brother, but the Klansmen were wearing hoods and robes to conceal their identities.[34] On the day of the murder, Fisher worked a hot and grueling ten-hour shift repairing a boiler from the inside. He left work at 8:01 p.m., more than two hours before the shooting.[35] On June 15, thirteen days after the attack on the deputies, Fisher, like Saxon Farmer and Ray McElveen, refused to be interviewed by the FBI.[36]

At White Knight meetings in 1966 and 1967, Fisher boasted that he could supply the Klan with ammunition from Mississippi sources and discussed how to make explosives with ammonium nitrate, fertilizer, and diesel fuel. Fisher wanted to "create a little excitement" in Bogalusa by lighting a cross and firing explosives all at once to show the populace that the Klan was still around.[37] On December 3, 1966, five crosses were burned in town. One of the crosses flamed at city hall and another at the home of Mayor Jesse Cutrer.[38] Fisher built the crosses and assigned members to torch them across town. He also showed Klansmen how to make brass knuckles.[39]

During several nights in 1966 and 1967, the White Knights distributed leaflets that contained false stories of police conducting illegal searches of the homes of citizens and claiming the Census Bureau would begin issuing numbers to taxpayers rather than use names in order to create a communist state. It urged whites to support conservative groups, Christianity, and private schools for whites, or otherwise to "register your white children in a Nigger School." When two newly hired Black policemen arrested a white man in 1967, the leaflet asked: "So what are these Niggers doing arresting white people anytime, anywhere?" Then it warned, "It could be dangerous."[40]

But things grew more tense in June 1967 when a Black male entered a Bogalusa drug store, cursed an employee, refused to pay, and left owing $5.48. Reportedly, the man later accosted two teenage white girls. He was arrested on a charge of simple battery and taken to the St. Tammany Parish jail because Bogalusa police felt he would be safer there. A short time later, on June 15, the Klan distributed literature criticizing police: "Your daughters are not safe on the streets of Bogalusa. . . . Black Animals molested white girls, kissed them, tore off their clothes. . . . Why were the Niggers spirited out of town?" Klansmen wanted to kill the Black man who was arrested, but while Saxon Farmer overruled them, he said Klansmen would later castrate him. A new police chief and a new mayor went looking for the distributors of the pamphlets. Multiple citizens, mostly whites, complained to police and city officials about the leaflets that were strewn across their driveways and lawns. Many whites were sick of the onslaught of Klan propaganda that included the typical untrue allegations of government welfare programs, personal attacks on individuals, and distorted half-truths.[41]

Later that night, police found Jim Fisher in possession of the pamphlets. In all, Bogalusa police confiscated more than five thousand mimeographed copies as evidence. As a result, Fisher and other White Knights were charged with violating a city ordinance against littering, and each was released on a bond of fifty dollars. The ordinance stated that no person "while a driver or passenger in a vehicle, shall throw or deposit any litter upon any street or other public place within the city, or upon private property." Conviction for the offense brought a maximum one-hundred-dollar fine and/or ninety days in jail. There was also talk in legal circles as to whether Klansmen should be charged for violating the federal court order prohibiting the Klan from harassing and intimidating the populace.[42] One man arrested in addition to Fisher was Bogalusa city attorney Robert T. Rester, who a few days later entered a motion in court to dismiss the charges, arguing that the town law was unconstitutional.

Robert Thomas Rester at age of thirty-four was elected city attorney in the spring of 1964 during a special election that saw only 32 percent of registered voters turn out. He replaced the former city attorney, who had resigned after a year and a half in office.[43] At the time of his election, Rester was the exalted cyclops of the Original Knights Unit 1 in Bogalusa before later joining the White Knights in 1966. In 1965, he would represent Bogalusa during federal court proceedings against the town and the Klan. When in 1967 the *Bogalusa Daily News* suggested that the city attorney position be appointive, the Klan attacked the paper in one of its late-night pamphlet drops, calling it the "Dirty News."[44]

On the night of the shooting of the deputies, at approximately 11:30 p.m., a radio dispatcher for the Bogalusa Police Department received a visit from Rester at the police station only minutes before the department had knowledge that McElveen had been arrested or that he was a suspect in the shooting. "He [Rester] asked me if I knew of any plot to kill the Negro deputies about one year ago," the dispatcher told FBI agents. The dispatcher answered he was not aware of such a plot although the FBI had been told by an informant a month before the shooting that three Klansmen were plotting to kill the deputies. Rester then told the dispatcher that "Ray McElveen has a truck that fits the description of the truck used in the shooting and that Ray McElveen's truck was not now at home because he just drove past the McElveen home." Minutes later, a report came in that McElveen had been arrested in Tylertown, Mississippi.[45]

Rester's action regarding McElveen raises questions.

Why did this Klansman and city attorney implicate his Klan brother by casting suspicion upon McElveen even before he was arrested?

Was Rester hiding his own involvement with another wrecking crew that was prepared to kill the deputies if they had gotten to them first? Bobby Lang had indicated there were two wrecking crews out that night and that McElveen's got to the targets before the other crew. Elmo Breland said there were two or more trucks out that night.

And why did McElveen in a few spontaneous remarks after his arrest in Tylertown express fear that once it was learned in Bogalusa that he had been arrested "they would kill him"? He did not identify "they," but was he referring to other Klansmen upset with McElveen for getting caught? Or did he fear elimination by the Klansmen who feared a confession would implicate them?

An hour or so before daylight on the night of the shooting, Rester contacted the police station again, this time by phone. Now he offered even more potentially incriminating evidence against McElveen. He said his son had spent the night with one of McElveen's sons both nights prior to the shooting and that on the morning of the shooting, according to Rester's son, McElveen had loaded shotguns into his pickup before leaving.[46] That story, however, was not true. Rester's son made no such statement.

In his phone call to police, Rester also said his son reported that a tall slim white man visited the McElveen home that morning. The dispatcher asked if the man was Jim Fisher. Rester said no. Rester also reported that his son said McElveen was going to his camp that day. When the dispatcher asked for the location of the camp, Rester said he would find out and call back. When he failed to do so, the dispatcher called him. Rester said he could not talk then because FBI agents were at his home.[47] However, there is no record that agents were at his home at that time.

By 1967, the hard-drinking attorney, one of the Klansmen arrested for passing out Klan leaflets, filed suit against the town he represented, challenging the legality of its ordinance on littering. In his argument, Rester cited the first amendment regarding freedom of speech and freedom of the press. Judge A. J. Jones dismissed the charges, giving Rester and the Klan a victory.[48]

When the mayor and city commission originally considered the matter, Rester had dodged any discussion of it. When a city representative went to Rester's office, his secretary said he was at home sleeping and would not be in for another three hours. By then, frustrated town officials went to other lawyers, and a new ordinance was prepared and later passed.[49]

On September 9, 1967, the *Bogalusa Daily News* reported that six lawyers had signed off on the legality of the new ordinance.[50] The law stood and Rester's days as city attorney were numbered. In October, the *Daily News* reported that "an extreme right-wing conservative" group was plotting to kill the mayor and city officials. The FBI learned from a source that the Whites Knights, seeking revenge over the littering charges, planned to kill a Black policeman and others in the event of a racial disturbance, including new city attorney Bascom Talley. Klansmen believed that if such a racial disturbance occurred, police would be so busy subduing it that a policeman could be shot, and the shooter could disappear into the crowd. Although the plot was thwarted and no arrests were made, the new police chief said that interest in the KKK was declining although there would likely always be a small core group.[51]

According to the Department of Justice's notice to close the Oneal Moore case file in 2016, the department and the FBI had launched a grand jury investigation in 1990 centering on Saxon Farmer, Jim Fisher, and Robert Rester. In recorded conversations gained through wired FBI sources and informants, Farmer "denied everything" involving the shooting and advised the others to take the Fifth Amendment, which Farmer had done before the House Un-American Activities Committee's probe into the Klan in 1966.[52]

Fisher, who never provided an alibi for his whereabouts the night of the shooting, was implicated directly in the murder when, in 1989, the bureau received a postmarked anonymous letter that said Fisher was with McElveen on the wrecking crew project and at one point had shouted, "Ray, slow down! You're going to throw us out of the truck!" Through handwriting analysis, the FBI identified the person believed to have written the letter, but the individual denied it.[53]

However, Rester, in one recorded conversation, told Fisher that he (Rester) "pulled the trigger from the back of the truck" and that Virgil Corkern and another man, whose name was redacted in the Department of Justice's case closure letter, were involved. Agents interviewed Rester in 1990. He claimed he did not remember confessing but said if he did, he was probably drunk and likely "looking for sympathy." Agreeing to a polygraph, he denied involvement in the shooting and said he did not know who did it. The polygrapher reported Rester's "reactions 'inconclusive,' determining that he was 'not a fit subject for the polygraph technique in his current state' because he had been drinking 12 beers a day for the past several days."[54]

One retired Washington Parish police officer said that after Rester retired, his drinking escalated and occasionally police would get calls from neighbors complaining about Rester's behavior and drinking. For the safety of everyone, Bogalusa police always sent two officers. "We'd have to be careful because we never knew how far he may go," said the retired officer. "He'd get a little crazy when drinking."[55]

EPILOGUE

Ernest Ray McElveen

In 2002, a year before Ernest Ray McElveen's death, a reporter for the *Los Angeles Times,* writing a story on the murder of Oneal Moore, contacted McElveen, who was then seventy-eight and often seen shopping in downtown Bogalusa. The reporter found McElveen to be good-natured and polite but not talkative. "Nope, no comment," McElveen said. "No comment. Not a thing. I just don't have anything to say. Goodbye."[1]

In 1965, McElveen did not have much to say to police either. He provided a few scant comments, just enough to cause confusion. He never granted the FBI an interview but told others he did not shoot the deputies. That may be the truth. He could not have shot anyone if he were the one driving his pickup at the time the shooters were firing. Even his lawyer, Ossie Brown, could not get McElveen to talk, once remarking, "What do you think of a man who would not even tell his attorney what happened?" FBI special agent Frank Sass, a lead agent on the case during the 1960s, said in 2002 that if "we in the Bureau could have gotten to McElveen before they [Mississippi authorities] turned him over" to Louisiana, "we might have gotten something out of him."[2] Maybe.

McElveen will forever remain a shadow. We know much about him, but we do not really know him. He was ultimately a loner but remembered as fierce in his beliefs as an American on a foreign battlefield of World War II and as a domestic terrorist in his homeland, disguised in a KKK hood and stained by blood.

In cases of violent Klansmen who displayed an extraordinary hatred for African Americans, one always wonders the source of that hate. In McElveen's case, it seems a candle of vengeance was lit when he was quite young; he was told the family story of an alleged attack on his mother in Mississippi when she was young. It was a longtime friend of McElveen's who shared the story with the FBI. Whether the story was true does not seem to matter. McElveen believed it.

Reggie Adams, another decorated war hero in Bogalusa, told the FBI that

McElveen's mother had been assaulted by a Black man when she was sixteen and that soon a vigilante mob was organized by McElveen's grandfather. When the Black man was caught, McElveen's grandfather hesitated in killing the alleged rapist, but friends of the family quickly committed the murder. Adams indicated that news of the episode devastated McElveen and that he never got over it. Adams framed it this way: McElveen "had to live" every moment of his life "with the knowledge" his mother had been molested by a Black man. This was the spark that flamed after the war and it fueled McElveen's lifelong hatred of Black men. Before he was jailed for the shooting and after the charges were dropped, he posted bond for white men accused in racial crimes. He and one of his best friends, Bogalusa Klan leader Saxon Farmer, were the go-to men in these cases.

Another powerful experience in McElveen's life was his service as a US Marine during World War II, when he fought on the Pacific Island of Saipan, seventy-five hundred miles from Bogalusa. He arrived there in summer 1944 as part of the Allied invasion to defeat the Japanese. Taking Saipan was strategically crucial. From there the United States could launch B-29 bombers that could reach Japan, sixteen hundred miles to the north. It took three weeks to force the Japanese to surrender the island. Japan lost some twenty-seven thousand men on the battlefield, while the United States suffered three thousand deaths and more than thirteen thousand wounded, including McElveen, who rushed onshore in mid-June of 1944. American supplies for the combat troops, particularly food and ammunition, were delivered by eight hundred Black marines under heavy fire from the enemy. Saipan was home to thirty thousand civilians, most of them Japanese, who worked in the sugar cane industry, the island's biggest crop. It is a tiny place—12.5 miles long and 5.5 miles at its widest point. Mount Tapochau, at 1,554 feet, is the highest point.[3]

Five years before his death, McElveen penned an account of his experience on Saipan in a marine magazine, explaining that at 2:00 p.m. on June 27, 1944, his platoon was halfway up Mount Tapochau shielded in foxholes as they watched Japanese soldiers walk about on the summit. From his position McElveen could see a cornfield with stalks as high as four feet about two hundred feet away, an excellent position for the enemy to lie in wait. As he scanned the area, McElveen had a premonition of death. He saw no place for cover. "For the first time in my life I felt I was making a decision to forfeit my life. I felt the odds of my making it were totally nil." Ordered to move out, the marines were halfway to the cornfield when they received orders to stop. They stood in place for a minute before being told to withdraw. Soldiers like McElveen, who were armed with Browning automatic rifles, were instructed to cover the withdrawal and at that moment "bullets started raining on us."[4]

McElveen "dropped to one knee and started firing along the ridge and into the corn field. Suddenly, a bullet hit me in the upper left shoulder and exited at my back bone," he said. He was knocked unconscious. "When I came to, I was lying with my face on the ground blowing bloody foam, and coughing up blood when I breathed." He could move his legs but was paralyzed in his upper body. He called for help but felt "nothing could save me even if I could be pulled out of the area." But soon a fellow marine, Edward Thomas Grant, came to his rescue and eventually dragged McElveen to safety. Wounded slightly, Grant rode with McElveen to the hospital, their ambulance under fire as they moved down the mountain. McElveen spent five days on the hospital ship *Bountiful* and wrote that his doctor told him that "the bullet missed my spinal cord by less than one-eighth of an inch." Edward Grant was killed days later during the assault on nearby Tinian Island. McElveen named his oldest son Grant in honor of the marine who saved his life.[5]

McElveen's action earned him military honors, and the wound left him with chronic back pain. Neighbors reported seeing him walking at night, partly due to physical pain and partly due to horrific memories of war. He suffered from stomach ulcers, too, and friends recalled that while they drank coffee he ate ice cream. But he also smoked and drank beer. Most remember him as a quiet man, but others, particularly Klansmen, remember him as someone who often advocated violence in the war against civil rights for Blacks.

McElveen returned home after the war, married, and began a family. By the middle of the 1950s, the decorated war veteran, like his grandfather, took on the role of a vigilante when he and two other men abducted Stanley Carl Bickham for a shotgun wedding. Bickham told FBI agents that in June 1954 the three men "kidnapped him in Bogalusa and claimed he was responsible for the pregnancy" of McElveen's relative, who was five months pregnant. "They drove to Columbia, Mississippi, where an unknown man who they told him was a justice of the peace performed a marriage ceremony," Bickham said. Bickham stated that he "[had] never seen a marriage license or any other type of marriage certificate" and remained uncertain whether the person who performed the ceremony was in reality a justice of the peace. Bickham "contacted authorities at Bogalusa concerning this kidnapping but nothing was done." In fact, McElveen was charged with simple battery and kidnapping, but the charges were dropped. McElveen told authorities the matter was a "family affair." The FBI investigated the case at the time since Bickham was kidnapped and his kidnappers crossed state lines. But the feds declined to prosecute, deferring to local prosecution.[6]

Vigilante justice had been born in Mississippi and Louisiana during the frontier days. The Justice Department's top civil rights lawyer in the 1960s, John Doar, who spent time in Bogalusa in the summer of 1965 after the shooting, said the two states had long been troublesome for federal law enforcement due to the Wild West mentality. In McElveen's case, it was something of a family tradition.

A couple of years after the kidnapping, McElveen and Saxon Farmer began work through the white Citizens' Council to purge Black voters from the rolls in Washington Parish, in part to help a Klan candidate defeat Sheriff Dorman Crowe. This was a massive campaign, resulting the purge of hundreds of Black voters before a federal judge ordered them returned to the rolls.

Then, in 1960, McElveen and his lifelong friend Russell Magee, head of the Washington Parish Klan, had a falling out over money collected by Klansmen to support Louisiana segregationist gubernatorial candidate Willie Rainach. Magee accused McElveen of mishandling the money. They argued. From then on their friendship cooled and McElveen's association with Saxon Farmer grew stronger.

In 1962, McElveen became president of the Washington Parish Citizens' Council. By 1963, he was an Original Knight. Many of his coworkers at the Crown-Zellerbach paper mill, where McElveen worked most of his adult life, indicated that he was a quiet man and rather standoffish. But Klansmen said he would go off the deep end at meetings, raging against civil rights and preaching violence as a means of stopping the movement. He took part in the planning and execution of vigilante beatings of white men the Klan felt were immoral, poor husbands and providers, supportive of civil rights, or simply, in the judgment of Klansmen, lazy and of no account. On one wrecking crew mission to beat a white man, McElveen's target punched him in the eye.

Despite the vigilante history, McElveen was only arrested twice—once for the kidnapping of Stanley Carl Bickham and once for the murder of Oneal Moore. He served eleven days in jail after his arrest in Moore's murder. That was the extent of his punishment.

Dorman Crowe

The man who charged McElveen with murder, Sheriff Dorman Crowe, died at age eighty in 1996. He had hired deputies Moore and Rogers as fulfillment of a campaign promise to the Black community for their support in the 1963–64 election. Without the Black vote, the Klan candidate, Elmer Smith, would have won. Provided a list by community leaders of five names of Black men to consider for deputies, Crowe had chosen Moore and Rogers.

Their hiring enraged the Klan and led to the shooting. State Klan leader Robert Fuller from Monroe visited Crowe at his office in Franklinton a short time afterward and admonished the sheriff for hiring the Black deputies and told him to fire them. Crowe showed Fuller the door. When a white man bumped into the back of their patrol car, the two deputies arrested the intoxicated driver. It was the first and only white man they had ever arrested. The sheriff refused to drop the charges. As a result, the man, who had two previous DWI offenses, was sent to the state prison. This, too, infuriated the Klan, and later they asked Governor John J. McKeithen to get the man out of jail. He refused.

Later, when state Wildlife and Fisheries agent Levert Strahan, a Klan leader, accosted the two deputies and accused them of night hunting, Crowe accused Strahan of trying to intimidate them. He wrote a letter to Strahan's boss, outlining his grievance against the agent and requesting that he be reassigned outside Washington Parish. The sheriff also emphasized that his deputies had done nothing wrong and that he was not going to stand for them being harassed by anyone.

In May 1965, when the FBI received a tip that three men might try to shoot the Black deputies, they relayed the information to the sheriff. Crowe told both Moore and Rogers to beware that Klansmen might attack them. Neither man told their wives or relatives to save them anxiety.

In the 1990s, Creed Rogers paid for an ad in the local newspaper thanking Crowe for hiring the two men and expressed his love for the Crowe family. Milton Graham and Ted Gardner, two retired FBI agents, praised Crowe as a capable, honest, and hardworking sheriff who did all he could to solve the case. They said he was always cooperative with the FBI and continuously provided the bureau with tips and leads. The FBI's Oneal Moore case file also reflects this. Crowe lost his reelection bid for a sixth term in 1968, but his five straight victories over twenty years remain a record in Washington Parish.

Race is an issue that defines this case, but the fact that the Klan shot two law enforcement officers and killed one is something that should have angered anyone who wears a badge. At Moore's funeral, the program noted: "Oneal Moore possessed all the qualities required for becoming a member of the Sheriff's Department. Such qualities were Honesty, Dependability, Courage, Interest and the like. He was employed June 1, 1964, by the Washington Parish Sheriff's Department under the leadership of Sheriff Dorman A. Crowe. He was one of the two Negro deputies to be hired in Washington Parish. He served well his post of duties and was admired, respected and deeply appreciated by those who really knew him."

Moore was survived by his wife, four daughters, his father and mother, five brothers, three sisters, and many relatives and friends.

Nine Prime Suspects

The weapons used in the shooting of Oneal Moore and Creed Rogers were never found. A latent fingerprint taken from McElveen's pickup was never identified.

The evidence seems to clearly indicate that at least two trucks with Klansmen abroad were prowling the roads on the night of the shooting waiting for a chance to shoot the deputies, while a third vehicle, a car, was employed by Klansmen to stop traffic on a bridge on Highway 21 a mile south of Varnado and five miles north of Bogalusa at the time of the attack.

Although there were multiple suspects and persons of interest over the fifty-one-year FBI investigation, no one other than McElveen was ever arrested. Nine Klansmen appear to be most likely candidates to have been physically involved with McElveen in the shooting.

Two of these men confessed to others their involvement, and the FBI had those confessions on tape.

Two other suspects told their wives they were involved in the shootings and threatened to kill them if they told anyone.

Five were from Bogalusa, and four from Varnado.

All are dead.

Bogalusa Suspects

James Wilford Moore, a shipping clerk who headed up the Mitch unit in Bogalusa, left town in a hurry two days after the murder and vomited several times during the first leg of the trip, fearing he was being followed. His traveling companion said Moore, who was forty-five, sold his M-1 Garand before leaving Bogalusa on June 4, 1965. Although the weapon in general was described as a hunting rifle, the FBI believed an M-1 was used in the shooting based on the land and groove markings on the five expended .30.06 shell casings found at the murder scene. The FBI never found the weapon, which Moore appears to have sold to raise money to leave Bogalusa. Like McElveen, Moore had been kicked out of the Klan because of his reckless, violent actions against whites and Blacks that drew criticism of the Klan and from the white community. When he was arrested in 1964 for the Klan beating of a white man, McElveen bailed him out of jail. Years after his death, Moore's ex-wife said he had confessed to her his involvement in the shooting. She said her fear of her husband and the Klan were the reasons she told agents in the 1960s that he never left home on the night of the shooting.

Robert Rester, the Bogalusa city attorney and exalted cyclops of a local KKK klavern, confessed to several individuals that he was one of the shooters. He also did an odd thing on the night of the murder by calling the police station less than an hour after the deputies were shot to tell an officer that Ray McElveen's truck was not parked at his house. Rester, who was thirty-five, made the call before news reached Bogalusa that McElveen had been arrested in Tylertown. If two trucks with shooters were prowling the parish roads looking for a chance to shoot the deputies, was Rester in the second truck and not McElveen's?

Saxon Farmer, the Klan leader of Bogalusa who recruited white male teens to attack Blacks during protests, was the only Klan leader at the May 31, 1965, meeting with Louisiana governor John McKeithen who did not agree to his request to give up efforts to recall Mayor Jesse Cutrer. The mayor infuriated Farmer, McElveen, and others when days earlier he agreed to many demands made by the Bogalusa Voters and Civic League to integrate local government and provide equal city services to Black neighborhoods. Farmer also refused to agree to McKeithen's request that Klansmen back off the violence. According to Klansman Elmo Breland, shortly before the shooting, Farmer, speaking of the deputies, told him, "We're going to get them damn niggers!"

Jim Fisher, age forty-four, was a close friend of McElveen's and Farmer's. He remained in the Klan in Bogalusa for many years, at first as an Original Knight before following Farmer into the White Knights. Fisher never provided an alibi for the night of the shooting. The FBI thought, but could not prove, that Fisher was among the men invited to McElveen's home the night prior to the murder, apparently to discuss the wrecking crew project against the two deputies. Fisher had been with other Klansmen the night before that at the meeting with Governor McKeithen. If Farmer were outraged by the governor's requests, so would have been Fisher and McElveen. In an anonymous letter received by the FBI in 1989, the writer said Fisher was with McElveen during the attack in Varnado and at one point yelled, "Ray, slow down! You're going to throw us out of the truck!"

Virgil "Crowbar" Corkern once pointed a pistol at a fellow Klansman's head over a dispute concerning Klan records. He was also implicated in violence against demonstrators in Bogalusa. A month before the shooting, an informant told the FBI there was a plan in development for a three-man wrecking crew, including the forty-two-year-old Corkern, to drive up beside the deputies' patrol car and shoot them. A salesman passing by Varnado heard the shots fired by Oneal Moore's killers while stopped on a bridge on the outskirts of town. The man who stopped him had a pistol, and his car, parked on the bridge, had a whip antennae on the back, adding to the FBI's belief that the attack was a military-style operation in which the participants used various means to communicate. The salesman was told to move on. Later, the salesman identified Corkern as the man on the bridge, but like many other witnesses discovered during the FBI investigation, he got weak kneed when he realized he might have to testify in court. At that point, he became less certain of what he saw.

Varnado Suspects

Bobby Lang, the thirty-five-year-old employee of a construction company, served as exalted cyclops of the Varnado Klan. He was known as a hothead with an extreme hatred of African Americans. One source told the FBI that Lang considered assassinating James Farmer, national head of the Congress for Racial Equality, who was in Bogalusa at the time of the shooting. A friend of Lang's backed up his alibi that he was frogging at the time of the murder. (FBI agent Sass said the Klansmen suspected in the murder formulated alibis and had other people support those alibis.) Lang said his son was also on the frog hunt, but he refused to let agents talk with him. Interviewed several times, Lang was on edge, perspiring heavily and trembling. He was fingerprinted, but when his print was compared to a latent print found in McElveen's truck, it was not a match. Arriving at the crime scene forty-five minutes after the shooting, Lang asked if the guns appeared to be "flashing fire." If so, he said, one of the weapons may have been an M-1 rifle, which, he said, "throws a flash from the muzzle of the gun for eight to twelve inches." Agents believed an M-1 was the murder weapon and learned from sources that McElveen had approached Lang about taking part in an attack on the deputies. Grilled by agents about McElveen, Lang said, "I'm sure you have the right man." Lang's brother told the bureau that Elmer Smith, the Klan's candidate for sheriff in 1963, planned to name Lang as his chief deputy. Sheriff Dorman Crowe's victory over Smith, however, devastated Lang.

Archie Roy Seals, brother-in-law and best friend of Bobby Lang, was known as an enforcer for the Varnado Klan. A barber in Bogalusa, Lang drew immediate suspicion from the bureau when agents first interviewed him after the murder. He lied, claiming he was home asleep at the time of the shooting. He said that before midnight Lang called with news of the attack. Agents knew from their sources, however, that Seals was not at home at that time. He later admitted he lied but then clouded his activities further by claiming to have been with others violating game laws. An anonymous caller claimed Seals had buried the murder weapons beneath the slab of his newly constructed house in 1965. In 1966, agents asked if they could "cut into the concrete slab foundation on his property." Seals said no. Three decades later, the agents again sought permission to search the foundation. This time, he let them look. They found nothing.

James Burch, a thirty-four-year-old carpenter, volunteered to take part in any action against the two deputies, according to FBI sources. In 1985, his wife, Irene, shot him to death inside the Washington Parish courthouse in Franklinton. She had accused him of hitting her. Stunned that the judge found him not guilty of assaulting her, she exited the courtroom and returned with a pistol and shot her husband to death. Four years later while serving time in the women's penitentiary at St. Gabriel, she told the FBI her husband had confessed his involvement in the shooting and threatened her life if she told anyone. She said he left home the night of the attack, and when he returned, he burned his KKK robe and hood and the next morning removed the white sideboards from his blue Chevrolet pickup and burned them in the backyard. Irene told agents that Burch had told her that McElveen's truck was a decoy. In 2020, James and Irene's daughter, Dianne, told me she asked her father once if he had killed the deputies. He told her no, adding that he was in the "other" truck, not McElveen's.

Elmo Breland, a thirty-five-year-old commercial painter, grew up poor and lived in poverty much of his life. During World War II, he served in Guam, but he had such trouble with authority and getting along with others that he was dishonorably discharged in 1950 after a court-martial for bad conduct. He moved about the South after his discharge. By the time he returned to Washington Parish, he was an ex-con, having served hard time in both Arkansas and North Carolina for forgery and false pretenses. Once he joined the Varnado Klan in 1963, he was appointed a special investigator, who would have the power to set up wrecking crew projects. Breland went to prison in 1972 for manslaughter in Louisiana. In the 1990s, he bragged to coworkers in North Carolina that he was involved in the shooting of Black law enforcement officers in Louisiana. The FBI recorded conversations of him telling FBI sources in Washington Parish of his involvement. Questioned about his statements, Breland told agents he was "just bullshitting." The FBI determined that Breland's statements "lacked credibility" because there was no evidence supporting his claims. Yet one FBI agent who spent more than four years working on the case believed Breland likely was involved in the murder. Breland, too, said McElveen's truck was a decoy, and he claimed that Saxon Farmer had told him the Klan was going to kill the two deputies.

FBI Investigations

1965–1967

In 2016, the Justice Department issued a notice that it was closing the Oneal Moore murder investigation, having exhausted all leads. In this notice, the department outlined the four major phases of the investigation, beginning with 1965–67. During this era, the New Orleans bureau assigned seventy-one agents, most from outside Louisiana, to investigate the case. More than fourteen hundred persons were interviewed, some multiple times, resulting in more than two thousand reports. The primary roadblock for agents was that witnesses were too terrified to talk, fearful that the Klan might later come calling. This was a healthy fear. Governor John J. McKeithen's $25,000 reward for information leading to the arrest and conviction of the killers resulted in no leads to break open the case.[7]

FBI director J. Edgar Hoover was "intimately and actively involved in minute details of investigation," communicated regularly with the special agent in charge of the New Orleans field office and sent "detailed questions" while directing "certain investigative leads, such as polygraphing certain witnesses or checking certain places for the murder weapon." Hoover emphasized that the case "be given top priority" and "receive continuous vigorous investigative attention."[8]

None of the weapons found in McElveen's truck were used in the shooting. The murder weapon was never found despite the FBI's extensive efforts to follow leads for a half century. During the 1960s, agents searched roadways, ditches, creek beds, and beneath bridges from Varnado, the site of the murder, to Tylertown, where McElveen was arrested less than an hour after the shooting. They broke through concrete patios and peeked into pits in search of the weapons based on tips from informants but had no luck there either.[9]

Daniel "Scraps" Fornea, the first person to arrive at the scene of the shooting, said he thought the shots were fired from the truck's cab, but that seems problematic. Pickups today dwarf those of the 1950s. The idea that a driver and two shooters—one with a rifle and one with a shotgun—could have positioned themselves to fire their weapons from the passenger window while crossing over bumpy railroad tracks seems highly unlikely.

Another mystery concerns what happened to the sideboards that Creed Rogers saw on the back of McElveen's pickup on the night of the shooting. Sideboards were common in the 1960s. They were called different names. Farmers and ranchers who hauled cattle in the back of their pickups had cattle rails on the bed of the truck—but these were a few feet high to keep the animal from jumping out. Sideboards are typically a few inches to a few feet high and used for various purposes—to wall in cargo, to haul hunting dogs, etc. Two posts frame a sideboard, and those posts fit into holes at each end of the bed rails. They were easily inserted and easily removed.

Rogers, who saw the black pickup up close three times prior to the shooting, was emphatic that the truck had sideboards. But when McElveen was arrested, the sideboards were missing. When asked where the sideboards on his truck were, McElveen refused to answer although he acknowledged his truck once had sideboards. In fifty-one years of searching, the FBI never found them.

Neither Scraps Fornea nor the other witness to the shooting, Mrs. Jesse Belle Thigpen, saw sideboards on the truck. But they were a long distance from the shooting—more than fifty yards—and each had a different perspective. There were few streetlights in Varnado, and the shooting scene was poorly lit at best. Fornea's view was of the driver's side of the pickup. The shooters fired from the passenger side. Additionally, Thigpen had a view of the rear of the vehicles and thought the sides of McElveen's pickup bed were six to twelve inches higher than a standard truck bed. Maybe from the distance in the poor lighting, she could not distinguish the sideboards from the side of the truck bed. Creed Rogers thought the sideboards on the pickup were about six inches high.

The case was closed in October 1967 "because of insufficient probable cause to sustain a grand jury indictment against any of the suspected perpetrators."[10]

1989–1991

While several tips were investigated during the early 1980s, the period of 1989 to 1991 resulted in a "confluence of leads," prompting the FBI to reopen the investigation. Among the leads were new allegations implicating Bobby Lang and his brother-in-law Archie Roy Seals. In June of 1989, as the FBI began following new leads, the New Orleans field office opined that the "majority of the Varnado white community had some affiliation with the KKK" during the 1960s. Because no one had yet been convicted in the case, agents found the Black community believing "the entire investigation was a coverup. The black community feels cheated and they feel that law enforcement, including the FBI, cannot be trusted."[11]

One of the most promising leads of this era involved that of a former Washington Parish sheriff's deputy, Vertrees Adams, certainly Sheriff Crowe's most controversial deputy and one who despised by the Black community. Adams was working as an investigator for the St. Tammany district attorney in the 22nd Judicial District office in Covington in 1989, when he and a coworker were arrested for assault in Florida. On their way to a law enforcement conference in Jacksonville, Adams and his coworker stopped at a rest area on Interstate 10, where they came upon four Mexican migrant workers whose car had broken down en route to southern Florida for the tomato harvest. According to police, Adams called one of the migrant workers over to him, and when the man arrived, Adams pulled him into his car and pounded him three times in the head with his fists. When a second migrant worker walked over to help his friend, Adams got out of the car and slammed the men's heads together three times. Adams then pretended to be an immigration officer and took one of the men's wallets. One of the workers wrote down the license plate of Adams's car and reported the number and the incident to police. Adams and his coworker were quickly arrested. Police found the wallet in Adams's possession.[12]

While Adams was not a suspect in the shooting of the two deputies in 1965, the FBI had great distrust and disdain for him because of his reputation for police brutality and his well-known hatred of Black people. Adams had been charged in federal court in some of these brutal attacks in the 1960s but was never convicted. However, despite this background, the FBI New Orleans division decided to "use the Florida robbery case as leverage against Adams" to assist in the Oneal Moore murder case, specifically by wiring him to talk with Russell Magee, Archie Roy Seals, and other suspects. Additionally, Florida authorities would consider offering probation in the migrant workers case if Adams pleaded guilty to all charges, got out of law enforcement for the rest of his life, cooperated with the FBI in the Oneal Moore investigation, and provide information that led to an indictment.[13]

First, however, Adams had to come clean on his past. He admitted he had joined the Klan in the early 1960s and was recruited by Jim Fisher and sworn in by Saxon Farmer. He claimed that was the only Klan meeting he attended and that neither Sheriff Crowe nor Deputy Doyle Holliday knew this.[14]

Adams admitted doing "a lot of wrong things in his early days in law enforcement," such as unprovoked beatings of at least ten to twenty Black men "for no reason at all." Adams admitted "taking 'niggers' out and 'whooping' them up in the Crown-Zellerbach Pasture." He said he could not remember the names of the Black men he had beaten but said he did recall assaulting Arthur Ray Mingo with a blackjack in the early 1960s. He claimed that "times are different now and things were much different back then," also claiming that he "truly regret[ted] all that he had done."[15]

Saying he had no knowledge as to who shot the deputies, he expressed concern the FBI might consider him a suspect. He agreed to a polygraph exam, to be wired, and to contact suspects. However, despite his attempts to draw incriminating statements from others, he was unsuccessful and was prosecuted for his Florida offense, receiving ten years for assault and robbery in 1991.[16]

As a deputy, Adams had no jurisdiction in Bogalusa but operated there with the permission of Police Chief Claxton Knight. "White people didn't want the niggers and niggers didn't want the white people and it was just a scrimmage," Knight said about the 1960s while also referring to Adams as "a good officer." Asked whether Adams liked Black people, Knight said, "No, he sure didn't. I don't either."[17]

The Justice Department reported that although during this era of the investigation "none of the leads resulted in a prosecutable case (or even a single coherent theory of who committed the crime and how), it was not for lack of effort," noting that the FBI hypnotized one witness to "jog" his memory of the shooting, while the FBI's Behavioral Science Investigative Support Unit assisted the bureau by providing "psychological profiles of suspected conspirators and subjects, their assessment of the case, and interview strategies and techniques." These behavioral experts traveled to New Orleans in 1989 to assist in the investigation. Even eyewitness Scraps Fornea was under suspicion for a time because agents wondered if he was holding back information or if he was involved. Born at the end of World War I, Fornea served multiple terms as mayor of Varnado in the years following the shooting of the two deputies. Ultimately, the FBI, including the longtime lead agent on the case, did not believe Fornea was involved or holding back information.[18]

During this period, the bureau "monitored key witnesses and subjects" and placed numerous suspects under surveillance. They also monitored telephone numbers registered to McElveen, Bobby Lang, Archie Roy Seals, Earl Stringer, Leroy "Slick" Seal, and Shellie James Seals. Additional conversations were recorded between FBI informants and Lang, Saxon Farmer, Jim M. Fisher, and Robert Rester.[19]

In preparing for a federal grand jury investigation in 1990, the Department of Justice focused on Farmer, Fisher, and Rester. In conservations secretly recorded by the bureau, Farmer "denied everything, and advised people to take the Fifth Amendment. Fisher also denied being involved, but did not provide an alibi for where he was that night. Rester, however, claimed to be involved" but later told the bureau he had no memory of being involved.[20]

Also in 1990, the FBI worked with the *Unsolved Mysteries* television show to present the case to a national audience. The show generated thirty-five calls but "none led to any major developments." In connection with the airing of the show, the FBI, as Louisiana governor John McKeithen had done in the 1960s, offered a $25,000 reward. But once again nothing came of it.[21]

On the program, Deputy Doyle Holliday, whose home was shot into two days after the shooting of Moore and Rogers, said he did not know why he was targeted "because had they shot me down, which they didn't, they still had the FBI and State Police to contend with." Holliday told the FBI that the sheriff's department had focused on two suspects who were not identified on the show. He said the two in the presence of Klansmen were overheard by a witness as they planned the attack on Holliday's home. A Bogalusa police officer had placed a call to Holliday around dusk that day to warn him of the possible attack, but Holliday was out in a remote area of the parish investigating the shooting of the two deputies.[22]

Concerning Moore and Rogers, Holliday believed that one day there would be arrests and convictions, thinking the suspects would not want to "face the Almighty with that on their conscience. And I think before the final day, somebody's gonna get it off of their chest."[23]

Creed Rogers said on the program that he would never stop wondering who "could have done it. And that'll be with me forever. Who could have done that, you know, when people try to kill you and you haven't done anything to them? Why? That never leaves your mind. Sometimes you wonder if they're still out there, still wanting to try it. It's a bad feeling." One other guest on the program, FBI agent Michael Heimbach, said he believed the Klansmen involved did it on their own and did not tell others "what they were going to do." This adds to the belief that most of these suspects were men who fully understood that a fish would never get caught if it did not open its mouth.[24]

The bureau also sent out press releases hoping to nudge witnesses forward, while numerous fingerprints were taken during this era of the investigation and sent to the FBI lab to see if they matched with fingerprints collected during the 1960s probe. There were no matches with the major suspects, and many of the fingerprints were never identified.[25]

Two substantial admissions during this era added volumes to the understanding of the case. Sidney Brock, the cattleman and rancher from the Franklinton area who served as the exalted cyclops of the local Klan unit, placed a mole, on the direction of his Klan superior Russell Magee, in the courthouse jail while McElveen was lodged there. During the 1960s, Brock denied that he planted an informant for the Klan, but in 1991, facing heat from the FBI, he admitted he had indeed done so but that nothing was learned. After taking a polygraph, he was told that he "was not completely truthful." Brock, like Magee and others, told agents that McElveen was a decoy on the night of the murder and was not directly involved in the shooting.[26]

During the 1960s, FBI agents believed the mole was planted to see if McElveen, once jailed at the courthouse, was talking about the shooting with other prisoners and implicating other Klansmen. But could there have been another reason? Maybe Russell Magee was trying to find out who was involved with McElveen because he and Brock did not know the shooting was going to take place on the night of June 2, 1965. Two days earlier, Magee had given his word to Governor McKeithen that he would work to get Klansmen off the streets of Bogalusa and order them to avoid violence. He also promised to end the recall petition against the mayor of Bogalusa, and this position created a rift with Saxon Farmer. By 1966, Magee and Farmer had gone their separate ways.

According to all accounts, Magee considered himself a big man and wanted to be bigger. Having an audience with the governor would have swelled his head. But having made a promise to the governor, only to see his promise evaporate, would have embarrassed him and eroded his credibility. Most likely, he would have been furious that Klansmen acted without his knowledge.

For a long while in 1967, the bureau followed leads that on the night of the shooting numerous vehicles were parked at Brock's house, apparently in preparation for the shooting that night. Rumors floated that "three separate groups had departed Sidney Brock's residence on the evening of June 2, 1965. Each group had a truck, and the alleged plans were that the first group which found the negro deputies would shoot them and then immediately leave the scene and tell no one in the other groups that they had actually done the shooting. This was so that it could be kept a secret from the others so that no persons in any of these three groups would actually know who had done the shooting except the actual participants."[27]

But it was never proven that the killers moved out after a meeting at Brock's house on the night of the shooting. It seems likely, however, that such a plan was in place. More likely the plan originated the day after the McKeithen meeting, possibly at McElveen's home, and a day before the shooting. At that point it appears an alliance was made between Klansmen from Bogalusa and Varnado to get the deputies once and for all and to warn the Bogalusa city government, which was preparing to hire Black policemen.[28] The agreement also points to a common pattern by violent Klansmen: if their leaders begin to compromise and seek to avoid all-out war, then it is time to break off into a renegade group.

Another Klansman, Louisiana Wildlife and Fisheries agent Levert Strahan, also cleared up one piece of the puzzle. Strahan had harassed the Black deputies, claiming they were night hunting. This drew the ire of Sheriff Crowe, who tried to have Strahan relocated out of Washington Parish. Strahan also served as the Klan's investigative head for Washington Parish, a position that gave him authority to approve or organize wrecking crew projects. Strahan told

FBI sources that the brush fire on the night of the shooting had been set by Klansmen to cause the deputies to stop to investigate. The original plan was to shoot them once they emerged from their vehicle. It was when the deputies saw the fire that they observed for the first time the black pickup tailing them. It appeared to come out of nowhere and may have been parked off the highway and awaiting the deputies' arrival. Strahan also told an FBI source that the "shooters had to amend their plans for the ambush when Moore and Rogers did not get out of their car to investigate the fire."[29]

That would explain why the pickup slowed almost to a stop and then passed the deputies at a snail's pace before slowly moving south on Highway 21. The deputies, having passed the fire, turned around and went back to the scene. Realizing the fire would not spread, they turned back south for Varnado without ever losing sight of the pickup. During this time, members of the wrecking crew may have been communicating by CB radio. Bobby Lang had one in his car. The man on the bridge at Varnado who stopped the Florida salesman bypassing the town at the time of the shooting was driving a car with a whip antenna on the back.

During this phase of the investigation, anonymous letters pointing to suspects were received by the bureau, and many persons of interest and suspects were polygraphed.

1992–1996

There was only one significant lead during this period, which involved Elmo Breland, the commercial painter from Varnado who had confessed to coworkers and others that he was one of the shooters. He also was caught on tape making the same assertions. But the FBI did not have any evidence to corroborate his statements according to the Justice Department.[30]

2001–2016

The "biggest development" during this era was the news from Mary Moore that she had lied previously about her husband, James Wilford Moore, being home at the time of the murder. In 2007, not long before she died, Mary said she had lied in the 1960s because she feared her husband and the Klan. But apparently trying to clear her conscious, she said her late husband had left home the night of the murder and around that time hid weapons in a cache at their Bogalusa home. The FBI investigated the site in the 1960s and in the early 2000s but found no weapons.[31]

There were more searches for the alleged murder weapon, but it was not discovered. "The Ghosts of Bogalusa," an episode of *The Injustice Files* a crime program that aired on Investigation Discovery in 2011, featured the case, but no "leads of value were developed from the broadcast."[32]

In 2002, the FBI announced a new reward—this one for $40,000—for information leading to the indictment and arrest of the killers. It was no more successful than previous attempts to use cash to lure viable witnesses forward.[33]

The FBI and Department of Justice concluded in 2016 that the FBI was "no closer to solving" the case "than they were fifty years ago. Many of the subjects and witnesses have passed away, taking their secrets with them." The bureau "devoted significant time and resources toward solving the case, but has yet to gather credible, admissible evidence to prove beyond a reasonable doubt who committed the crime. In addition, even if someone were to confess to having committed this crime, this case would not be prosecutable unless there was significant corroborating evidence, including physical evidence such as the murder weapon, to support any witness testimony. There is significant Brady information in this case because numerous people have allegedly confessed to this crime, and in addition . . . the FBI has gathered numerous, uncorroborated (and in many cases, uncorroborate-able) 'confessions,' admissions, or leads, none of which were substantiated but all of which could be used to cast reasonable doubt on any prosecution."[34]

Despite a herculean effort, the Oneal Moore murder case was never solved. In the announcement of the closure of the case, the Department of Justice wrote:

> This laundry list of alleged perpetrators demonstrates the virtual impossibility of prosecuting this case even if someone were to confess to the crime. . . . This is why Breland and Rester could not be prosecuted despite the fact that the FBI had recorded 'confessions' from them—there was simply no physical evidence that backed up their accounts, and the FBI had collected significant conflicting information that other subjects had committed the crime.
>
> Moreover, even if the FBI were able to develop sufficient evidence to prove beyond a reasonable doubt that a particular individual had killed Moore, the applicable statute of limitations would preclude prosecu-

tion under the federal criminal civil rights statutes. . . . While the Civil Rights Division has used non–civil rights statutes to overcome the statute of limitations challenge in certain cases, such as those occurring on federal land and kidnapping resulting in death when the victim is transported in interstate or foreign commerce, the facts here do not indicate that federal prosecution is available under these other statutes. The FBI has devoted significant resources through the years in developing and pursuing several credible theories. Investigators unfortunately have been unable to gather independent corroborating information to verify any of them. No viable leads remain, and therefore, this matter should be closed.[35]

But when a suspect admits to his wife, as two did, that he was involved in the murder, and when two other suspects are on tape admitting they pulled the trigger, it is impossible to believe that all four were lying. The actions and beliefs and comments made by the other leading suspects make it hard to ignore their likely involvement. There can be no doubt that a conspiracy to kill the deputies was under way at least a month before they were shot because an informant told the FBI that a wrecking crew of three planned to drive beside the deputies' patrol car and kill them.

The most haunting question will forever be, Who pulled the trigger?

The Families

Creed Rogers, who survived his partner Oneal Moore by forty-two years, died in a Franklinton nursing home on March 4, 2007, at the age of eighty-four. He had retired from the sheriff's office in 1988 as a captain and was survived by one son, Larry, two grandchildren, and a great-grandchild.

"I made up my mind," Rogers said before his death, "I'm never going to find out who did this."[36] His house was along the route McElveen took to his fishing camp, and on many occasions Rogers saw McElveen pass by.

Rogers would often recur to that terrible night in 1965. He was burdened with the memory, tortured by guilt that he survived while his partner died, and perpetually buttonholed by one person after another giving him their unsolicited opinions of who shot the two deputies.

In 1965, despite his wounds and initial uncertainty as to whether his partner was dead or alive, he radioed the sheriff's office describing the pickup truck that held the escaped shooters. Rogers had three opportunities to look over that pickup—when the deputies stopped for the fire and the truck slowly passed them, when the deputies passed the truck as they neared Varnado, and when the truck began firing at them as they crossed the railroad tracks in town. He radioed the sheriff's office that the pickup was a mid-1950s Chevrolet, dark colored, maybe dark blue, dark green, or black. He said the truck had a white grill across the front. He also added one other piece of information—that on the front of the pickup offset to the right was a rebel flag license plate.

Many trucks in the parish and that region of Louisiana and Mississippi were similar to McElveen's, and many had rebel flag emblems or license plates. But the process of elimination during the FBI investigation showed that only one truck—the one McElveen was driving through Tylertown when he was pulled over less than an hour after the shooting—had a rebel flag placed to the right of center on the front.

Only one.

In 2017, I met Maevella Moore for the first time at her home in Varnado, the same house she and Oneal shared with their four daughters in 1965, located a half mile from the crime scene. At eighty-two, Maevella used a walker, but she was in good health, full of energy and constantly displaying a vibrant smile. In that house, where she lived with her parents and later with her husband, she reared her daughters—Tresslar, Regenia, Veronica, and Sheronda—in the aftermath of the great tragedy of her life.

Tresslar led me through the house showing me photos hanging on the walls of her father and her family. When they married in 1954, Maevella was nineteen. Oneal was twenty-three. It was not love at first sight, Maevella said, but after two years of dating both were ready to marry.

She told a reporter once that her husband "was not afraid of anything. He was not a scaredy-cat." Like Creed Rogers, she resigned herself long ago to the fact that there would be no justice in her lifetime. "If you did a terrible thing, you should be brought forth," she said. "I'm not going to feel sorry for them. They didn't feel sorry for me and my daughters. . . . Old men, young men, gotta pay. They're going to pay, one way or another."[37]

"Man might not know," she added, "but God knows what's been going on."[38]

At her home in 2017, she pointed out a photograph of Oneal in his army uniform and commented on how handsome he was before closing her eyes and smiling as she recalled that he was "a good kisser."

Silent for a while, she looked up again at the photo.

"I loved him," she said. "I still love him."

ACKNOWLEDGMENTS

During a series of telephone conversations more than a decade ago, retired FBI agent Ted Gardner told me about his time investigating the 1965 Ku Klux Klan attack on Washington Parish, Louisiana, deputies Oneal Moore and Creed Rogers. Moore died during the nighttime ambush while Rogers survived.

My central focus at that time was on other Klan murder cases in northeastern Louisiana and southwestern Mississippi. Occasionally, during our many conversations, the Moore murder would come up. In 2012, I recorded Gardner's recollections about the FBI investigation into the attack on the Black deputies. Three years after his death, I listened to that recording again and this time my mind was not cluttered by other cases. I realized Gardner had left me a trail to follow.

After Gardner died, his widow, Karen, told me about another retired agent, Milton Graham, who also had worked on the case. While scores of agents were sent to Bogalusa during the 1960s, few of these men are still alive. Finding Graham, a former professional football player and mountain climber, was a godsend. In 2018, Graham explained he was one of the first agents on the ground in Washington Parish investigating the attack on the deputies. With Graham's account of the first two years of the investigation and Gardner's remembrances from 1967, I was presented a fascinating glimpse of Bogalusa and Washington Parish as well as details of the agents' frequent encounters with Klansmen, including Ernest Ray McElveen. Both agents had conversed with McElveen, the lead suspect and only man arrested for the attack.

Graham remembered many of the policemen and deputies of the era, as well as Sheriff Dorman Crowe, the man who hired the Black deputies. Gardner and Graham respected Crowe, and FBI documents indicate the sheriff was cooperative with the bureau and wanted nothing more than to put the men who attacked his deputies behind bars.

In 2014, the LSU Manship School of Mass Communications Student Cold Case Project began receiving hundreds of pages on another Klansman who was connected to the case through the Freedom of Information Act. In 1960, Robert "Shotgun" Fuller shot five of his Black employees, killing four, during a violent altercation. Although he was charged with murder, a grand jury refused to indict him. Because Fuller became one of the earliest leaders of the Original Knights of the Ku Klux Klan, which was organized in late 1960 in Shreveport-Bossier, his FBI file chronicles the rise of this Klan and the competing Klan groups that crisscrossed much of the state in the 1960s. Fuller was of interest in the FBI's investigation into the Oneal Moore murder because he had previously attempted to persuade Sheriff Crowe to fire Moore and Rogers. Also, in the Fuller file are FBI informant reports involving multiple Klan meetings held by the Washington Parish and Bogalusa Klan klaverns.

In 2017, I began work on a project for Reveal, an initiative of the Center for Investigative Reporting (CIR), based in Emeryville, California. CIR is the nation's oldest nonprofit investigative news organization. Dating back to 2008, CIR has been a dependable and generous supporter of my work, beginning during the leadership of Robert "Rosey" Rosenthal, who though now retired, remains a member of the CIR board of directors. I have also worked with CIR's Amanda Pike, director of TV and documentaries, and executive producer.

A few years ago, I visited with Barbara Hicks Collins in Bogalusa. Barbara's father was Robert Hicks, one of the most effective civil rights leaders during the era. Barbara was an eyewitness to the civil rights movement in Bogalusa, her home was a busy place where her father met and strategized with other Black leaders as well as heads of the Congress for Racial Equality and the Deacons for Defense and Justice.

In Barbara's youth, her family dodged bullets and saw activists bloodied by Klan assaults. Now she is busy developing a civil rights museum in the family home where she was reared. We drove to Varnado, Louisiana, in the fall of 2017 and Barbara introduced me to Maevella Moore, the widow of Oneal Moore. It was at this point that I asked Amanda Pike to determine whether CIR could obtain the complete Oneal Moore file through the Freedom of Information Act and take an additional step, if need be, to file suit to expedite the process. Obtaining FBI civil rights–era cold case murder and/or Klan files is a tedious and long ordeal that often takes years and, due to heavy redactions, is a frustrating endeavor.

Pike agreed to proceed, enlisting the assistance of CIR's in-house general counsel, Victoria Baranetsky, and CIR producer Rachel de Leon. In November 2017, de Leon made the initial Freedom of Information request, claiming that obtaining these documents was in the public interest. But days later the request was denied, with Department of Justice claiming it needed more information from CIR to understand "the urgency to inform" by "a person primarily engaged in disseminating information." To help our case, I asked Maevella Moore if she would sign a privacy waiver, which would help reduce redactions of many documents relating to the investigative file. She readily agreed. CIR then filed a lawsuit in U.S. District Court, Northern District of California—the case *The Center for Investigative Reporting vs. U.S. DOJ No. 1389729-000*—to expedite the release of the file. CIR was successful, and in June 2018 the first batch of documents arrived.

The Moore file includes almost 40,000 pages (many still heavily redacted and some essentially blank), and it will take possibly three more years for all the material to be processed and released. This includes 13,500 pages of FBI special agent interviews of witnesses, 4,600 pages of memoirs, handwritten notes, public source material, case summaries, transcripts from consensual monitoring and other administrative documents, as well as photographs. However, the bulk of the files from the 1960s—those filled with the reports of agents like Ted Gardner and Milton Graham, and the most crucial investigative years—were in my hands by the time my work on this book was drawing to a close.

I also have relied on two newspapers in Washington Parish, the *Bogalusa Daily News* and the *Franklinton Era-Leader,* located in the parish seat of Franklinton. The *Era-Leader*'s front pages contain colorful and informative stories about politics, particularly the election of Sheriff Dorman Crowe at the end of World War II and his reelection campaigns through 1968, when he was defeated for the first time. When he gave up the badge, Crowe had served five terms, still a record in the parish. But the newspaper coverage also provided great insight into the long-term efforts of the sheriff's political opponents to unseat him, the most vocal being members of the White Citizens Council and the Original Knights of the Ku Klux Klan. Two times the Klan pulled out all the stops in an attempt to beat the sheriff and during both elections the Klan failed.

In Bogalusa, the newspaper, led by publisher Lou Major, provided consistent coverage of the civil rights movement in the region and of the Klan. Major was a longtime victim of Klan intimidation attempts (and the target of cross burnings), but not once did he back down. These two publications, while neither perfect, are examples of the importance of the hometown newspaper, its coverage of everyday events, and the metamorphosis from a hot news story one day to a crucial record of historical events a half century later. The loss of newspapers in many communities across the country is monumental.

Certainly, no entity has been more supportive of my work over the years than the LSU Manship School of Mass Communications, including its deans, professors, and students. I am appreciative to the late Martin Johnson, the dean who hired me as an adjunct professor to work with students in investigating civil rights–era cold cases. I thank interim dean Josh Grimm for his support as well. I am indebted to former LSU professor and former head of the student cold case program, Jay Shelledy, for many things, including reading the rough draft of this manuscript. I am also grateful to Chris Drew, who followed Shelledy and now holds the Fred Jones Greer Jr. Endowed Chair, and is responsible for heading up the cold case work and the Statehouse Bureau, the Manship School's experiential journalism program focusing on racial and criminal justice.

Students who worked on Student Cold Case Team over the years include Matthew Albright, Natalie Anderson, Matt Barnidge, S. Rene Barrow, Alyssa Berry, Chelsea Brasted, Courtney Brewer, Gordon Brillon, Lynne Bunch, Ryan Buxton, Zachary Carline, Karli Carpenter, Brett Christensen, Matthew Clark, Jake Clapp, Ward Collin, Kaitlan Darby, Sydni Dunn, Tessalon Felician, Caroline Fenton, Andrea Gallo, Evan Garrity, Abigail Hendren, Joshua Jackson, Alaysia Johnson, David LaPlante, Sarah Lawson, Minjie Li, Katie Macdonald, Jace Mallory, Justin McAcy, Olivia McClure, Rachel Mipro, Lara Nicholson, Willborn Nobles III, Brianna Piche, Madeline Reineke, Sydney Reynolds, Patrick Richoux, Liz Ryan, Paromita Saha, Matthew Schaeffer, Morgan Searles, Brian Sibille, Jay Stanford, Robert Stewart, Kevin Thibodeaux, Jennifer Vance, Ben Wallace, Drew White, Amy Whitehead, Bailey Williams, Mary Lee Williams, Foster Willie, Xerxes Wilson, and Dena Winegeart.

I thank the Concordia Parish Library, including library director Amanda Taylor, and Hattie Neal from the Vidalia branch. The Concordia public library system is one of the best in the state and one of the most visionary. The staff at the Washington Parish Library in Bogalusa was generous in their assistance as well.

Thanks, too, to Heather Kaplan Card of the *Ouachita Citizen* and Lesley Hanna Capdepon of the *Concordia Sentinel.*

Robert "Bobby" Crowe, a former Washington Parish sheriff and son of Sheriff Dorman Crowe, provided me with much information about his late father and to him I am grateful.

I greatly appreciate Paul R. Dotson and the kind and professional staff of LSU Press for their support of this book from beginning to end.

Finally, I am grateful to Maevella Moore and her daughters—Tresslar, Regenia, Veronica, and Sheronda—for their time and for sharing memories. They have been kind and accommodating. It has been a joy to spend time with them.

NOTES

INTRODUCTION

1. Adam Fairclough, *Race & Democracy: The Civil Rights Struggle in Louisiana, 1915–1972,* (Athens: University of Georgia Press, 2008).

2. Bob Lawrence, *Bogalusa Memories: A Conversation with Bob Lawrence* (Lucien, FL: Mill City, 2018) 189.

CHAPTER ONE

1. Maevella Moore, interview by author, November 11, 2017.

2. Duncan Nichols, interview by FBI special agents Curtis L. Perryman and W. J. Danielson Jr., June 17, 1965, FBI Civil Unrest, Oneal Moore file, 44-NO-2594.

3. David Creed Rogers, interview by FBI special agents Jack Evans Mehl and Kevin McCarthy, June 12, 1965, FBI Civil Unrest, Oneal Moore file, 44-NO-2594.

4. Relative of David Creed Rogers (name redacted), interview by FBI special agents Curtis L. Perryman and W. J. Danielson Jr., June 17, 1965, FBI Civil Unrest, Oneal Moore file, 44-NO-2594.

5. David Creed Rogers, interview by FBI (agent name redacted), June 12, 1965.

6. David Creed Rogers, interview by Mehl and McCarthy, June 17, 1965.

7. Ibid., June 5, 9, 1965.

8. Ibid.

9. Ibid.

10. Olin Q. Harmon, interview by FBI special agent Kenyon D. Bowles Jr., June 14, 1965, FBI Civil Unrest, Oneal Moore file, 44-NO-2594.

11. David Creed Rogers, interview by Mehl and McCarthy, June 5, 9, 1965.

12. Statement of Deputy Doyle Holliday, June 11, 1965, FBI Civil Unrest, Oneal Moore file, 44-NO-2594.

13. Daniel R. "Scraps" Fornea, interview by FBI special agent Frank Sass Jr. and (two agents names redacted), June 4, 6, 14, 1965, FBI Civil Unrest, Oneal Moore file, 44-NO-2594.

14. John Fahey, "Witness Reported to Deputy Slaying: Saw Truck, Heard Shots from Yard, He Says," *New Orleans Times-Picayune,* June 5, 1965, A1.

15. Daniel R. "Scraps" Fornea, interview by Sass.

16. Jessie Bell Thigpen, interview by FBI special agent L. M. Shearer Jr., June 13, August 6, 23, FBI Civil Unrest, Oneal Moore file, 44-NO-2594.

17. Daniel R. "Scraps" Fornea, interview by FBI special agent Frank Sass Jr., Oneal Moore file, 44-NO-2594.

18. Statement of Doyle Holliday, June 11.

19. Robert J. "Bobby" Crowe, interview by author, March 30, 2019.

20. Statement of Doyle Holliday, June 11.

21. "Murder of Negro Deputy, Varnado, La.," Mississippi Highway Safety Patrol, June 3, 1965, FBI Civil Unrest, Oneal Moore file, 44-NO-2594.

22. Ibid.

23. Ibid.

24. Ibid.

25. Ibid.

26. Ibid.

27. Statement of Doyle Holliday, June 11, 1965.

28. "Murder of Negro Deputy, Varnado, La."

29. Ibid.

30. Ibid.

31. Memo from US Attorney General to FBI Director, June 3, 1965, FBI Civil Unrest, Oneal Moore file, 44-NO-2594.

32. FBI Director, urgent memo to New Orleans, June 9, 1965.

33. Airtel from New Orleans Special Agent-in-Charge to FBI Director, August 10, 1965, Oneal Moore file, 44-NO-2594.

34. Milton Graham, interview by author, February 8, 2018.

35. Milton Graham, interview by John P. DeCourcy, Society of Former Agents of the FBI, July 6, 2006, FBI Oral History Project.

36. US v. Original Knights of the Ku Klux Klan, US District Court for the Eastern District of Louisiana, December 1, 1965.

37. Memo from FBI Jackson to FBI Director and New Orleans FBI, June 3, 1965, FBI Civil Unrest, Oneal Moore file, 44-NO-2594.

38. US v. Original Knights of the Ku Klux Klan, December 1, 1965.

39. Memo from FBI Jackson to FBI Director and New Orleans FBI, June 3, 1965.

40. Urgent Message from FBI New Orleans to FBI Director, June 3, 1965, Oneal Moore file, 44-NO-2594.

41. Urgent Message from FBI New Orleans to FBI Director, June 5, 1965, Oneal Moore file, 44-NO-2594.

42. Ibid.

43. Washington Capital News Service, "Bogalusa," June 3, 1965, Oneal Moore file, 44-NO-2594.

44. "McKeithen View Given in Killing: Misguided, Saw Peace Coming, Belief," *New Orleans Times-Picayune,* June 4, 1965, A1.

45. Ibid.

46. John Fahey and Joseph A. Lucia, "Tuesday Hearing Slated for Slay Case Suspect," *New Orleans Times-Picayune,* June 10, 1965, A8.

47. Funeral Program for Oneal Moore, June 9, 1965, Oneal Moore file, 44-NO-2594.

48. Maevella Moore, interview by author.

49. Funeral Program for Oneal Moore.

50. John Fahey, “Witness Reported to Deputy Slaying: Saw Truck, Heard Shots from Yard, He Says,” *New Orleans Times-Picayune,* June 8, 1965, A1.

51. Ibid.

52. Memo from R. I. Shroder to Mr. Rosen, June 8, 1965, Oneal Moore file, 44-NO-2594.

53. Dr. George E. Ellis, “To Whom It May Concern,” New Orleans, June 8, 1965, Oneal Moore file, 44-NO-2594.

CHAPTER TWO

1. “Bogalusa Man Is Beaten by 3 Black-Hooded Men,” *Bogalusa Daily News,* April 1965, A1.

2. Klansman (name redacted), interview by FBI special agent Ernest C. Wall Jr., July 6, 1965, FBI Civil Unrest, Oneal Moore file, 44-NO-2594.

3. “Bogalusa Man Is Beaten by 3 Black-Hooded Men.”

4. Teletype from FBI New Orleans to FBI Director, June 9, 1965, FBI Civil Unrest, Oneal Moore file, 44-NO-2594.

5. Stanley Carl Bickham, interview by FBI special agent Louis F. Caputo, June 28, 1965, FBI Civil Unrest, Oneal Moore file, 44-NO-2594.

6. Rilanders L. Little, interview by FBI special agent Louis F. Caputo, June 8, 1965, FBI Civil Unrest, Oneal Moore file, 44-NO-2594.

7. FBI St. Louis to FBI Director, June 7, 1965, FBI Civil Unrest, Oneal Moore file, 44-NO-2594.

8. Neighbor of Ray McElveen (name redacted), interview by FBI special agent Louis F. Caputo, June 22, 1965, FBI Civil Unrest, Oneal Moore file, 44-NO-2594.

9. Report of FBI special agent John T. Reynolds, July 5, 1965, FBI Civil Unrest, Oneal Moore file, 44-NO-2594.

10. Tylertown doctor (name redacted), interview by FBI, June 22, 1965, FBI Civil Unrest, Oneal Moore file, 44-NO-2594.

11. Robert Deck, interview by FBI, June 18, 1965, FBI Civil Unrest, Oneal Moore file, 44-NO-2594.

12. Louisiana Commissioner of Insurance, June 17, 1965, FBI Civil Unrest, Oneal Moore file, 44-NO-2594.

13. Charlie J. Talbert, interview by FBI, June 17, 1965, FBI Civil Unrest, Oneal Moore file, 44-NO-2594.

14. Ibid.

15. Joseph Edward Gerniglia, interview by FBI special agent Ernest Wall, August 7, 1965, FBI Civil Unrest, Oneal Moore file, 44-NO-2594.

16. Report of FBI special agent John T. Reynolds, July 5, 1965, FBI Civil Unrest, Oneal Moore file, 44-NO-2594.

17. “Klansmen Threaten Daily News Publisher: Reporter is Beaten,” *Bogalusa Daily News,* April 20, 1964, A1.

18. Urgent teletype from FBI New Orleans to FBI Director, July 9, 1965, FBI Civil Unrest, Oneal Moore file, 44-NO-2594.

19. Testimony of Ralph Blumberg, House Un-American Activities Committee, January 5, 1966, 2415–38, National Archives and Records Administration (NARA).

20. Ibid.

21. Ibid.

22. Teletype from FBI New Orleans to FBI Director, June 6, 1965, FBI Civil Unrest, Oneal Moore file, 44-NO-2594.

23. John Walters, interview by FBI, June 9, 1965, FBI Civil Unrest, Oneal Moore file, 44-NO-2594.

24. Statement of Deputy Doyle Holliday, June 11, 1965, FBI Civil Unrest, Oneal Moore file, 44-NO-2594.

25. Teletype from FBI New Orleans to FBI Director, June 18, 1965, FBI Civil Unrest, Oneal Moore file, 44-NO-2594.

26. Statement of Friend (name redacted) of Grant McElveen, FBI Cincinnati, June 18, 1965, FBI Civil Unrest, Oneal Moore file, 44-NO-2594.

27. Otis Slocum, interview by FBI, June 18, 1965, FBI Civil Unrest, Oneal Moore file, 44-NO-2594.

28. S. D. Crain, interview by FBI, June 19, 1965, FBI Civil Unrest, Oneal Moore file, 44-NO-2594.

29. Teletype from FBI New Orleans to FBI Director, June 28, 1965, FBI Civil Unrest, Oneal Moore file, 44-NO-2594.

30. Lindsey-Feiber Chevrolet Company employee, interview by FBI special agent Frank Sass Jr., July 10, 1965, FBI Civil Unrest, Oneal Moore file, 44-NO-2594.

31. Report of FBI special agent John T. Reynolds, July 5, 1965, FBI Civil Unrest, Oneal Moore file, 44-NO-2594.

32. Bobby Rester, interview by FBI special agent Frank Sass Jr., July 6, 1965, FBI Civil Unrest, Oneal Moore file, 44-NO-2594.

33. Sergeant Joe Passaro, interview by FBI, June 6, 1965, FBI Civil Unrest, Oneal Moore file, 44-NO-2594.

34. Oneal Autopsy Report by Dr. A. B. Fredrichs, June 4, 1965, FBI Civil Unrest, Oneal Moore file, 44-NO-2594.

35. FBI Laboratory Examinations, June 21, 1965, FBI Civil Unrest, Oneal Moore file, 44-NO-2594.

36. Benjamin Miller, interview by FBI special agent Merriman D. Diven, June 25, 1965, FBI Civil Unrest, Oneal Moore file, 44-NO-2594.

37. FBI Laboratory Examinations, June 21, 1965.

38. Teletype from New Orleans FBI to FBI Director, June 11, 1965, FBI Civil Unrest, June 11, 1965, FBI Civil Unrest, Oneal Moore file, 44-NO-2594.

39. Ibid.

40. Ibid.

41. Ibid.

42. "Suspect in Deputy Sheriff Slaying Released on Bond," *New Orleans Times-Picayune,* June 12, 1965, A1.

43. Teletype from FBI New Orleans to FBI Director, June 13, 1965, FBI Civil Unrest, Oneal Moore file, 44-NO-2594.

44. Saxon Farmer, interview by FBI, June 14, 1965, FBI Civil Unrest, Oneal Moore file, 44-NO-2594.

45. Teletype from FBI New Orleans to FBI Director, June 6, 1965, FBI Civil Unrest, Oneal Moore file, 44-NO-2594.

46. Teletype from FBI New Orleans to FBI Director, June 16, 1965, FBI Civil Unrest, Oneal Moore file, 44-NO-2594.

47. Testimony of Saxon Farmer, House Un-American Activities Committee, January 5, 1966, 2464, NARA.

CHAPTER THREE

1. Robert J. "Bobby" Crowe, interviews by author, March 30, June 21, 2019.

2. Ibid.

3. "Seven Candidates in Primary," *Franklinton Era-Leader,* January 22, 1948, A1.

4. Robert J. "Bobby" Crowe, interview by author, March 30, 2019.

5. "Blackjacks Are Reissued to Police: Wild Night on 4th St. Brings Orders from Police Head," *Bogalusa Daily News,* December 15, 1947, A1.

6. "Negroes Run White Man Off Own Land with Guns," *Bogalusa Daily News,* December 30, 1947, A1.

7. Dorman Crowe advertisement, *Franklinton Era-Leader,* January 22, 1948.

8. "Rayburn, Crowe, Bateman Win in Parish 2nd Race," *Bogalusa Daily News,* January 22, 1948, A1.

9. Dorman Crowe advertisement, *Bogalusa Daily News,* February 26, 1948.

10. "Sheriff Crowe Warns Would Be Slot Machine Operators," *Bogalusa Daily News,* March 27, 1948, A1.

11. Robert J. "Bobby" Crowe, interview by author, March 30, 2019.

12. Dorman Crowe advertisement, *Bogalusa Daily News,* January 2, 1952.

13. "Primary Election Next Tuesday: Much Interest Being Centered on Primary Election as Time Nears," *Franklinton-Era Leader,* January 12, 1952, A1.

14. "Crowe and Bateman Win Easy Victories," *Bogalusa Daily News,* January 16, 1952, A1.

15. "Bateman Elected; Crowe in Run-off," *Franklinton Era-Leader,* January 19, 1956, A1.

16. Charles E. Tullos advertisement, *Franklinton Era-Leader,* February 2, 1956, A4.

17. Charles E. Tullos advertisement, *Franklinton Era-Leader,* February 16, 1956, A9.

18. Ibid.

19. "Dorman Crowe Elected Sheriff for Third Term," *Bogalusa Daily News,* February 23, 1956, A1.

20. "Registrar Hospitalized after Bogalusa Affair," *Bogalusa Daily News,* May 25, 1950, A1.

21. "Negroes Bring Registrar of Voters to Court; Charge Prejudice Exist in Voter Registration," *Franklinton Era-Leader,* June 8, 1950, A1. Members of the group included Joe Dean, Pauline Brumfield, William Baily Jr., Earl Sanders, Nina Dean, Rev. Abraham Williamson, Charles Otis, Albert Barnes, and H. T. Torence.

22. "Federal Judge Orders Qualified Parish Negroes Registered to Vote," *Franklinton Era-Leader,* July 27, 1950, A1.

23. "Two Negroes Selected to Serve on Grand Jury," *Franklinton Era-Leader,* June 8, 1950. The two men were identified as Murray Tate and Hollis Huft.

24. "Kennon Says State Will Continue Segregation in La.," *Franklinton Era-Leader,* May 27, 1954, A1.

25. "Negroes Present Petition to the School Bd., Asking Hearing on Attending School," *Franklinton Era-Leader,* October 21, 1954, A1.

26. "Don't Be Brainwashed: We Don't Have to Integrate Our Schools!," pamphlet produced by the State Sovereignty Commission and the Joint Legislative Committee on Segregation, 1956.

27. Willie Rainach segregation advertisements, *Franklinton Era-Leader,* November 1, 1956.

28. "Supreme Court Orders Little Rock Integration: Arkansas School Board Directed to Admit Negro Students Monday," *Bogalusa Daily News,* September 12, 1958, A1.

29. "No Leads in Kidnapping of Poplarville Prisoner: Accused Negro Rapist Seized by Hooded Men," *Bogalusa Daily News,* April 26, 1959, A1.

30. Milton Graham, interview by John P. DeCourcy, Society of Former Agents of the FBI, July 6, 2006, FBI Oral History Project.

31. Teletype from FBI Jackson to FBI New Orleans and FBI Director, June 3, 1965, FBI Civil Unrest, Oneal Moore file, 44-NO-2594.

32. Drew Pearson, "Long's Race Betting Is Big Problem," *Washington Post,* July 6, 1959.

33. Interviewee name withheld, interview by FBI, June 28, 1965, FBI Civil Unrest, Oneal Moore file, 44-NO-2594.

34. "More Registered Voters Challenged," and "17 More Voters Challenged," *Bogalusa Daily News,* March 12, 1959, A1.

35. United States of America, Plaintiff, v. Diaz D. McElveen, E. Ray McElveen, Saxon Farmer and Eugene Farmer, Individually and as Members of the Citizens Council of Washington Parish, Louisiana, Curtis M. Thomas, Registrar of Voters of Washington Parish, Louisiana, and the Citizens Council of Washington, Parish, Louisiana, Defendants, US District Court of the Eastern District of Louisiana, January 11, 1960.

36. "Elmer Smith for Crowe in Runoff," *Bogalusa Daily News,* January 23, 1956, A1.

37. Robert J. "Bobby" Crowe, interview by author, March 30, 2019.

38. Elmer Smith advertisements, *Franklinton Era-Leader,* November 19, 1959.

39. "First Primary Election Returns Made Public," *Franklinton Era-Leader,* December 10, 1959, A1.

40. Ibid.

41. "To the Voters of Washington Parish, Crowe for Sheriff," Dorman Crowe advertisement, *Franklinton Era-Leader,* December 17, 1959, A6.

42. "Shame-Shame, Mr. Dorman Crowe," Elmer Smith advisement, *Franklinton Era-Leader,* December 17, 1959, A6.

43. "An Open Letter to the Voting Parents of Washington Parish," Dorman Crowe advertisement signed by Mrs. Pickney Crowe, *Franklinton Era-Leader,* January 7, 1960, A7.

44. "1,377 Negroes Are Restored to Voting Rolls by Registrar," *Franklinton Era-Leader,* January 14, 1960, A1.

45. "US Supreme Court Orders Negroes Reinstated to Registrar of Voters Rolls," *Franklinton Era-Leader,* March 3, 1960, A1.

46. "Smith Petition to Be Heard by Court Saturday Morning," *Franklinton Era-Leader,* January 21, 1960, A1.

47. Smith v. Washington Parish Democratic Committee, Supreme Court of Louisiana, February 15, 1960.

CHAPTER FOUR

1. Varnado, Louisiana, resident (name redacted), interview by FBI, June 17, 1965, FBI Civil Unrest, Oneal Moore file, 44-NO-2594.

2. Elmer Smith, interview by FBI special agent Frank Sass Jr., June 28, 1965, FBI Civil Unrest, Oneal Moore file, 44-NO-2594.

3. Numan V. Bartley, *The Rise of Massive Resistance: Race and Politics in the South during the 1950's* (Baton Rouge: Louisiana State University Press, 1997), 83.

4. Teletype from FBI New Orleans to FBI Director, August 27, 1965, FBI Civil Unrest, Oneal Moore file, 44-NO-2594.

5. "Negro Killed by Deputy: 15 Arrested," *Bogalusa Daily News,* December 1, 1960, A1.

6. "Franklinton Economy Is Based on Dairying," *Bogalusa Daily News,* May 24, 1963, A1.

7. "Racial Trouble Remains Nation's First Problem," *Bogalusa Daily News,* June 2, 1963, A1.

8. "Governor Denies Negroes to Enter," *Bogalusa Daily News,* June 11, 1963, A1.

9. William Branham Historical Research, william-branham.org.

10. Jim Leslie, "Klan Leader Picked Up, Warned by Police Here," *Shreveport Times,* April 7, 1961, A1.

11. Stanley Nelson, "FBI's Lancaster Sought 'Dying Declaration' from Frank Morris," *Concordia Sentinel,* May 20, 2009, A1.

12. FBI special agent Paul Lancaster, "Report Regarding Objectives, Activities, Observations and List of Members of OKKKK at West Monroe, Alexandria and State Meeting of OKKKK at Alexandria, La., 1964," May 31, 1964, FBI Civil Unrest, Robert Fuller file, 157-NO-1300, NARA.

13. Thomas Simon Fontenot, interview by FBI special agents Eugene E. Bjorn and W. J. Danielson Jr., January 11, 1965, FBI Civil Unrest, Robert Fuller file, 157-NO-1300, NARA.

14. Ibid.

15. Ibid.

16. Ibid.

17. Ibid.

18. Ibid.

19. Ibid.

20. FBI special agent Steve Callender, Report on Zennie Robert "Shotgun" Fuller, January 14, 1964, FBI Civil Unrest, Robert Fuller file, 157-NO-1300, NARA.

21. Charlottie Dent, unpublished recollections provided to author.

22. Ibid.

23. Callender, Report on Zennie Robert "Shotgun" Fuller.

24. Dent, unpublished recollections provided to author.

25. Ibid.

26. Callender, Report on Zennie Robert "Shotgun" Fuller.

27. "3 Slain, 2 Wounded By La. Employer," *New Orleans States-Item,* July 13, 1960; "5 Armed Negro Men Shot by Employer, *Monroe News-Star,* July 13, 1960; FBI Civil Unrest, Robert Fuller file, 157-NO-1300, NARA.

28. Ibid.

29. Ibid.

30. "Hint Injustices Behind Mass Slaying of 3 Men," *Louisiana Weekly,* July 23, 1960, FBI Civil Unrest, Robert Fuller file, 157-NO-1300, NARA.

31. Callender, Report on Zennie Robert "Shotgun" Fuller.

32. "3 Slain, 2 Wounded."

33. Notice to Close File, US Department of Justice, April 22, 2010.

34. "3 Slain, 2 Wounded."

35. Dent, unpublished recollections provided to author.

36. "Ku Klux Klan Removes Secrecy Cloak in Book," *Ouachita Citizen,* March 1, 1973, A3.

37. "Elmer Smith Announces," *Franklinton Era-Leader,* September 9, 1963, A1.

38. "Crowe Makes Announcement of Re-Election," *Bogalusa Daily News,* September 26, 1963, A1.

39. Dorman Crowe advertisement, *Franklinton Era-Leader,* November 14, 1963.

40. Ibid.

41. "Crowe is Re-Elected in Close Win over Smith," *Bogalusa Daily News,* January 12, 1964, A1.

42. "Washington Parish Has One of Closest Contested Elections in Parish's History," *Franklinton Era-Leader,* December 17, 1963, A1.

43. Ibid.

44. FBI special agent Steve Callender, Report on Zennie Robert "Shotgun" Fuller, February 2, 1964, FBI Civil Unrest, Robert Fuller file, 157-NO-1300, NARA.

45. "Washington Parish Has One of Closest Elections."

46. "Crowe is Re-elected."

47. Patrick Richoux, "FBI Docs Reveal Rumors That Gov. McKeithen Paid KKK to Avoid Violence," *Concordia Sentinel* website, www.hannapub.com/concordiasentinel, April 28, 2016.

48. FBI special agent John Hanlin to special agent in charge, New Orleans, March 27, 1964, FBI Civil Unrest, Oneal Moore file, 44-NO-2594.

49. FBI special agent Earl Cox, "Special Meeting of OKKKK Officers, December 12, 1963, Monroe, La.," December 16, 1963, FBI Civil Unrest, Oneal Moore file, 44-NO-2594.

50. Hearing of the Joint Legislative Committee on Un-American Activities, June 16, 1965.

51. United States v. Original Knights of the Ku Klux Klan, US District Court for Eastern District of Louisiana, December 1, 1965.

CHAPTER FIVE

1. James Austin Kennedy, interview by FBI special agent Ernest Wall Jr., July 6, 1965, FBI Civil Unrest, Oneal Moore file, 44-No-2594.

2. "Witness Tells Details of Shooting in Angie: Charges Pending," *Bogalusa Daily News,* January 21, 1964, A1.

3. Ibid.

4. "Murder Charge Is Filed against Kennedy," *Bogalusa Daily News,* January 22, 1964, A1.

5. James Austin Kennedy, interview by Wall.

6. John Hugh Gipson, testimony before the House Un-American Activities Committee, US Government Printing Office, Washington DC, January 11, 1966, 2609–26, NARA.

7. Ibid.

8. Ibid.

9. Ibid.

10. FBI New Orleans to FBI Director, November 4, 1965, FBI Civil Unrest, Robert Fuller file, 157-NO-1300, NARA.

11. Stanley Nelson, *Devils Walking: Klan Murders along the Mississippi in the 1960s* (Baton Rouge: Louisiana State University Press, 2016), 135–41.

12. Henry A. Kennedy, interview by FBI special agent Merriman D. Diven, June 30, 1965, FBI Civil Unrest, Oneal Moore file, 44-No-2594.

13. Milton Graham, interview by John P. DeCourcy, Society of Former Agents of the FBI, July 6, 2006, FBI Oral History Project.

14. Creed Rogers advertisement, *Bogalusa Daily News*, 1994, copy provided to author by Robert J. "Bobby" Crowe.

15. Ibid.

16. Informant reports, FBI special agent Vincent B. Coyle, September 28, 1965, and FBI special agents James A. Theisen and Tony J. Seabaugh, September 9, 1965, FBI Civil Unrest, Robert Fuller file, 157-NO-1300, NARA.

17. Sheriff Dorman Crowe, interview by FBI special agent Frank Sass Jr., August 8, 1965, FBI Civil Unrest, Robert Fuller file, 157-NO-1300, NARA.

18. Memo on Howard Lee, FBI special agent Roy H. McDaniel, November 12, 1964, FBI Civil Unrest, White Knights file, 157-JN-63.

19. James "Buster" Ellis, testimony before the House Un-American Activities Committee, US Government Printing Office, Washington DC, January 6, 1966, 2525–29, NARA, Washington, DC.

20. Informant report, FBI special agent Steven Callender to special agent in charge, New Orleans, August 8, 1964, FBI Civil Unrest, Robert Fuller file, 157-NO-1300, NARA.

21. Sheriff Dorman Crowe, interview by FBI special agent Frank Sass Jr.

22. Ibid.

23. James "Buster" Ellis, interview by FBI special agents Donald C. Steinmeyer and Stephen Callender, September 29, 1965, FBI Civil Unrest, Robert Fuller file, 157-NO-1300, NARA.

24. Ibid.

25. OKKKK Meeting in Bogalusa, special agent in charge, News Orleans to FBI Director, October 31, 1964, FBI Civil Unrest, Robert Fuller file, 157-NO-1300, NARA.

26. "Washington Parish Has One of Closet Elections in Parish's History," *Franklinton Era-Leader,* December 17, 1965, A1.

27. Washington Parish School Board member (name redacted), interview by FBI special agent Frank Sass Jr., August 14, 1965, FBI Civil Unrest, Oneal Moore file, 44-No-2594.

28. Urgent teletype from special agent in charge, New Orleans to FBI Director, July 5, 1965, FBI Civil Unrest, Oneal Moore file, 44-No-2594.

29. Washington Parish School Board member (name redacted), interview by FBI special agent Frank Sass Jr.

30. Ed Anderson, "Longtime State Sen. B. B. 'Sixty' Rayburn dead at 91," NOLA.com, March 5, 2008.

31. Senator B. B. "Sixty" Rayburn, interview by FBI special agent Donald C. Steinmeyer, November 29, 1965, FBI Civil Unrest, Oneal Moore file, 44-No-2594.

32. Urgent teletype from FBI New Orleans to FBI Director, June 19, 1965, FBI Civil Unrest, Oneal Moore file, 44-No-2594.

33. Russell Magee, interview by FBI special agent Steve Callender, October 8, 1965, FBI Civil Unrest, Robert Fuller file, 157-NO-1300, NARA.

34. Teletype from FBI New Orleans to FBI Director, June 18, 1965, FBI Civil Unrest, Robert Fuller file, 157-NO-1300, NARA.

35. Teletype from FBI New Orleans to FBI Director, September 27, 1965, FBI Civil Unrest, Robert Fuller file, 157-NO-1300, NARA.

36. James "Buster" Ellis, interview by FBI special agents Donald C. Steinmeyer and Steve Callender.

CHAPTER SIX

1. Ted Gardner, interview by author, April 13, 2012. Gardner was twenty-seven when he arrived in Louisiana. He had gotten an education in Concordia Parish, a place agents called a "maggot-infested mess." The FBI had received multiple reports that more than a dozen Black men had either been killed or were missing in the parish. Gardner and fellow agent John Pfeifer had arrived in Concordia with orders to put the Klan out of business and to investigate the Concordia Parish Sheriff's Office. That investigation resulted in the federal conviction of Sheriff Noah Cross for his role in the operation of a brothel. Deputy Frank DeLaughter was also implicated in that case and was convicted in another federal case for police brutality.

2. Ibid.

3. Murl A. "Bill" Rogers, Case records from Washington Parish Sheriff's Office, Washington Parish District Attorney's, Louisiana State Penitentiary, 1964–65, FBI Civil Unrest, Oneal Moore file, 44-NO-2594.

4. Ibid.

5. Ibid.

6. Murl A. "Bill" Rogers, interview by FBI special agents Alexander Jamieson and Milton Graham, November 24, 1965, FBI Civil Unrest, Oneal Moore file, 44-NO-2594.

7. Russell Magee, interview by FBI special agent Frank Sass Jr., June 28, 1965, FBI Civil Unrest, Oneal Moore file, 44-NO-2594.

8. Murl A. "Bill" Rogers, interview by Jamieson and Graham.

9. Ibid.

10. Teletype from FBI New Orleans to FBI Director, June 13, 1965, FBI Civil Unrest, Oneal Moore file, 44-NO-2594.

11. Levert Strahan, interview by FBI special agent Frank Sass Jr., June 28, 1965, FBI Civil Unrest, Oneal Moore file, 44-NO-2594.

12. Levert Strahan, interview by Sass, June 24, 1965.

13. Sheriff Dorman Crowe, interview by FBI special agent Frank Sass Jr., June 23, 1965, FBI Civil Unrest, Oneal Moore file, 44-NO-2594.

14. Original Knights of the Ku Klux Klan Informant Report, October 31, 1965, FBI Civil Unrest, Robert Fuller file, 157-NO-1300.

15. Memo from FBI special agent Stephen Callender to Inspector J. A. Sullivan, September 17, 1965, Robert Fuller file, 157-NO-1300.

16. Original Knights of the Ku Klux Klan Informant Report.

17. Bogalusa OKKKK Meeting on November 9, 1965, FBI special agent Steve Callender, November 11, 1965, Robert Fuller file, 157-NO-1300.

18. Baton Rouge State Meeting of Four OKKKK Factions on March 12, 1965, FBI special agent William Dent, March 15, 1965, FBI Civil Unrest, Robert Fuller file, 157-NO-1300; Meeting of Swartz Unit of UKA & Citizen Council Rally in Monroe, La., FBI special agent John McCurnin II, September 10, 1965, FBI Civil Unrest, Robert Fuller file, 157-NO-1300.

19. "White Knights of the Ku Klux Klan Bogalusa July 1966," FBI special agent Steve Callender, July 14, 1966, FBI Civil Unrest, White Knights file, 157-NO-1962.

20. "Deacons for Defense and Justice," special agent in charge, New Orleans to FBI Director, February 26, 1965, FBI Civil Unrest, Deacons for Defense file, 157-NO-2466.

21. "Mayor Announces Appeal for Civic Responsibility," *Bogalusa Daily News,* March 26, 1965, A1.

22. "Committee Calls for Composure," *Bogalusa Daily News,* March 30, 1965.

23. Robert "Buck" Lewis Jr., interview by author, August 6, 2014.

24. Ibid.

25. "Former Mayor Jesse Cutrer Junior, Who Gained National Attention," July 20, 1987, United Press International website archives, www.upi.com.

26. "Deacons for Defense and Justice," special agent in charge, New Orleans to FBI Director, February 26, 1965, FBI Civil Unrest, Deacons for Defense file, 157-NO-2466.

27. Ibid.

28. Ibid.

29. Ibid.

30. Ibid.

31. Ibid.

32. "Thousands in Rally Here," *Bogalusa Daily News,* May 9, 1965, A1.

33. "McKeithen Expresses Support for Cutrer," *Bogalusa Daily News,* May 28, 1965, A1.

34. "Responsibility of Peace Cited by Gov. McKeithen," *Bogalusa Daily News,* April 16, 1965, A1.

35. "Talks Opened on Racial Issues," *Bogalusa Daily News,* May 17, 1965, A1.

36. "Thousands in Rally Here," A1.

37. "New Rights Policy Announced by Mayor Here," *Bogalusa Daily News,* May 24, 1965, A1.

38. "Number of Pickets to Be Increased," *Bogalusa Daily News,* May 27, 1965, A1.

39. "McKeithen Expresses Support for Cutrer," A1.

40. "New Rights Policy Announced by Mayor Here."

41. "Violence Erupts on Columbia Street Again," *Bogalusa Daily News,* A1.

CHAPTER SEVEN

1. Jack E. Davis, *Race against Time: Culture and Separation in Natchez since 1930,* (Baton Rouge: Louisiana State University Press, 2001) 9.

2. Fairclough, *Race & Democracy,* 345.

3. Ibid.

4. Joy J. Jackson, "The Piney Woods—Tangipahoa, St. Helena, and Washington Parishes," Folklife in the Florida Parishes: Louisiana's Living Traditions, Louisiana Folk Life Program, Louisiana Division of the Arts and the Center for Southeast Louisiana Studies at Southeastern Louisiana University, http://www.louisianafolklife.org/LT/Virtual_Books/Fla_Parishes/book_florida_piney.html, 1988.

5. Fairclough, *Race & Democracy,* 346.

6. Ibid., 347, 354.

7. Barbara Hicks, email to author, February 2020.

8. Elmer Smith, interview by FBI special agent Frank Sass Jr., June 30, 1965, FBI Civil Unrest, Oneal Moore file, 44-NO-2594.

9. Ibid.

10. Ibid.

11. Ibid.

12. US v. Original Knights of the Ku Klux Klan, US District Court for the Eastern District of Louisiana, December 1, 1965.

13. Edward Davis Burkett, interview by FBI special agent Furman G. Boggan, June 16, 1965, Oneal Moore file, 44-NO-2594.

14. Ibid.

15. FBI New Orleans to FBI Director, June 6, 1965, FBI Civil Unrest, Oneal Moore file, 44-NO-2594.

16. FBI New Orleans to FBI Director, June 9, 1965, FBI Civil Unrest, Oneal Moore file, 44-NO-2594.

17. Rayford Lamar Dunaway, interview by FBI director Michael Baron, June 22, 1965, FBI Civil Unrest, Oneal Moore file, 44-NO-2594.

18. Edward Paul Dubuisson, interview by FBI special agents Frank Sass Jr. and Joseph Peggs, June 13, 1965, FBI Civil Unrest, Oneal Moore file, 44-NO-2594.

19. FBI New Orleans to FBI Director, June 5, 1965, FBI Civil Unrest, Oneal Moore file, 44-NO-2594.

20. Bogalusa Acting Captain Wilson Richardson, June 7, 1965, FBI Civil Unrest, Oneal Moore file, 44-NO-2594.

21. FBI Special Agent John T. Reynolds Informant Report, June 25, 1965, FBI Civil Unrest, Oneal Moore file, 44-NO-2594.

22. FBI New Orleans to FBI Director, June 2, 1965, FBI Civil Unrest, Oneal Moore file, 44-NO-2594.

23. Mervin Taylor, interview by FBI special agent Donald C. Steinmeyer, November 6, 1965, FBI Civil Unrest, Oneal Moore file, 44-NO-2594.

24. Jessie Bell Thigpen, interview by FBI special agent L. M. Shearer Jr., June 15, 1965, FBI Civil Unrest, Oneal Moore file, 44-NO-2594.

25. Mrs. Cecil Rester, interview by FBI Inspector Joe Sullivan, August 31, 1965, FBI Civil Unrest, Oneal Moore file, 44-NO-2594.

26. James "Jimmy" Lang, interview by FBI special agent L. M. Shearer Jr., June 24, 1965;

interview by FBI special agents Joseph G. Engelhardt and James L. Theisen, September 28, 1965, FBI Civil Unrest, Oneal Moore file, 44-NO-2594.

27. Ibid.

28. Milton Graham, interview by John P. DeCourcy, Society of Former Agents of the FBI, July 6, 2006, FBI Oral History Project.

29. Glenn Reid, interviews by FBI special agents Richard Knock, James A. McBride, Daniel D. Dreiling, Donald P. McDermott, Merriman D. Diven, and Brooke Roberts, June 6, 23, July 1, 6, 1965, FBI Civil Unrest, Oneal Moore file, 44-NO-2594.

30. Ibid.

31. Mervin Taylor, interview by FBI special agent Donald C. Steinmeyer.

32. Tommy Smotherman, interview by FBI special agents Joseph G. Peggs and Timothy M. Casey Jr., June 23, 1965, FBI Civil Unrest, Oneal Moore file, 44-NO-2594.

33. Daniel "Scraps" Fornea, interviews by FBI special agents Frank Sass Jr., June 14, 1965, and James L. Theisen, October 13, 1965, FBI Civil Unrest, Oneal Moore file, 44-NO-2594.

34. Alvin "Snow" Walker, interview by FBI special agent Merriman Diven, August 11, 1965, FBI Civil Unrest, Oneal Moore file, 44-NO-2594.

35. Name redacted, interview by FBI special agent Merriman Diven, June 21, 1965, FBI Civil Unrest, Oneal Moore file, 44-NO-2594.

36. FBI New Orleans to FBI Director, June 9, June 13, 1965, FBI Civil Unrest, Oneal Moore file, 44-NO-2594.

37. Ibid.

38. John T. Reynolds Informant Report, June 25, 1965, FBI Civil Unrest, Oneal Moore file, 44-NO-2594.

39. Daniel "Scraps" Fornea, interview by FBI, June 26, 1965, FBI Civil Unrest, Oneal Moore file, 44-NO-2594.

40. FBI New Orleans to FBI Director, October 2, 1965, FBI Civil Unrest, Oneal Moore file, 44-NO-2594.

41. Ibid.

42. Robert "Bobby" Lang, interview by FBI special agent Merriman Diven, October 1, 1965, Oneal Moore file, 44-NO-2594.

CHAPTER EIGHT

1. FBI Case Inspector Joe Sullivan to FBI Director, July 2, 1965, FBI Civil Unrest, Oneal Moore file, 44-HQ-29287.

2. Varnado witness 1 (name redacted), interview by FBI special agents Joseph G. Englehart and James L. Theisen, 1965, FBI Civil Unrest, Oneal Moore file, 44-NO-2594.

3. Varnado witness 2 (name redacted), interview by FBI special agents Joseph G. Englehart and James L. Theisen, 1965, FBI Civil Unrest, Oneal Moore file, 44-NO-2594.

4. Velma Seals, interviews by FBI special agents Joseph G. Englehart and James L. Theisen, October 9, 15, 1965, FBI Civil Unrest, Oneal Moore file, 44-NO-2594.

5. Velma Seals demeanor, interview by FBI special agent Clement J. Hood, October 21, 1965, FBI Civil Unrest, Oneal Moore file, 44-NO-2594.

6. Minnie Lee Seals, teletype from FBI New Orleans to FBI Director, June 14, 1965, FBI Civil Unrest, Oneal Moore file, 44-NO-2594.

7. FBI Case Inspector Joe Sullivan to FBI Director, July 2, 1965.

8. Wilbert Hodge, interview by FBI special agent L. M. Shearer Jr., June 21, 1965, FBI Civil Unrest, Oneal Moore file, 44-NO-2594.

9. FBI New Orleans to FBI Director, June 12, 1965, FBI Civil Unrest, Oneal Moore file, 44-NO-2594.

10. Fielding Crain, June 14, 1965, interview by FBI special agent Frank Sass Jr., FBI Civil Unrest, Oneal Moore file, 44-NO-2594.

11. FBI New Orleans to FBI Director, June 12, 1965.

12. Glenn Reid, interviews by FBI special agents Richard Knock, James A. McBride, Daniel D. Dreiling, Donald P. McDermott, Merriman D. Diven, and Brooke Roberts, June 6, 23, July 1, 6, 1965, FBI Civil Unrest, Oneal Moore file, 44-NO-2594.

13. FBI Case Inspector Joe Sullivan to FBI Director, July 2, 1965.

14. Dr. Robert Rollins Jr., interview by FBI special agents Joseph G. Peggs and Timothy M. Casey Jr., FBI Civil Unrest, Oneal Moore file, 44-NO-2594.

15. Ibid.

16. Deputy Percy C. Thomas, interview by FBI, March 13, 1967, FBI Civil Unrest, Oneal Moore file, 44-NO-2594.

17. Ibid.

18. Sidney Brock, interview by FBI, June 30, 1965, FBI Civil Unrest, Oneal Moore file, 44-NO-2594.

19. Franklinton chief of police Carruth Miller, interview by FBI special agent Frank Sass Jr., FBI Civil Unrest, Oneal Moore file, 44-NO-2594.

20. Ted Gardner, interview by author, April 13, 2012.

21. Notice to Close File, US Department of Justice, March 10, 2016.

22. FBI New Orleans to FBI Director, February 16, 17, 1965, FBI Civil Unrest, Oneal Moore file, 44-NO-2594.

23. Larry Ryals, interview by FBI special agent Nathan Brown, March 3, 1967, FBI Civil Unrest, Oneal Moore file, 44-NO-2594.

24. Urgent message from FBI New Orleans to FBI Director, August 23, 24, 1965, FBI Civil Unrest, Oneal Moore file, 44-NO-2594.

25. Ossie Brown obituary, *Advocate,* August 29, 2008.

26. FBI New Orleans to FBI Director, August 23, 24, 1965.

27. Ibid.

28. Milton Graham, interview by John P. DeCourcy, Society of Former Agents of the FBI, July 6, 2006, FBI Oral History Project.

29. Jack Nelson, *Scoop: The Evolution of a Southern Reporter* (Jackson: University Press of Mississippi, 2013), 113–14.

30. Bond for Ernest Ray McElveen, FBI New Orleans to FBI Director, June 13, 1965, FBI Civil Unrest, Oneal Moore file, 44-NO-2594.

31. Testimony of Dewey Bernard Smith, House Un-American Activities Committee, 2415–38, January 5, 1966, NARA.

32. Dewey Bernard Smith, interview by FBI special agent Merriman D. Diven, June 25, 1965, FBI Civil Unrest, Oneal Moore file, 44-NO-2594.

33. Dewey Bernard Smith advertisement, *Franklinton Era-Leader,* February 24, 1964.

34. Testimony of Dewey Bernard Smith.

35. Ibid.

36. Dewey Bernard Smith, interview by Diven.

37. Ibid.

CHAPTER NINE

1. "Doar Confers with City Officials," *Bogalusa Daily News,* July 16, 1965, A1.

2. Seldon Albert Lang, interview by FBI special agent Ralph J. Leiwer, September 19, 1965, FBI Civil Unrest, Oneal Moore file, 44-NO-2594.

3. "Rights Worker's Testimony Denied," *Bogalusa Daily News,* July 2, 1965, A1.

4. John Doar and Dorothy Landsburg, "The Performance of the FBI in Investigating Violations of Federal Laws Protecting the Right to Vote—1960–1967," *Hearings before the Select Committee to Study Governmental Operations with Respect to Intelligence Activities of the United States Senate,* Ninety-Fourth Congress, vol. 6, attachment 4, Washington, DC, 944.

5. Ibid., 945.

6. "Five Suits Filed by Justice Department," *Bogalusa Daily News,* July 16, 1965, A1.

7. "Contempt Action Threatened against Officials," *Bogalusa Daily News,* July 18, 1965, A1.

8. Milton Graham, interview by John P. DeCourcy, Society of Former Agents of the FBI, July 6, 2006, FBI Oral History Project.

9. Ibid.

10. "Crowd Jams Klan Rally," *Bogalusa Daily News,* July 22, 1965, A1.

11. Ibid.

12. "Contempt Action Threatened against Officials."

13. "Hurricane Stronger; Picking Up Speed," *Bogalusa Daily News,* September 2, 1965, A1.

14. "Bi-Racial Committee Looks for Director," *Bogalusa Daily News,* September 2, 1965, A1.

15. "Subpoenas Issued in Klan Suit," *Bogalusa Daily News,* September 5, 1965, A1.

16. "Judge Herbert William Christenberry," *Loyola University New Orleans,* http://magazine.loyno.edu/judge-herbert-william-christenberry.

17. Rupert Cornwell, "Obituary: John Minor Wisdom," *Independent,* https://www.independent.co.uk/arts-entertainment/obituary-john-minor-wisdom-1097913.html, June 3, 1999.

18. "Robert Andrew Ainsworth, Jr.," US District Court, Eastern District of Louisiana, http://www.laed.uscourts.gov/court-history/judges/ainsworth.

19. "Produce Klan's Records, Order: Amite, Bogalusa Men Directed by Court," *New Orleans Times-Picayune,* September 7, 1965, A1.

20. "71 Are Sworn In to Testify at Hearing," *Bogalusa Daily News,* September 7, 1965, A1.

21. "Winds Swirl into Gulf of Mexico," *Bogalusa Daily News,* September 8, 1965, A1.

22. "Seek to End Hearing before Hurricane Strikes," *Bogalusa Daily News,* September 9, 1965, A1.

23. "Klan Officer May Be Jailed: Judges Give Last Chance to Produce Records," *New Orleans Times-Picayune,* September 10, 1965, A1.

24. Ibid.

25. "Alleged Klan Names Listed by Attorneys: Bogalusa Case Evidence Is Concluded," *New Orleans Times-Picayune,* September 12, 1965, A1.

26. "Klan List Submitted," *Bogalusa Daily News,* September 12, 1965, A1.

27. Milton Graham, interview by John P. DeCourcy, Society of Former Agents of the FBI, July 6, 2006, FBI Oral History Project.

28. "McElveen Hearing Request Withdrawn," *Bogalusa Daily News,* September 17, 1965, A1.

29. "Grand Jury Seeks McElveen Hearing," *Bogalusa Daily News,* November 4, 1965, A1.

30. Ibid.

31. Ibid.

32. Ibid.

33. Ibid.

34. FBI New Orleans to FBI Director, State Prosecution against Ernest Raphael McElveen, October 26, 1965, FBI Civil Unrest, Oneal Moore file, 44-NO-2594.

35. United States v. Original Knights of Ku Klux Klan, US District Court, Eastern District of Louisiana, New Orleans Division, December 1, 1965.

36. Ibid.

37. Ibid.

38. Ibid.

39. Ibid.

40. "Court to Issue Injunction against Klan in Bogalusa Area," *Bogalusa Daily News,* December 2, 1965, A1.

41. FBI New Orleans to FBI Director, September 16, 17, 1965, FBI Civil Unrest, Oneal Moore file, 44-NO-2594.

42. Ibid.

43. Special agent in charge, New Orleans to FBI Director, September 11, 1965, FBI Civil Unrest, Oneal Moore file, 44-NO-2594.

CHAPTER TEN

1. FBI New Orleans to FBI Director, September 10, 1965, FBI Civil Unrest, Oneal Moore file, 44-NO-2594.

2. Milton Graham, interview by John P. DeCourcy, Society of Former Agents of the FBI, July 6, 2006, FBI Oral History Project.

3. Leroy "Slick" Seal obituary, Poole-Ritchie Funeral Home and Crematory, February 5, 2016.

4. Leroy "Slick" Seal, interviews by FBI, June 12, August 28, 1965, FBI Civil Unrest, Oneal Moore file, 44-NO-2594.

5. Ibid.

6. FBI New Orleans memo, June 1, 1989, FBI Civil Unrest, Oneal Moore file, 44-HQ-49207.

7. Leroy "Slick" Seal, interviews by FBI, June 12, August 28, 1965.

8. FBI New Orleans memo, June 1, 1989.

9. "The Ghosts of Bogalusa," *The Injustice Files,* Investigation Discovery, February 25, 2011.

10. FBI New Orleans memo, June 1, 1989.

11. Archie Roy Seals, interviews by FBI, October 7, 22, 25, 1965, FBI Civil Unrest, Oneal Moore file, 44-NO-2594.

12. Ibid.

13. Notice to Close File, US Department of Justice, March 10, 2016.

14. William James "Dick" Williams Jr., interview by FBI, October 10, 1965, FBI Civil Unrest, Oneal Moore file, 44-NO-2594.

15. FBI New Orleans to FBI Director, October 6, 1965, FBI Civil Unrest, Oneal Moore file, 44-NO-2594.

16. "Area Men Take 5th Amendment in Hearing," *Bogalusa Daily News,* January 6, 1966, A1.

17. Congressman Charles L. Weltner, "The Terror of Bogalusa: A Case in Point," *Congressional Record,* vol. 111, part 21, 28485–86, October 22, 1966.

18. "Branch Offers to Go to Court to Disprove Klan Membership," *Bogalusa Daily News,* February 9, 1966, A1.

19. "Why? Why? Why? An Open Letter to the District Attorney and Sheriff of Washington Parish," advertisement for Mrs. D. D. McElveen Sr., *Bogalusa Daily News,* January 10, 1966, A10.

20. Ibid.

21. Ibid.

22. "Covington to Get FBI Branch Office," *Bogalusa Daily News,* October 24, 1965, A1.

23. "Burke Found Guilty of Attacking Agent," *Bogalusa Daily News,* September 21, 1966, A1.

24. "Reggie G. Adams," *Military Times,* Hall of Valor Project, http://valor.militarytimes.com/recipient.php?recipientid=6243.

25. "Arrested after Shotgun Incident: Fired Blast at Feet of Agents, FBI Charges; Hearing Scheduled Monday in New Orleans," *Bogalusa Daily News,* March 1, 1966, A1.

26. Milton Graham, interview by author, February 1, 2018.

27. Milton Graham, interview by John P. DeCourcy, Society of Former Agents of the FBI, July 6, 2006, FBI Oral History Project.

28. Ibid.

29. Ibid.

30. Reggie Adams, interview by FBI special agent Paul F. Rowlands, FBI Civil Unrest, Oneal Moore file, 44-NO-2594.

31. "Shooting at Service Station Probed: Negro Army Captain Wounded at Close Range; Didn't See Assailant, Victim Tells Police," *Bogalusa Daily News,* March 11, 1966, A1.

32. "Suspect Confesses Sims Shooting," *Bogalusa Daily News,* March 13, 1966, A1.

33. Milton Graham, interview by John P. DeCourcy, Society of Former Agents of the FBI, July 6, 2006, FBI Oral History Project.

34. Milton Graham, interview by John P. DeCourcy, Society of Former Agents of the FBI, July 6, 2006, FBI Oral History Project; interview by author, February 1, 2018.

35. Ibid.

36. "Vietnam-Bound Negro Soldier Shot in Bogalusa," *Jet,* March 24, 1966, 4.

37. Milton Graham, interview by John P. DeCourcy, Society of Former Agents of the FBI, July 6, 2006, FBI Oral History Project.

38. Ibid.

39. "Defense Begins in Copling Trial," *Bogalusa Daily News,* July 15, 1967, A1, 8.

40. Ibid.

41. Ibid.

42. Ibid.

43. Ibid.

44. State v. Copling, Supreme Court of Louisiana, December 11, 1961.

45. "Copling Found Not Guilty in Triggs Shooting: Witness Admits Writing Letter Saying She Fired Fatal Shots," *Bogalusa Daily News,* July 15, 1967, A1.

46. Ibid.

47. Ibid.

48. Ibid.

49. Ibid.

50. "Sentenced to State Penitentiary: Former Court Clerk Fined $500; Kennedy Changes Plea to Guilty," *Bogalusa Daily News,* August 29, 1966, A1.

CHAPTER ELEVEN

1. James Wilford Moore, interviews by FBI, June 28, 30, 1965, FBI Civil Unrest, Oneal Moore file, 44-NO-2594.

2. FBI New Orleans to FBI Director, June 29, 1965, FBI Civil Unrest, Oneal Moore file, 44-NO-2594.

3. Mary Moore, interviews by FBI, June 29, 1965, February 4, 11, 1966, FBI Civil Unrest, Oneal Moore file, 44-NO-2594.

4. Claude W. Riles, interview by FBI special agents Milton Graham and Joseph E. Ondreila, February 24, 1966, FBI Civil Unrest, Oneal Moore file, 44-NO-2594.

5. John Pope, interviews by FBI, February 9, 15, March 3, 1965, FBI Civil Unrest, Oneal Moore file, 44-NO-2594.

6. Ibid.

7. FBI New Orleans to FBI Director, June 21, 1965, FBI Civil Unrest, Oneal Moore file, 44-NO-2594.

8. Claude W. Riles, interview by Graham and Ondreila.

9. Florine Pope, interview by FBI, February 9, 1966, FBI Civil Unrest, Oneal Moore file, 44-NO-2594.

10. Ibid.

11. Mary Moore, interviews by FBI.

12. John Pope, interviews by FBI.

13. Ibid.

14. Ibid.

15. Ibid.

16. Ibid.

17. James Wilford Moore, interviews by FBI, February 3, 14, 18, March 2, 1966, FBI Civil Unrest, Oneal Moore file, 44-NO-2594.

18. Ibid.

19. Memo from investigator Donald T. Appell to Director Francis J. McNamara, House Un-American Activities Committee, May 25, 1965, FBI Civil Unrest, Robert Fuller file, 157-NO-1300, NARA.

20. John Pope, interviews by FBI.

21. FBI New Orleans to FBI Director, April 12, 1966, John Pope, interviews by FBI, FBI Civil Unrest, Oneal Moore file, 44-NO-2594.

22. Nelson, *Devils Walking,* 135–41.

23. "Hooded Men Beat Father, Threaten Son," *Bogalusa Daily News,* August 10, 1964, A1.

24. Ibid.

25. Ibid.

26. Report on Beating of James Spears, FBI special agents Ernest Wall Jr. and Robert E. Bashum, June 21, 1965, FBI Civil Unrest, Oneal Moore file, 44-NO-2594.

27. "Hooded Men Beat Father, Threaten Son."

28. "First Arrest Reported in Beating of Bogalusan," *Bogalusa Daily News,* August 12, 1964, A1.

29. "Four More Charged in Spears Beating: Another Arrest Expected," *Bogalusa Daily News,* August 14, 1964, A1.

30. Report on Beating of James Spears, Wall and Bashum.

31. Ibid.

32. FBI New Orleans to FBI Director, February 22, 1966, FBI Civil Unrest, Oneal Moore file, 44-NO-2594.

33. John Pope, interviews by FBI.

34. Ibid.

35. James Wilford Moore, interviews by FBI.

36. Ibid.

37. John Pope, interviews by FBI.

38. James Wilford Moore, interviews by FBI.

39. Report of FBI special agent Donald C. Steinmeyer, February 3, 14, 18, March 2, 10, 1966.

40. Robert "Bobby" Lang, interview by FBI special agent James A. Theisen, March 18, 1966, FBI Civil Unrest, Oneal Moore file, 44-NO-2594.

41. Report of Steinmeyer.

42. Robert "Bobby" Lang, interview by special agent Donald C. Steinmeyer, March 20, 1966.

43. Special agent in charge, New Orleans to FBI Director, April 12, 1966, FBI Civil Unrest, Oneal Moore file, 44-NO-2594.

44. Report on Leroy "Slick" Seal, May 31, 1966, FBI Civil Unrest, Oneal Moore file, 44-NO-2594.

45. Gulf Breeze, Florida, salesman (name redacted), interview by FBI special agents James L. Theisen and Donald C. Steinmeyer, April 4, 1966.

46. Ibid.

47. Ibid.

48. Ibid.

49. Will Jones, interview by FBI special agent J.P. Hufford, April 5, 1965, FBI Civil Unrest, Oneal Moore file, 44-NO-2594.

50. Gulf Breeze, Florida, salesman.

51. Dewey Norsworthy, letter to FBI, July 2, 1980, FBI Civil Unrest, Oneal Moore file, 44-NO-2594.

52. Notice to Close File, US Department of Justice, March 10, 2016.

53. Ibid.

54. Ibid.

CHAPTER TWELVE

1. Dianne Burch Bass, interview by author, March 9, 2020.

2. Ibid.

3. Don Ferguson, "Woman Faces Murder Charge in Shooting: Husband Died of Gunshot," *Franklinton Era-Leader,* August 14, 1985, A1.

4. Dianne Burch Bass, interview by author.

5. Notice to Close File, US Department of Justice, March 10, 2016.

6. FBI New Orleans to FBI Director, October 6, 1965, FBI Civil Unrest, Oneal Moore file, 44-NO-2594.

7. James Eldon Burch, interview by FBI special agent Paul F. Rowlands Jr., July 2, 1965, FBI Civil Unrest, Oneal Moore file, 44-NO-2594.

8. FBI New Orleans to FBI Director, November 20, 1965.

9. James Eldon Burch, interview by FBI, October 15, 1965, FBI Civil Unrest, Oneal Moore file, 44-NO-2594.

10. Dianne Burch, interview by author.

11. James Eldon Burch, interview by FBI, October 21, 1965, FBI Civil Unrest, Oneal Moore file, 44-NO-2594..

12. Dianne Burch, interview by author.

13. FBI special agents Terry M. Scott and Michael J. Heimbach to special agent in charge, New Orleans, March 5, 1965, FBI Civil Unrest, Oneal Moore file, 44-NO-2594.

14. Elmo Breland Military Record, FBI Civil Unrest, Oneal Moore file, 44-NO-2594.

15. Elmo Breland Arrest Record, FBI Civil Unrest, Oneal Moore file, 44-NO-2594.

16. Informant Report Received by FBI special agents James L. Theisen and Tony J. Seabough, September 18, 1965, FBI Civil Unrest, Robert Fuller file, 157-NO-1300.

17. Ibid.

18. Elmo Breland Inmate Record, Louisiana State Penitentiary, Angola, Louisiana, August 3, 1972, FBI Civil Unrest, Oneal Moore file, 44-NO-2594.

19. Sheriff Willie Blair, letter to Secretary of Corrections, Louisiana State Penitentiary, Angola, Louisiana, March 27, 1979, FBI Civil Unrest, Oneal Moore file, 44-NO-2594.

20. Gail Verberne McClendon v. Louisiana Department of Corrections, Third Circuit Court of Appeals, March 20, 1978.

21. Computation of Sentence to Fifteen Years for Elmo Breland, Governor Edwin Edwards, July 31, 1969, FBI Civil Unrest, Oneal Moore file, 44-NO-2594,

22. FBI New Orleans to FBI Director, February 8, 1995, FBI Civil Unrest, Oneal Moore file, 44-NO-2594.

23. Notice to Close File, US Department of Justice, March 10, 2016.

24. Charlotte Paint Company employees, interviews by FBI, July 27, August 31, 1994, FBI Civil Unrest, Oneal Moore file, 44-NO-2594.

25. FBI special agent (name redacted), memo to special agent in charge, New Orleans, December 19, 1994, FBI Civil Unrest, Oneal Moore file, 44-NO-2594.

26. FBI Behavior Science Services Accomplishment Report, July 13, 1995, FBI Civil Unrest, Oneal Moore file, 44-NO-49207.

27. Elmo Breland, interview by FBI, July 19, 1996, FBI Civil Unrest, Oneal Moore file, 44-NO-49207.

28. Notice to Close File, US Department of Justice, October 17, 1996, FBI Civil Unrest, Oneal Moore file, 44-NO-49207.

29. Ibid.

30. Klan informant (name redacted), interview by FBI special agent Frank Sass Jr., June 19, 1965, FBI Civil Unrest, Oneal Moore file, 44-NO-2594.

31. FBI special agent Steve Callender reports, July 7, 14, 1966, July 13, 1967, FBI Civil Unrest, White Knights file, 157-HQ-1552.

32. Ibid.

33. FBI New Orleans to FBI Director, June 6, 1965, FBI Civil Unrest, Oneal Moore file, 44-NO-2594.

34. Sister of Jim Fisher (name redacted), interview by FBI, June 19, 1965, FBI Civil Unrest, Oneal Moore file, 44-NO-2594.

35. Coworker of Jim Fisher (name redacted), interview by FBI, June 15, 1965, FBI Civil Unrest, Oneal Moore file, 44-NO-2594.

36. Jim Fisher, interview by FBI, June 15, 1965, FBI Civil Unrest, Oneal Moore file, 44-NO-2594.

37. Report of Informant T-2, January 25, 1967, FBI Civil Unrest, White Knights file, 157-HQ-1552.

38. Report of Informants T-1, T-2, T-3, and T-4, December 4, 1966, FBI Civil Unrest, White Knights file, 157-HQ-1552.

39. Report of Informant T-2, December 7, 1966, FBI Civil Unrest, White Knights file, 157-HQ-1552.

40. White Knights of the Ku Klux Klan (Bogalusa, Louisiana, unit) Informant Report, May 2, 1967, FBI Civil Unrest, White Knights file, 157-HQ-1552.

41. Bogalusa chief of police Haynes Wascom, interview by FBI, June 16, 1967, FBI Civil Unrest, White Knights file, 157-HQ-1552.

42. Mayor Curt Siegelin and City of Bogalusa press release, July 27, 1967, FBI Civil Unrest, White Knights file, 157-HQ-1552.

43. "Robert Rester Defeats Henry Richardson; New City Attorney Is Elected," *Bogalusa Daily News,* May 17, 1964, 1.

44. Haynes Wascom, interview by FBI.

45. Statement of Bogalusa Police Officer (name redacted), June 13, 1965, FBI Civil Unrest, Oneal Moore file, 44-NO-2594.

46. Ibid.

47. Ibid.

48. Haynes Wascom, interview by FBI.

49. Ibid.

50. "Seal Says Six Lawyers OK'ed New Law: Arrests Will Be Made," *Bogalusa Daily News,* September 9, 1967, A1.

51. "Alleged Plot to Assassinate Bogalusa, Louisiana, Civic and Police Officials," T. E. Bishop memo to Mr. DeLoach, October 11, 1967, FBI Civil Unrest, Oneal Moore file, 44-NO-2594.

52. Notice to Close File, US Department of Justice, March 10, 2016.

53. Ibid.

54. Ibid.

55. Retired Washington Parish police officer, interview by author, May 29, 2020.

EPILOGUE

1. Richard A. Serrano, "Answers Elusive in 1965 Slaying," *Los Angeles Times,* June 26, 1965, www.latimes.com/archives/la-xpm-2002-jun-26-na-deputies26-story.html.

2. Kristine Meldrum Denholm, "Chasing Ghosts in a Civil Rights Era Cop Killing," *Los Angeles Times,* October 22, 2010.

3. James H. Hallas, *Saipan: The Battle That Doomed Japan in World War II* (Guilford, CT: Stackpole Books, 2019).

4. E. R. McElveen, "Never Forgotten," *Marine Corps Gazette,* November 1998, 37.

5. Ibid.

6. Stanley Carl Bickham, interview by FBI, June 28, 1965, FBI Civil Unrest, Oneal Moore file, 44-NO-2594.

7. Notice to Close File, US Department of Justice, March 10, 2016.

8. Ibid.

9. Ibid.

10. Ibid.

11. FBI special agents Terry M. Scott and Michael J. Heimbach to special agent in charge, New Orleans, June 1, 1989, FBI Civil Unrest, Oneal Moore file, 44-NO-2594.

12. Michael McClelland, "Louisiana Lawmen Held for Beating Migrant Workers," UPI Archives, February 20, 1989.

13. Vertrees Adams, interview by FBI special agents Terry M. Scott and Michael J. Heimbach, August 23, 1989, FBI Civil Unrest, Oneal Moore file, 44-NO-2594.

14. Ibid.

15. Ibid.

16. Ibid.

17. James Varney and Ronette King, "Ex-Deputy Gets 10-Year Term in Beating, Robbery of Workers," *New Orleans Times-Picayune,* February 22, 1991, 1A.

18. Notice to Close File, US Department of Justice, March 10, 2016.

19. Ibid.

20. Ibid.

21. Ibid.

22. *Unsolved Mysteries,* National Broadcasting Company, November 1990.

23. Ibid.

24. Ibid.

25. Notice to Close File, US Department of Justice, March 10, 2016.

26. Ibid.

27. FBI special agent Report to special agent in charge, New Orleans, April 12, 1967, FBI Civil Unrest, Oneal Moore file, 44-NO-2594.

28. Ibid.

29. Notice to Close File, US Department of Justice, March 10, 2016.

30. Ibid.

31. Ibid.

32. Ibid.

33. Ibid.

34. Ibid.

35. Ibid.

36. "David Creed Rogers, 84; Deputy Shot in Suspected Racist Attack in 1965," *Los Angeles Times,* March 4, 2007.

37. Allen G. Breed, "Family Still Dreams of Justice for '65 Civil Rights Murder," *Los Angeles Times.* September 6, 1998.

38. Ibid.

BIBLIOGRAPHY

PRIMARY SOURCES

Archival Documents

FBI Records

FBI Civil Unrest Archives, National Records and Archives Administration, College Park, MD

Deacons for Defense file, 157-NO-2466

Oneal Moore file, 44-NO-2594

Robert Fuller file, 157-NO-1300

White Knights file, 157-NO-1962

House Un-American Activities Committee Records

Center for Legislative Archives, National Archives Records Administration, Washington, DC

Records of the US House of Representatives, Record Group 233.

Shamel, Charles E. Records of the House Un-American Activities Committee, 1945–1969 / House Internal Security Committee, 1969–1976. July 1995.

Court Cases

United States v. Original Knights of the Ku Klux Klan, December 1, 1965 (US, DC, LA)

United States of America, Plaintiff, v. Diaz D. McElveen, E. Ray McElveen, Saxon Farmer and Eugene Farmer, Individually and as members of the Citizens Council of Washington Parish, Louisiana, Curtis M. Thomas, Registrar of Voters of Washington Parish, Louisiana, and the Citizens Council of Washington Parish, Louisiana, Defendants, January 11, 1960 (US, DC, LA)

Smith v. Washington Parish Democratic Committee and Dorman Crowe, February 15, 1960 (Supreme Court of Louisiana)

State v. Copling, December 11, 1961 (Supreme Court of Louisiana)

Interviews and Personal Correspondence

Bass, Dianne Burch. Phone interview, March 9, 2020.

Crowe, Bobby. Personal interview, Bogalusa, LA, March 30, 2019. Phone interviews, June 21, July 19, 2019.

Dent, Charlottie. Phone interview, September 2015.

——. Unpublished recollections.

Graham, Milton. Phone interviews, February 8, 22, March 29, 2018.

——. Interview by John P. DeCourcy, July 6, 2006. Society of Former Special Agents of the FBI, Inc.

Gardner, Ted. Phone interview, April 13, 2012.

Hicks, Barbara. Phone interview and email, February 2020.

Lewis, Robert "Buck" Jr. Personal interview, Ferriday, LA, August 6, 2014.

Moore, Maevella. Personal interview, Varnado, LA, November 11, 2017.

Newspapers

Baton Rouge Advocate

Bogalusa Daily News

Concordia Sentinel

Franklinton Era-Leader

Los Angeles Times

Louisiana Weekly

Ouachita Citizen

Shreveport Times

States-Item

New Orleans Times-Picayune

Washington Post

Other Primary Sources

US Department of Justice, Notice to Close Oneal Moore file, 44-NO-2594, March 10, 2016.

SECONDARY SOURCES

Bartley, Numan V. *The Rise of Massive Resistance: Race and Politics in the South during the 1950's.* Baton Rouge: Louisiana State University Press, 1997.

Davis, Jack E. *Race against Time: Culture and Separation in Natchez since 1930.* Baton Rouge: Louisiana State University Press, 2001.

Fairclough, Adam. *Race & Democracy: The Civil Rights Struggle in Louisiana, 1915–1972.* Athens: University of Georgia Press, 1995.

"The Ghosts of Bogalusa." *The Injustice Files,* Investigation Discovery, February 25, 2011.

Hallas, James H. *Saipan: The Battle That Doomed Japan in World War II.* Guilford, CT: Stackpole Books, 2019.

Jackson, Joy J. "The Piney Woods—Tangipahoa, St. Helena, and Washington Parishes." Folklife in the Florida Parishes: Louisiana's Living Traditions, Louisiana Folk Life Program, Louisiana Division of the Arts and the Center for Southeast Louisiana Studies at Southeastern Louisiana University, http://www.louisianafolklife.org/LT/Virtual_Books/Fla_Parishes/book_florida_piney.html, 1988.

Lawrence, Bob. *Bogalusa Memories: A Conversation with Bob Lawrence.* Lucien, FL: Mill City, 2018.

McElveen, E. R. "Never Forgotten." *Marine Corps Gazette,* November 1998.

Nelson, Jack. *Scoop: The Evolution of a Southern Reporter.* Jackson: University Press of Mississippi, 2013.

Nelson, Stanley. *Devils Walking: Klan Murders along the Mississippi in the 1960s.* Baton Rouge: Louisiana State University Press, 2016.

"Vietnam-Bound Negro Soldier Shot in Bogalusa." *Jet,* March 24, 1966.

Weltner, Charles A. "The Terror of Bogalusa: A Case in Point." *Congressional Record,* vol. 11, part 21, Washington, DC, 1966.

INDEX